DISTANT NEIGHBORS

Distant Neighbors

THE SELECTED LETTERS OF
WENDELL BERRY AND
GARY SNYDER

Edited by Chad Wriglesworth

COUNTERPOINT

BERKELEY

Library of Congress Cataloging-in-Publication Data is available

ISBN 978-1-61902-305-5

Interior design by VJB/Scribe

COUNTERPOINT
1919 Fifth Street
Berkeley, CA 94710

www.counterpointpress.com

Printed in the United States of America
Distributed by Publishers Group West

10 9 8 7 6 5 4 3 2 1

CONTENTS

Dear Gary,[†]
I think it would be both surprising and disappointing if we
agreed more than we do. If we agreed about everything, what
would we have to say to each other? I'm for conversation.

Wendell Berry

Dear Wendell,[†]
… I'm not sure if anything is [between you and me] except distance and differing plant communities and climates. That's how
it feels to me, anyhow.

Gary Snyder

In contemporary American literature and environmental thought,
Wendell Berry and Gary Snyder are often mentioned among the
most important writers and public intellectuals of our day. Gary
Snyder was born in 1930 and grew up on the West Coast in a politically active household of timber workers and dairy farmers during
the 1930s and 40s. He studied literature and anthropology at Reed
College and emerged in San Francisco as a central figure in the
counterculture movement. He went on to travel throughout Japan
and across the globe, before settling down in 1970 with his young
family at Kitkitdizze, a homestead built with friends in the Sierra
Nevada foothills. While living there, Snyder has written more than
twenty works of prose and poetry that explore connections among
ecology, Eastern philosophy, and indigenous anthropology. On the
opposite side of the nation, Wendell Berry was born in 1934 and also
grew up in a family committed to economic reform through the
Burley Tobacco Growers Cooperative, a regional initiative begun in
the 1920s to secure marketplace parity for local farmers, and established finally under the New Deal in 1941. After studying English at
the University of Kentucky, Berry attended the Stanford Creative

Writing Program in the late 1950s. His first novel, *Nathan Coulter,* was published in 1960. In 1965, after an extended period of travel, Berry moved with his family to Port Royal, Kentucky, where he has written more than fifty works of poetry, fiction, and nonfiction. He continues to live and work alongside his wife, Tanya Berry, at Lanes Landing Farm.

For the past two years, I have had the pleasure of working with nearly 250 letters exchanged between Wendell Berry and Gary Snyder from the early 1970s to the present. When these two men began writing to each other, neither could have imagined the impact their lives would have on American literary and political culture, nor how their lives would link them to distinct places, as well as to one another. The letters tell a story of friendship between men committed to restoring ecological, cultural, and economic health in two different American regions. They speak of shared experiences at their respective homesteads—Lanes Landing Farm and Kitkitdizze—their influence on each other's numerous writing projects, and their participation in groups such as the Lindisfarne Association, The Land Institute, and the Schumacher Society. But even more important, the letters exchanged between Berry and Snyder provide a lived example of something increasingly scarce in American culture—two people working to recover and maintain the art of dialogue—namely, the practice of sustaining a meaningful conversation that is both critical and hospitable, particularly when ideological tensions run high enough to spark division.

When reading the works of Wendell Berry and Gary Snyder, it can be tempting to stress points of difference, setting Snyder's radical countercultural commitment to reinhabiting the Sierra Nevada foothills as a Zen Buddhist against Berry's agrarian practice of land stewardship that is shaped by Christian thought. However, focusing on differences alone clouds the unifying power of fidelity. The beauty and witness of this complex friendship exists in the men's expressions of particularity more than stark points of division. Snyder remains a practicing Zen Buddhist committed to principles of animism and hunting-and-gathering in the Sierra Nevada foothills, even as Berry works from Port Royal, equally dedicated to revising rural economies in relation to the inheritance of Western culture. Neither man practices a superficial—what Berry calls "feckless"— expression of religiosity, but instead weaves the ecological rhythms and patterns of the places they inhabit into their lives. Their distinct cultural upbringings, educations, and commitments to particular regions shape where they stand and how they write. Yet the shared practice of restoring the health of wounded places remains intact in the work of both men.

When differences arise between Wendell Berry and Gary Snyder, the two writers remain in conversation, benefiting from what Berry calls "binocular vision,"[†] the art of gaining clarification of thought by perceiving through the other person's way of being. This leads to an awareness of their mutual existence in an expansive and generous source of energy that Snyder calls "mind." For example, in 1980, after reading Snyder's *The Real Work: Interviews & Talks, 1964–1979,* Berry sent a letter acknowledging key differences between himself and Snyder, yet was also moved to write the following:

> ...I read this book with a delight and gratitude that I
> rarely feel for the work of a contemporary. Given our obvious differences of geographic origin, experience, etc., it is
> uncanny how much I feel myself spoken for by this book
> —and, when not spoken for, spoken *to*, instructed. It is a
> feeling I have only got elsewhere from hearing my brother
> speak in 'environmental' controversies—the realization
> and joyful relief of hearing someone speak well out of
> deeply held beliefs that I share. And this always involves a
> pleasant quieting of my own often too insistent impulse
> to speak.[†]

In that same collection of interviews, Snyder—in spite of any differences—also spoke of the common bond he shared with Berry. While stating the importance of Eastern philosophy in his life and work, he insisted that Berry's commitment to practicality and Western culture "draws on the best of American roots and traditional mindfulness . . . to teach us something that we're not going to learn by studying Oriental texts."† In this spirit, Berry and Snyder retain their particular ways of being, but through hospitable acts of perceiving beyond the self are also enlarged into a common existence of work and hope.

Wendell Berry and Gary Snyder knew about each other long before they met in the early 1970s. After Berry and Tanya Amyx were married in 1957, the couple spent a summer living in the Camp, a family cabin on the Kentucky River. That fall, they moved to nearby Georgetown, where Berry taught English at Georgetown College. Following the birth of their first child, Mary, the growing family headed west to California, where Berry attended the Stanford Creative Writing Program on a Wallace Stegner Fellowship (1958-60). It was then, while living in Mill Valley at what is now the O'Hanlon Center for the Arts, that Berry was reading *Poetry* magazine and took interest in the work of Robert Creeley, Denise Levertov, and Gary Snyder. Before long, he went to City Lights Books and bought a copy of *Riprap* (1959), Snyder's first book of poems that was published in Kyoto, Japan, by Origin Press. The poems made a substantial impression on Berry, who, a few years later, spoke of Snyder's work in "A Secular Pilgrimage," a lecture given through United Campus Ministry at University of Kentucky, before it was published in *The Hudson Review* (1970) and *A Continuous Harmony* (1972).

By the late 1950s, Gary Snyder was already something of a legend in the San Francisco poetry scene. After graduating from Reed College, he worked several jobs for the U.S. Forest Service, the U.S. Park Service, and the Warm Springs Indian Reservation. Between periods of work, writing, and hitchhiking up and down the West Coast as an itinerant laborer, Snyder also studied Chinese and Japanese at University of California, Berkeley. Then, in 1955, after meeting Kenneth Rexroth in San Francisco, he read "A Berry Feast" alongside Allen Ginsberg's *Howl* at the now famous Six Gallery event. At the time, Snyder was living in Mill Valley with Jack Kerouac, who went on to cast him as Japhy Ryder in *The Dharma Bums* (1958). A year after the Six Gallery reading, Snyder departed again, this time on a marine freighter to study Zen Buddhism in Japan. For nearly fifteen years, he lived in Buddhist communities, worked on an oil tanker, explored India, and made several trips back to San Francisco.

The 1960s proved to be a decade of travel for both Wendell Berry and Gary Snyder, ultimately leading to conscious decisions to settle down and raise families at specific homesteads. After the publication of *Nathan Coulter*, Berry spent a year with his family, mostly in Florence, Italy, on a Guggenheim Fellowship (1961–62). When they returned to Kentucky their second child, Den, was born—and the family moved again—this time for a teaching opportunity in New York City. Two years later, Berry took an appointment at the University of Kentucky, and the family purchased a small farm in Henry County, where Berry's ancestors had lived and farmed for seven generations. While the family was restoring an old farmhouse above the Kentucky River, Snyder was living in Japan, making plans to return to the West Coast with his wife, Masa Uehara, and their first son, Kai. Upon returning to California, their second child, Gen, was born and the family settled into the Sierra Nevada foothills where they built a homestead called Kitkitdizze. With Berry and Snyder now rooting themselves in very different places, it did not take long for these like-minded neighbors to find each other across the miles and cultures between them.

Jack Shoemaker, an editor and publisher in the Bay Area, proved to be a catalyzing link between Wendell Berry and Gary Snyder. Shoemaker had met Snyder in the early 1960s, when the poet agreed to do a reading for the opening of the Unicorn, a bookstore that Shoemaker started with friends near the University of California at Santa Barbara. A few years later, in 1969, Shoemaker read Gary Snyder's *Earth House Hold* and "a book by a young writer [he'd] barely heard about, *The Long-Legged House* by Wendell Berry." Enamored by both works, Shoemaker remembers that "where Snyder's book celebrated the exotic and otherness of life, from Zen in Japan to working as a merchant mariner and a fire lookout in the Sierras, Berry's book explored and celebrated the familiar, the possible, an American life that [he] could imagine living."† While traveling through Kentucky the next year, Shoemaker visited Port Royal and spent a few days at Lanes Landing Farm. The two men talked about writing and publishing, as well as Sand Dollar Books, an independent bookstore and press that Shoemaker was starting in Berkeley. Within a few years, Shoemaker had further extended his literary friendship to both Snyder and Berry by publishing Howard McCord's *Some Notes to Gary Snyder's* Myths & Texts (1971) and *An Eastward Look* (1974), a book of poems about Chinese paintings that Berry entrusted to him.

In 1973, while Jack Shoemaker and Wendell Berry worked through the production details for *An Eastward Look*, Snyder stepped into the conversation, and a correspondence began to take shape. Snyder's first letter to Berry expressed thanks for *A Continuous Harmony* (1972), a book that mentions Snyder as a contemporary poet with "an impulse of reverence moving toward the world, toward a new pertinence of speech and a new sense of possibility."† Berry responded to Snyder's letter with words of mutual appreciation. He wrote of purchasing additional acreage and farming with horses, as well as "reading with pleasure several booklets by you that Jack Shoemaker sent me."† Berry closed the note by wishing Snyder prosperity at Kitkitdizze, and in this polite exchange a journey of more than forty years of friendship had begun.

Within a few months, Wendell Berry and Gary Snyder were making plans to meet in person. Snyder was giving several readings in Ohio and Texas and hoped to stay in Port Royal a couple of days "to help with work around [Berry's] place. And talk some."†

Subsequent letters say very little about that first meeting, but the encounter made a lasting impression on both men. Snyder returned to Kitkitdizze and sent back several books, along with updates on poetry and politics in the Bay Area. The positive energy felt by Snyder was mutual. A few years later, at an event organized by Jack Shoemaker at the San Francisco Museum of Modern Art, Berry and Snyder read poetry together for the first time. Before the reading, Berry called the evening a "moving event"† and remembered the pleasure of welcoming Snyder to Port Royal some years ago. He had felt "close to [Snyder] for a long time from his work" and told the crowd that "to have an orderly head visit you from the other side of your subject" was certainly "a welcome event" and cause for excitement.

After that initial visit, Gary Snyder returned to Kitkitdizze and continued working with bioregional poets in the Bay Area, while Wendell Berry resumed the patterns of life at Lanes Landing Farm. Letters traveled between California and Kentucky over the winter. Then, with the onset of spring, Snyder received a warm letter from Berry, who wrote, "I have been keeping you and your place and things you told me about it a good deal in mind."† He had hoped to visit Kitkitdizze soon, but farming obligations and the recent death of friend and neighbor, Owen Flood, would postpone any trip out west. He regretted the distance between them, but encouraged Snyder to bring his family back to Port Royal. With that invitation, Berry enclosed the poem "To Gary Snyder," a memory about their previous visit together.

A few years later, when Wendell Berry and Gary Snyder read poetry together at the San Francisco Museum of Modern Art, Berry told listeners the story behind "To Gary Snyder" in a tone that was both lighthearted and serious. He said:

> The day that Gary left to go to the airport, my boy Den
> and I went on up to visit the neighbor up a creek. The

river was up and we were going along the edge of a backwater and we became aware that we were coming up on a
rather large flock of mallards that had come down on the
backwater. So we began to ease along to see if we could get
up close to them. And we did. We got very close, crawling
along on our bellies. And we stayed and watched a long
time, got into that companionable spirit that you can get
into with creatures—especially ducks, who are very conver-
sational. And then, for some reason, we did a thing neither
one of us anticipated. We said, "Well, we got to be going
now" and the ducks didn't move.... The reason we had
spoken, I think, was because we hated to break it up....
And we were walking along together, being sort of amazed
at ourselves and pleased, and Den said, "I wish Mr. Snyder
had been here." And I knew exactly what he meant and I
wrote a poem about it.[†]

Berry and his son, Den, had set out to check on a local neighbor cut
off by backwater, but instead stepped into an unexpected encounter
with nature that stirred longings for a new and distant companion
still present in their minds despite his physical absence.

The language and structure of "To Gary Snyder" connect Wendell Berry and Gary Snyder together as distant neighbors—allies
with a common stance in the world—while still acknowledging
the geographic space and cultural differences between them. The
poem reads:

To Gary Snyder

After we saw the wild ducks
and walked away, drawing out
the quiet that had held us,
in wonder of them and of ourselves,

Den said, "I wish Mr. Snyder
had been here." And I said, "Yes."
But many fine things will happen here
that you will not see, and I
am resigned to ignorance of many
that will happen in your hills.
It cannot often be as it was
when we heard geese in the air
and ran out of the house to see them
wavering in long lines, high,
southward, out of sight.
By division we speak, out of wonder.

The poem begins with a moment of intimacy shared between a father and son, yet by the concluding lines this community of affection has expanded to also include Snyder. Wendell and Den are connected to a place, but also within a memory. They recall the presence of a new friend, one who was drawn into their home—and then released again—to return to the responsibilities and pleasures of his own place.

With distance set between Wendell Berry and Gary Snyder, the pattern of migrating geese becomes the metaphor that links the two men across any geographic or cultural divide. In a moment of shared wonder, Berry and Snyder watched the geese "wavering in long lines, high, / southward, out of sight." Snyder's time at Port Royal came and went quickly, like the geese that passed over the farm and called both men outdoors with eyes set to the sky. Now enclosed with a letter, Berry's own poetic "lines" are sent across the miles—like geese in flight—to offer an affectionate hello and good-bye, a gesture of friendship that speaks fidelity across the distance. When read from this perspective, the concluding moment of the poem does not speak of "division" as separation. Instead, the final line communicates the existence of two lives within a mutual vision, separated by nothing more than a comma that holds two distinct expressions of being together: "By division we speak, out of wonder."

A few months after Gary Snyder visited Port Royal, the publication and critical success of *Turtle Island* (1974) brought new opportunities for teaching and travel, including an appointment as poet-in-residence at the University of Cincinnati. The possibility of the Snyder family staying near Port Royal "delighted"[†] Wendell and Tanya Berry and "set [them] to thinking" about living arrangements at Lanes Landing Farm. Ultimately, Snyder and his family stayed in Cincinnati but still made several visits to the farm. After nearly three months away, Snyder returned home and wrote to Berry about the pleasures of San Juan Ridge. Writing by the pond and fireside, he described the pleasant "music"[†] of Kitkitdizze: the slashing and swooping bats, the bullfrogs booming, and the crickets chirping. He had reunited with the rhythmic energies of the Sierra Nevada foothills, but memories of Lanes Landing Farm were also crisscrossing his mind. The "soft rustling of the fire" and music of home conjured harmonious patterns of a nightscape at Berry's place, "when the lightning was flashing all night and the firebugs were ecstatically responding to that apparently thinking that the absolute principle in the sky was a firebug like themselves." By way of closing the letter, Snyder enclosed the poem "Berry Territory," a memory about time spent at Lanes Landing Farm.

In 1977, at the San Francisco Museum of Modern Art poetry reading, Gary Snyder told the story behind "Berry Territory" and then dedicated the poem to his friend. He said:

> Well, last spring my family and I were all in Cincinnati for a couple of months.[†] And we had the pleasure of going for a walk one morning up in the hills back of Wendell Berry's farm above the Kentucky River. So I wrote this poem called "Berry Territory." This is really my poem for Wendell.

Before reading the poem, Snyder playfully wagered, "I bet [Wendell] has no idea how I read this." He then took a breath and began to read, diving deeply into the rich ecology of the Kentucky River woodlands.

Berry Territory

Many soft leaf structures, bush or tree
All, angiosperms, blossoms pinched by frost

Under dead leaves Tanya finds a tortoise
    matching leaves—legs pulled in—

And woodchuck holes that dive in
    under limestone ledges
    seabottom strata
    (brush their furry backs
    on shell and coral).

Most holes with dry leaves scattered at the door
    nobody there.

A Beech, silvery, smooth, "FJ '45"
    deep carved.
A Chestnut Oak—tall—in the woods on heights
    above Kentucky River, this one born
    back in Dream Time:
    it has a shining being in it,
    with eternal life!

Wendell, crouched down,
    Sticks his face in a woodchuck hole
    "Hey, smell that, it's a fox!"
    I go on my knees,

Put the opening to my face
like a mask. No light;
All smell: sour—warm—
Splintered bones, scats? feathers?
Wreathing bodies—wild—

Some home.

Throughout the poem, all residents of Lanes Landing Farm are described as homemakers, various types of burrowers and divers who set down roots in an ecosystem they know as home. Early in the poem, Tanya Berry looks under dead leaves to find a neighboring tortoise, an animal that evokes connections to *Turtle Island*, an indigenous name for North America and the title of Snyder's Pulitzer Prize–winning book of poems about learning how to reinhabit the earth. In Native creation stories, a giant turtle carries the continent on its back, or in some cases dives through primordial waters to recover ancient materials to form the place we call home. In a similar way, Wendell and Tanya Berry are portrayed as stabilizing guides, those who have reached down to recover regional stories and materials from the past that can teach us how to live more responsibly in the present. After seven generations of ancestral farming in Henry County, their family has set down roots and become "native to this place."[†] The woodchuck, fox, plants, timber, and humans all flourish within an ongoing cycle of life, death, and regeneration, a rhythm of homemaking that is both domestic and wild.

As previously mentioned, "To Gary Snyder" and "Berry Territory" were read together at the San Francisco Museum of Modern Art, when Wendell and Tanya Berry made their first visit to Kitkitdizze. Jack Shoemaker, who organized the reading and designed a broadside for the event, highlighted the similarities and differences between Berry and Snyder through side-by-side photographs. In one photo, taken in 1975, Berry is shown smiling in the afternoon

Wendell Berry & Gary Snyder

READING
San Francisco Museum of Modern Art
Thursday 8pm March 3
co-sponsored by The Poetry Center

Broadside for Wendell Berry and Gary Snyder reading at the San Francisco Museum of Modern Art, March 3, 1977. Gary Snyder Papers, Department of Special Collections at the University of California, Davis.

sun of Frankfort, Kentucky, where local citizens have rallied to oppose the construction of a dam on the Red River. He is a clean-cut protestor. He wears a sweater and has a blade of Kentucky bluegrass leisurely resting on his lower lip. The other photograph, taken at roughly the same time, shows Snyder working at Kitkitdizze. He is a long-haired voice of the counterculture. He wears a denim work shirt, an earring, and a goatee. He looks directly into the camera and—like Berry—is connected to place by a blade of grass held between his lips. The two men speak from different regions and backgrounds, yet the placement and content of the two photos illustrate their common bond.

In weeks leading up to the poetry reading, Wendell Berry sensed that the West Coast trip would be tightly scheduled and crowded by appointments and obligations. Yet he promised Snyder, "We *are* going to visit you ... and long enough to talk and look around responsibly.† I will want to see as much as time allows of what you will want to show me. I assume that will allow some insight into what is working there in your community." The trip went as planned and Wendell and Tanya Berry returned from Kitkitdizze feeling inspired and instructed by a place that felt something like home. Two weeks later, Berry sent Snyder a copy of "Life on (and off) Schedule," a reflective essay about his trip to California that included a commentary about Kitkitdizze and San Juan Ridge. To make his intentions and fidelity plain, Berry enclosed a letter with the essay that concluded, "It's clear from what I wrote, I hope, how much I was pleased and moved by what I saw there. I'm only sorry we couldn't stay longer, and will hope to come back again before too long. We are neighbors—*distant* neighbors."†

Wendell Berry begins "Life on (and off) Schedule"† by discussing the pleasures of Kentucky farm life, where work is directed by the rhythms and cycles of seasons. Farm work is patterned and loosely scheduled, but, as Berry observes, "one does not make an appointment with a milk cow or a garden, and so one's care for those things has a kind of margin of convenience." Once away from the farm, Berry contrasts a life of affection against the movement of people committed to making a living by "waking, eating, talking, sleeping on schedule." Work is no longer done with pleasure, but by an expectation to be somewhere, to meet a demand, and to ultimately stay on schedule. Comparing the two ways of life, Berry considers "how vulnerable schedules are," particularly to drastic changes and so-called "unscheduled" weather patterns. Berry's reference to weather was timely, as Kentucky was experiencing "the coldest winter on record" even as California was in the middle of "the driest winter on record." The two regions, although ecologically and culturally quite different, were united by the same unwarranted faith in assumed schedules. By imposing human will upon the land, rather than conforming to patterns of local ecology and economy, "the country was prepared to deal with the winter it expected, not the one it got."

By contrast to life lived on tight schedules, Wendell and Tanya Berry's visit to San Juan Ridge felt close to home, much like a return to the natural and cyclical rhythms of Lanes Landing Farm. While much of culture celebrates the superficial, Berry described Kitkitdizze as a place with roots "deepening into the continent." The people of San Juan Ridge, like Berry's farm back home, had made deliberate decisions to cultivate a "responsible local life, a life that lives by looking around where it is, discovering what is available there, and making *appropriate* changes in itself as well as in the place." Upon their arrival at San Juan Ridge, Wendell and Tanya Berry were taken into Kitkitdizze as friends and members of a community that paid little mind to haste. Berry described the first day there in the following way:

> Our arrival at Gary's place—welcomed by his wife, Masa, and his boys, Gen and Kai—was an emergence from schedules. It was like coming out of a tunnel. We were with the people we had come to see, and for a day and a half had no appointments. Natural and human events took place around us because of their own necessities—a kind of generosity in that, permitting rest. We had the deer stepping unafraid through the clearing, the windy light shimmering in the pines, good food, fire, laughter, the company of friends. Later, we slept in the new guest room in the barn.

The next day, Wendell and Tanya Berry were taken through pine trees, along ridges and pathways, and through clearings, where they observed a local settlement of people working to live within the patterns of the Sierra Nevada foothills. In a region once "partly devastated by hydraulic mining," excessive logging, and random grazing, the people of San Juan Ridge were attempting to live intelligently and modestly within the "ecological limits" the region offered to them. The settlement was only beginning to take shape and would surely be confronted with future questions, but Berry was certain that "the whole country" needed to know what they were learning.

Wendell Berry's first visit to Kitkitdizze marked a significant moment in a rich friendship that continued to evolve for decades. In years that followed, the two men became closer, and the frequency and complexity of their letters increased. Both continued to make return trips to California and Kentucky, where they gave readings at community and university gatherings and visited each other's homes. They also appeared at several venues together, including a conference sponsored by the Menninger Foundation; a Schumacher Society lecture in Bristol, England; a gathering at the University of Montana's Wilderness Institute; and in Santa Fe, New Mexico, where they participated in an interview for the Lannan Foundation with Jack Shoemaker. Between these visits, their letters continued to grapple with questions about particularities of religion, local economics, styles of writing, and the ongoing work of reinhabitation as practiced from two distinct regions. Though not always in agreement, their friendship is a testament to the power of fidelity in an increasingly sectarian culture. With grace and good humor they have lived out what Snyder calls "an ethical life," the principles and need for which are laid out in *The Practice of the Wild*:

> An ethical life is one that is mindful, mannerly, and has style. Of all moral failings and flaws of character, the worst is stinginess of thought, which includes meanness in all forms. Rudeness in thought or deed toward others, toward nature, reduces the chances of conviviality and interspecies communication, which are essential to physical and spiritual survival.[†]

By choosing paths of hospitality over mindless competition, these two men—known for giving us alternative models for living in place—have also left us a social map that leads to more generous and imaginative ways of existing together.

Nearly thirty years after Wendell Berry's first visit to Kitkitdizze, the Kentucky poet returned to visit Gary Snyder's place with Jack

Shoemaker. He had made the trip many times before. On the way back to Berkeley, while Berry and Shoemaker were driving through the winding turns of Highway 49, Berry's mind went into the past and he said, "I am amazed and moved by the connections in my life. When I sat in Mill Valley in 1959, I never imagined I would ever meet Gary Snyder. I am so grateful to him—he has helped me more then he'll ever know." Shoemaker, who was moved by the sincerity of Berry's words, wrote them down and passed them on. For years, Snyder has kept the words tucked away at Kitkitdizze, telling us that such feelings of wonder and gratitude have certainly been mutual.

While some of the letters collected in *Distant Neighbors* emerged from books and files at Kitkitdizze and Lanes Landing Farm, most of them are held at special collections and research libraries in California and Kentucky. Wendell Berry's letters are in the Department of Special Collections at the University of California at Davis, and Gary Snyder's letters are available through the Breckinridge Research Room at the University of Kentucky and the Kentucky Historical Society Martin F. Schmidt Research Library.

The letters that follow are arranged chronologically. Editorial notes are added to provide information about the context of specific letters, or to note places where an occasional letter is missing. Endnotes are included to reference names, key events, and particular writings mentioned or enclosed with the letters. For the most part, copies of enclosed poems and essays held at special collections libraries are not reproduced in the book, but are noted or described in the text. To help with locating these materials, references made to works by Berry and Snyder are noted by title and date of publication. These materials are readily available in print editions of each writer's works. Secondary works by other writers are noted with a complete citation, while materials unique to the archives are typically described. For purposes of readability, information such as phone numbers, addresses, and extraneous passages have been omitted from the book. In such cases, an ellipsis [...] inserted in the text indicates that information has been removed from a particular letter.

Distant Neighbors

THE SELECTED LETTERS OF
WENDELL BERRY AND GARY SNYDER

EDITOR'S NOTE: In the early 1970s, Gary Snyder had returned from a long residence in Japan to the Sierra Nevada foothills of Northern California. He built a home at Kitkitdizze, a homestead that he settled on with his wife and young family. On the other side of the country, after living in California, Italy, and New York, Wendell Berry's family had recently moved to Port Royal, Kentucky, where they were restoring an old house and settling a farm adjoining his grandfather's land. Gary Snyder and Wendell Berry had not yet met, but they were familiar with each other's writings and shared a common friendship with Jack Shoemaker, then editor of Sand Dollar Books in Berkeley, California.

GARY SNYDER [NEVADA CITY, CA]
TO WENDELL BERRY [PORT ROYAL, KY]

[*July 7, 1973*]†

Dear Wendell—

Am reading *Continuous Harmony*† in between building hen-house, tending bees, cutting firewood, and reading La Barre's *Ghost Dance*.† *Sanity*! Thank you for helping show that creativity and wisdom come from a base of sanity, not disorientation.

fraternally,
Gary Snyder

WENDELL BERRY [PORT ROYAL, KY]
TO GARY SNYDER [NEVADA CITY, CA]

7/24/73 [*July 24, 1973*]

Dear Gary,

I'm happy to know my book [*A Continuous Harmony*] meant something to you. It seems to have been lost, in the main, via publication.

I have been reading with pleasure several booklets by you that Jack Shoemaker[†] sent me. We bought an adjoining 40 acre farm[†] last winter to save it from a speculator—which, gives us about 52 acres, a lot of work, a big debt, all in the rainiest summer on record. We decided to farm with horses instead of a tractor. All this adds up to a profound event. We'll be years, I think, learning what to make of it.

Thanks. May your household prosper.

Your friend,
Wendell

◇◇◇◇◇

EDITOR'S NOTE: In the fall of 1973, Gary Snyder was scheduled to give poetry readings in Ohio and Texas. Berry and Snyder made plans to meet for the first time at Lanes Landing Farm between the readings in early December of 1973. During that visit Snyder also gave a poetry reading at the University of Kentucky.

GARY SNYDER [NEVADA CITY, CA]
TO WENDELL BERRY [PORT ROYAL, KY]

16. X: 73 [*October 16, 1973*]

Dear Wendell—

How I'd like to! From Cincinnati I go straight off, and am busy up til November 28—at Southern Methodist, in Dallas. But I could fly back to the nearest airport, and maybe visit you, do a reading on the 29th or 30th of November? Reading would be good to cover extra jog-back plane fare. Let me know possibilities—and if there's an ok, I'll schedule plane to yr. area. I want to speak w/ you of several things—

G

4

GARY SNYDER [NEVADA CITY, CA]
TO WENDELL BERRY [PORT ROYAL, KY]

1. XI.73 [*November 1, 1973*]

Dear Wendell—

Here's how I've worked it out: arrive on the 29th in Lexington
at 6.55 pm (having eaten something during the layover in Louisville) and doing the poetry reading [at the University of Kentucky]
directly. [...]

And if it's ok with you, stay at your place Fri. night too, and fly
from Louisville leaving 2:38 pm Saturday. I'd like to help with work
around your place. And talk some. [...]

best,
Gary

◇◇◇◇◇

EDITOR'S NOTE: Gary Snyder sent this letter after returning from his
first visit to Lanes Landing Farm. He also sent Wendell and Tanya
Berry several books.

GARY SNYDER [NEVADA CITY, CA]
TO WENDELL BERRY [PORT ROYAL, KY]

[*December 6, 1973*]†

Wendell, Tanya—†

Thank you. Stewart Brand† is talking about starting an "energy"
newsletter. Will read WHALE poems with Ferlinghetti,† McClure,†
others at S.F. Soviet Embassy December 12—try to make 'em quit
whaling—see you soon I hope—

Gary

Port Royal, Ky. 40058
April 9, 1974

Dear Gary,

Thank you for sending the books. Amidst my various hastes, I have been reading off and on with great pleasure in *Spring and Asura*.[†] The others I will get to in time.

I enclose two poems, written shortly after you were here. As you and Tanya were starting off for the airport, you remember, Den[†] and I were starting to see about two neighbors cut off by the backwater. That was when we had our meeting with the ducks. The poem ["To Gary Snyder"],[†] I'm afraid, falls far short of the experience. The other poem ["Poem for Den"][†] may be too much a sequel. Anyhow, I thought you might like to see them. Depending on how my feelings finally settle on them, I may try to publish them sometime, with your permission.

Our weather this spring has been generally bad—cold and wet, with enough unseasonably warm days to start the trees budding too early. The recent tornadoes missed us, but did severe damage all around us.

I have been keeping you and your place and things you told me about it a good deal in mind. I would like to pay you a visit, but it appears that obligations here are going to be very demanding for the foreseeable future. One of my neighbors[†]—my beloved friend and teacher for thirty years—just died; his boy, two months home from the service, is going to try to carry on the farm, and will need my help. But I do intend to come by your place *some day*.

Don't let my failure to return your visit stop you from coming to see us again as soon as possible. Bring your family.

Love,
Wendell

24.V.74 [*May 24, 1974*]

Wendell—

Glad you weren't blown away (or your barns) in the recent tornados
—and thanks for the poems.—I'm sure you'll be out this way sometime—of course no rush, so much work here, too (and mountain
weather—a sudden snowfall right now—big flakes)—

    best,
    Gary

[*November 5, 1974*]

Dear Wendell:

Nice poem in *Kayak* 36. "Its hardship is its possibility."†

    Gary

◇◇◇◇◇

EDITOR'S NOTE: Gary Snyder was going to be poet-in-residence at
the University of Cincinnati (1976), an appointment that Wendell
Berry had held in 1974. While in residence both poets delivered the
Elliston Lectures, which are available as digital recordings through
the University of Cincinnati Libraries. In months leading up to Snyder's position, the two writers considered the possibility of having
his family stay at Lanes Landing Farm.

2/17/1975 [*February 17, 1975*]†

Dear Gary,

I have read your new book [*Turtle Island*], for which I thank you. Your poems offer a sort of companionship that is of the greatest importance to me. I feel the differences of our origins and educations—and the similarity of our hopes and aims. That is *good*. Your phone call has delighted us, and set us to thinking. We will do our best to find you something. A house next door to ours is all we can see for sure right now, but it has *nothing* in the way of convenience. We'll look for something better. Our winter is wet, warm, muddy.

> Your friend,
> Wendell

17.III.75 [*March 17, 1975*]

Wendell—

For your agriculture book—†

[...] Liese Greensfelder (daughter of old comrade Bob G.)† is undergrad. in Agronomy at Davis—spent 2 years working on (running) a traditional farm in northern Norway. Super-bright. Made definite job at Cinc. next spring. What fun!

> edibly,
> Gary

GARY SNYDER [NEVADA CITY, CA]
TO WENDELL BERRY [PORT ROYAL, KY]

28 April 1975

Dear Wendell,

After some thought Masa† and I decided that it would be best for us to rent a place in Cinn. and be closer to the schools. We hope to drive down and visit you often. Thanks for thinking about it for us. Just got the book *People's Land*† from Rodale Press—it looks good.

Best,
Gary

GARY SNYDER [NEVADA CITY, CA]
TO WENDELL BERRY [PORT ROYAL, KY]

16. IX. 75 [September 16, 1975]

Dear Wendell—

A dear friend of this region will be in Kentucky in October, and he wonders if there's a chance he could come and spend a few days (2 or 3) with you watching and working? He's a solid grown man with 2 little ones, who built his own house here 4 years ago, and is slowly learning how to farm. He'd be by himself. You'd get on fine with him. *Richard Sisto*. I've told him to call you when he gets to Lexington, and you give him your answer. I know sometimes the last thing you (one) wants to see is another stranger's face—esp. when writing—so what's right for *you* (as I'm sure you will)—See you in spring. And thanks for *Old Jack*† Marvelous!

Gary

◇◇◇◇◇

EDITOR'S NOTE: This letter was written shortly after Gary Snyder's return home to Kitkitdizze, following his stay as poet-in-residence at University of Cincinnati. Snyder enclosed the poem "Berry Territory" with the letter.

GARY SNYDER [NEVADA CITY, CA]
TO WENDELL AND TANYA BERRY [PORT ROYAL, KY]

July 25, 1976

Dear Wendell and Tanya,

I'm sitting outside here by the fire by the pond listening to the sharp little slashing sound that bats make when they swoop down and hit the surface of the water after insects, along with the bull frog booming, the crickets in the background and the soft rustling of the fire, enough music for anybody. Makes me think of the night at your place when the lightning was flashing all night and the firebugs were ecstatically responding to that apparently thinking that the absolute principle in the sky was a firebug like themselves. We're getting back about on an even keel again, and I'm about where I was in February—on my book,† that is to say, everything else cleared off the deck and I'm ready to sit down and work with the actual text. I'm also finally ready to sit down and read the sheets that were sent me from the Sierra Club on your agriculture book.† When I get into that, I'll probably have some responses to make.

I was devastated to hear of the loss of the second foal and then the loss of the mare. Steve† wrote me about it, or actually I heard about it from his son Aaron who heard about it first; not much to say about it now except I think I know how it felt. Neighbor Richard Sisto got himself a pair of eight-year old white mares, one a bit larger than the other with blue eyes, they really show the red dust. They also take the saddle, they're not too big; so he and I rode back to his place from my place today with our two year old, used saddles. He's picked up some pretty good horse equipment, including a mower that works, a disc, a harrow and a plow. I guess he figures to sow oats this fall. He, as well as a number of others, are really looking forward to a little visit from you folks.

Gen[†] was much better—the asthma—as soon as he got here. Masa was tired, if not downright sick, took almost the whole three weeks gap of time before I got here, before she felt really strong again. I had a really nice drive with Kai,[†] just the two of us, west, going through the Nebraska sandhills where the cattle are fat and the windmills spinning, through the Black Hills, and visiting the Custer Battle Field—where the crickets sing in the grasses just like they did a couple of centuries ago. We went across the Snake River, Idaho, only a couple of days after the Teton Dam flood. There was mud all over the place and the radio was full of instruction on how to get relief. One of the banks kept making an announcement saying that all of your savings accounts and your records are safe.

Since being back here the main topic of attention is the extreme drought and the high fire hazard. A 1000-acre fire swept part of San Juan Ridge about five miles from here last month, burning about 20 houses to the ground. A lot of them were only semi-permanent shelters for itinerant yogis; but some of them were really fine little homesteads, with fruit trees, water tanks, pianos, Tibetan scrolls, potted plants, goat sheds, etc. There's a good spirit around here to get back in and rebuild, though. I'm in the process of hooking up a pumpjack and getting a little gas engine to run it to the force pump on my well, since the pond from which we usually irrigate our fruit trees and garden is far lower than ever before, and we can't siphon out of it to do the watering as we have in the past. The well is good, but simply operating it with a handpump is too much labor with all of that garden out there. The pumpjack unit is still obtainable, brand-new, for $200, and I guess the gas engine will run another $150; but then we'll be pumping 300–400 gallons an hour into the storage tank and if the well holds up that'll be just fine. Masa just woke up from a little nap and told me that she wrote a whole letter to you in her notebook when she first got back here in June, but then never wrote it into a letter and sent it to you, so this is really our first communication since we left Ohio—maybe she'll type it up and send it to you yet, I'm urging her to. It is so much work to communicate for her because English is a double-duty labor. New copy of *Kuksu*† is out; you should be getting a copy soon. I told Fred Martin† at New Directions that Rodale Press might be getting more interesting in the future and he answered back saying he hoped so because he'd dropped his subscription to *Organic Gardening* after he began getting the same information about the third time around. It would be exciting if you guys could do something with that.

Opening up my imagination to Mars is like a real extension of brain-habitat. The image of a whole planet of highly eroded rock, sand and boulder that may have once hosted a whole Gaia bio-sphere† now evaporated away—boggles something. Say hello to Steve [Sanfield] if he's anywhere nearby—I haven't heard from him for quite a while, though I did hear a rumor of being a deck hand on the river.

Love, from us both

Gary

◇◇◇◇◇

EDITOR'S NOTE: In this letter, Wendell Berry and Gary Snyder began an ongoing conversation about their participation in the Lindisfarne Association, an organization founded by cultural historian William Irwin Thompson in 1972. The group began as an association of artists, scientists, scholars, and contemplatives committed to exploring new ways for the humanities to develop within contexts of social sciences and economics. They started meeting in Southampton, New York, in 1973; then moved to Manhattan in 1976; and then to Crestone, Colorado, in 1979. In 2009, the association disbanded; however, some of the fellows still meet on an occasional basis.

At the Lindisfarne Annual Summer Conference (1976), Berry read the chapter, "The Body and the Earth," from *The Unsettling of America* (1977). The conference theme was "A Light Governance for America: The Cultures and Strategies of Decentralization." A digital recording of the talk is available through the Schumacher Center for a New Economics.

WENDELL BERRY [PORT ROYAL, KY]
TO GARY SNYDER [NEVADA CITY, CA]

September 1, 1976

Dear Gary,

I've let your letter go much too long. We were delighted to have it and to have the poems. To have a poem from you[†] about our place is a link that means a lot to us.

We hope Masa will send her letter. We understand the work she must put into English and, as Tanya says, we will be glad to work at it too.

My delay in answering has been caused by work. In addition to work on the place, I spent the summer on a 68 page chapter in my farming book[†] that came nearer to an ordeal than anything I've written. I think that was because it was tight up against so much of my own bewilderment from beginning to end. I have a draft of it now, and have asked Jon Beckmann[†] to send you a copy.

But you mustn't let this book of mine become a burden to you. Read it only as you would like to, for interest, and tell me nothing about it that you don't *want* to tell me.

Two days after I finished my chapter, I went to the meeting at Lindisfarne. I had a good time there and was moved and instructed. They are part of the puzzle we're trying to put together. Your friend Sim Van der Ryn[†] was there, and was for me one of the main contributors. I admire and like him.

Sim and I talked of the possibility that I might come to California to talk about farming—maybe in Feb., maybe later. Anyhow, it's getting plainer that I've *got* to make another errand to California. I want to *see* what you're doing, what Sim is doing, what Bob Callahan† is doing, maybe even visit with Stewart [Brand] if we can make any friendliness between us† in the meantime. The only practical considerations—beyond arranging to be gone—are when and how to get enough money so Tanya and I both can come.

Teaching has started again at the University† and work has begun coming from that direction—to wrench my mind around. And the tobacco harvest is on; I'll be helping my neighbors in that in the afternoons when I'm home. Then fall farm work, finishing my stone wall, building fence, etc. And I hope to finish my book [*The Unsettling of America*] by Christmas.

So the work is crowding in as usual, and I'll have to make this shorter than I would like. What I'd like would be to give you a digest of all I've *thought* of telling you since you left. But we'll sit down together again before too long, and then I will.

If you see Steve [Sanfield], tell him hello. He gave us some noble help while he was here. I hope he is working out his problems there. And tell Richard Sisto I'll answer his letters as soon as I can—though I have no way to help him locate land in the area he plans to move to.

A few drops of rain are hitting the roof. We would be glad to have a lot of them.

Our love to you, Masa, and the boys.

Wendell

25. XI [*November 25, 1976*]

Dear Wendell—

Hasty note on the book MS [of *The Unsettling of America*]—I've been reading—strong, *moral* work—but I think the ch. on energy is weak. It needs, simply, a better use of terms, and, I think there are some minor confusions.

-- "energy" and "power"

You don't get "energy" from machines (you run machines w/ energy) you get "power." *All* energy is either solar (=fusion) or gravity or electromagnetic (=gravity?)

Ok. If you had time it would clarify it for you to read quickly Odum's[†] *Environment, Power and Society* and the Scientific American *Energy* book.[†] Or something else, useful on basics.

I'll try and get into the chapter in more detail and write you again, but I wanted to send this off quick.

Sacramento people were very pleased to hear you speak—reports back—Sim [Van der Ryn] says the Berkeley gathering had its difficulties—

I'm glad I only get to Sacramento about 2 days a month—they're too frantic ...

i.e. what do you do about folks whose heart is in the right place —good ideas etc. —but who on one level are just *speeding* anyhow and they won't get their hands on it (anything). Brown's[†] good, he does *listen*. I hope he listened to you.

Looks like maybe you and I will read poesy *together*[†] in SF when you come out. OK?

yrs v sinc
Gary

[*December 8, 1976*]

Wendell—

Just wrote this for Sierra Club—they wanted something now—tho haven't read final chapter yet. If you don't like it just ask Jon Beckmann not to use it. I sure do like the way the book's going.

Gary

[PS] The chapter explicating the return of Odysseus is an extraordinary meeting of literary and social insight—

For W.B.'s *Unsettling of America*†

This book [is] about *culture* in the deep, ripe sense: a nurturing habitat. Our habitat is the planet in all its local specifics. This has meant, for most people, for centuries, "the farm." The farm not only grows food, it nourishes human character, is a challenge and a teacher, a source of insight and values. With unwavering focus, Wendell Berry shows what we lost of our real human American potential when we lost our commitment to living well, in place, on the land. An infinitely greedy sovereign is afoot in the universe, staking his claims. What's left, then, is the future—a future of declining agri-business and a necessary return to good farming. Wendell knows from his own life that this work—though not easy—need not dismay us: in the right spirit, it is mankind's "right livelihood"— and delight. The preserver of abundance is excellence.

Gary Snyder

6.XII.76

December 11, 1976

Dear Gary,

Thanks for the help—both kinds.

I think the language of that energy chapter can be changed fairly readily so it doesn't imply that the energy comes *from* the machines. My intended distinction is that between energy produced (made available) *by* machines and that produced *by* plants. I will attempt to be corrected by your criticism, and I will read some in Odum.

Your sentences for Sierra relieve me a good deal: you see what I'm trying to mean. Sometimes this book seems such a going off in all directions that even *I* can't see what I'm trying to mean. I'm getting to the end now of a chapter trying to say how the land grant college idea has been perverted. After that, a chapter on better possibilities. And then, I pray, the end.

I'm done with the fall semester teaching—a bust. I gave nearly ⅓ incompletes. That is to say, I'm afraid, that the impossibility of teaching has begun: there is nothing in or behind many students to hold them up against a discipline.

Tuesday we kill hogs, if the weather's right.

Wendell

12/23/76 [December 23, 1976]

Dear Gary,

We hope Masa's trip will please her—all the way there and back.

We'll get the schedule settled a little later. There's a chance I may read in Boise on the way out or on the way home. I'll let you know as soon as I know.

We *are* going to visit you, though, and long enough to talk and look around responsibly. I will want to see as much as time allows of what you will want to show me. I assume that will allow some insight into what is working there in your community. And I would love to read for your neighbors at the grade school. But will hope too not to be *crowded* by a schedule.

I just finished the next-to-last chapter and am relieved. It was rough.

I too am happy about the reading.

Wendell

◇◇◇◇◇

EDITOR'S NOTE: Wendell Berry sent Gary Snyder a copy of a letter addressed to David Ignatow, concerning the Statement on the Editorial Policy of *The American Poetry Review*. Berry's letter was addressed to Ignatow, with copies to Adrienne Rich, June Jordan, Stephen Berg, and others. He had declined signing the statement of policy because he found it to be offensive to the life and nature of poetry. The policy, among other things, addressed issues of affirmative action, namely, that the editors were using demographic statistics on race and gender to make decisions on whose work should or should not be published in the magazine.

In a postscript to the letter, Berry wrote the following note:

Dear Gary—

This is to David Ignatow, one of the signers or sponsors of the statement, which I suppose you have seen. If you have, what do you think of it?

W.

P.S. 5° and falling here at 8:00 p.m. We're having to cut a lot of wood this winter.

21. I. 40077 [*January 21, 1977*]†

Dear Wendell—

It must be very difficult to keep things together and working in the cold—I read the Ohio River might freeze across.† I hope your pipes are well wrapped.

Sierra Club sent chapter 8 and additions to introduction.

"*organization*" vs. "*order*" a fine discrimination! Very rich insight, throws light on civilization and its discontents.

About *APR* [*American Poetry Review*]. I appreciate your position but I also think if it's a national, cosmopolitan periodical (funded as such) it *should* undertake "affirmative action." From the last 15 years' experience we know affirmative action works—does bring out new things, new people, of quality. In a cosmopolitan society such as U.S. "quality" is a poor place to argue from too—my experience on the California Arts Council† has taught me "quality" is a smoke screen for all sorts of skullduggery but also, there is no one standard of quality for (for example) poetry, I believe. The Chicanos and the Indians are often doing something *else*. Not to be judged by European style (or avant-garde, or whatever) standards. Best route would be several editors—one for each tradition. I'm comfortable with such a device—American culture needn't be all the same cloth; but it could have several places the different streams converge. *APR could* have served such a function. So far, nothing does.

The drouth here is getting scary. Next summer may be a major agricultural disaster† for California. My little pond is the only free water in some miles—it has brought in 30-40 thirsty deer per 2-3 days. *Nine* bucks drink from here over any 2-3 day period—from a 5/4 point to spikes. I'm looking at 2 of them thru the window right now.

Have been delving into Tamil poetry—Ramanujan's translations†

and George Hart's[†] study— (Masa is in Tamil country) —what an
incredible tradition! I'll tell you about it when I see you.

Greetings to Tanya—

Gary

◇◇◇◇◇

EDITOR'S NOTE: This letter was written after Wendell and Tanya
Berry returned to Lanes Landing Farm following their first visit
to Kitkitdizze. During that visit, Snyder and Berry read poetry
together for the first time at the San Francisco Museum of Modern Art. A promotional broadside for the event was designed by Jack
Shoemaker and a recording is archived at The Poetry Center, San
Francisco State University. At this event, Berry told the backstory
of friendship behind the poem "To Gary Snyder," while Snyder did
the same with "Berry Territory." Wendell Berry's visit inspired his
essay titled "Life on (and off) Schedule," later published in *Organic
Gardening*, that told about his visit to San Juan Ridge.

WENDELL BERRY [PORT ROYAL, KY]
TO GARY SNYDER [NEVADA CITY, CA]

3/20/77 [*March 20, 1977*]

Dear Gary,

I enclose a first draft of an article[†] intended for *Organic Gardening*. It ends, as you'll see, with a brief sketch of our visit to San Juan
Ridge. Would you mind to look at it to see that it's free of errors? I
would be grateful for any suggestions or corrections.

It's clear from what I wrote, I hope, how much I was pleased and
moved by what I saw there. I'm only sorry we couldn't stay longer,
and will hope to come back again before too long. We are neighbors—*distant* neighbors.

The work of the new season has begun here. The other afternoon Tanya and I planted peas, onions, beets, chard, carrots,

spinach, lettuce, parsnips, salsify, radishes.

My love to you all.

Wendell

[PS] My apologies to Kai whose name I've been spelling wrong in my head (and on paper) for a while now! Love to you all. —Tanya

GARY SNYDER [NEVADA CITY, CA]
TO WENDELL BERRY [PORT ROYAL, KY]

27. III [*March 27, 1977*]

Wendell and Tanya—

What a fine little piece you wrote. Interesting to see thru other eyes. No additions or suggestions. We were pleased you could be here however short the time—speaking of distant neighbors, the next farm (another hop) is our group of friends on Suwa-no-se Island in the East China Sea. We'll go there someday.

Do you suppose I cd submit a short prose piece to *Organic Gardening* from time to time? I feel the need of some sort of place to appear that is neither *Atlantic* or *Kuksu*—

Gary

[PS] I hope J. Brown sees your comment on the Calif. drouth [in *Organic Gardening*].

WENDELL BERRY [PORT ROYAL, KY]
TO GARY SNYDER [NEVADA CITY, CA]

4/21/77 [*April 21, 1977*]

Dear Gary,

Thanks much for your note. I'm glad you liked the little essay. They are evidently going to use it.

Jerry Goldstein† says you should try something for *OGF* [*Organic Gardening and Farming*] by all means. Do you want suggestions as to possible subjects, he asks, or do you want to suggest your own. I assume the latter.

I hope you will send some things. They ought to be short. I've been trying to keep mine under 2000 words, and finding that a form that is both demanding and pleasant. Also I think the audience needs to be kept in mind—a diversity of kinds of people, inclined to listen to what people like ourselves have to say, but who are perhaps not well or widely read. My own rule has been to be as *plain* as possible without condescending or misrepresenting what I have to say. As you see, I'm interested in this as a writer. What it offers to me—as it may to you—is a chance to speak to people outside the "literary" audience.

You might want to communicate directly with Jerry. [...]

Let me hear what happens.

Work is going along here. We send our love to you all.

Wendell

◇◇◇◇◇

EDITOR'S NOTE: In 1977, Wendell Berry published *Three Memorial Poems* with Jack Shoemaker at Sand Dollar Books. Berry was pleased to find Gary Snyder's affirming comment printed on the book jacket, which began by echoing a line from Berry's poem "Rising" and then continued as follows:

Ancient knowledge seeking
its new mind[s].

> —poems that go off the
> edge of the world to visit the dead:
> our teachers still.
> Brave poems—they send me back to my own life.
> refreshed; work joyfully in impermanence!

Gary Snyder
4.V.77

7/12/77 [*July 12, 1977*]

Dear Gary,

Perhaps enough has passed between us by now that you will know, beyond my awkward effort to tell you, the depth of my thanks for your several recent kindnesses. Best of all was the surprise and happiness of finding your words on the back cover of the *Three Memorial Poems.*

But I hurry to say that I'm grateful to you for much more than your generosity to my writing. Your words, everywhere I find them, give me the sense of being spoken not just to, but *for*. What a relief! This is happening, I think, because our lives have forced us out of the *career* of poetry. To use the terms of your interview,† after you give up poetry, then poems become ways of speaking to and for other people, not acquisitions, like money, to get something with. In what you say I don't hear you speaking as a poet, but as a friend and fellow worker. And so you speak for me, and relieve me of the confining, isolating necessity to "speak for myself."

That doesn't do justice to what I *wanted* to say. The experience of reading your interview in the *East West Journal* (or the first two installments, which are all I've seen so far) suggested more powerfully than it has been suggested to me before that thought might proceed—instead of by argument, dialectic—by people speaking for, clarifying, confirming one another's experience. The model would be people telling each other stories of their *common* experience, something I've seen a lot among people who've known each other a long time. Argument is necessary, I guess, to provide correction, to keep the exchanges of talk from becoming false or foolish. We've paid little attention or honor to the sort of common, communal, community talk that I mean (I need a better term). But community surely depends on it. Argument is a disastrous substitute. So is gossip, carrying "news."

Several years ago I wrote an essay disapproving† among other things, the vogue of interviews with poets. I'm glad to make an exception of this one of yours. It's first rate—sound, settled, authoritative, well-spoken. I would give a good deal to be able to carry on some of the conversations with you that it suggests. Some day.

Steve [Sanfield] has been here and gone. It was good to be with him. We pump each other up, Steve and I do. He thinks I know the answers to his problems, which I don't. I think he has a lot of information, hard for me to come by, about Buddhism, Judaism, Indians, etc., which he does.

Our love to you all, and to your work.

Wendell

◇◇◇◇

EDITOR'S NOTE: Gary Snyder had returned from a Poetry Teaching Symposium sponsored by the Centrum Foundation at Fort Worden State Park in Port Townsend, Washington. Teaching poets included Snyder, Olga Broumas, Carolyn Kizer, William Pitt Root, Robert Hedin, Philip Whalen, Tree Swenson, and Sam Hamill. After discussing some writers and scholars committed to indigenous studies and anthropology, Snyder's letter initiated an ongoing conversation about re-inhabiting place, in this case, through the recovery of neolithic principles found in China. Berry extended the scope of this dialogue by considering the thought of agrarian teachers, the Bible, and Amish communities.

GARY SNYDER [NEVADA CITY, CA]
TO WENDELL BERRY [PORT ROYAL, KY]

November 3, 1977

Dear Wendell,

Belated response to last summer's letter from you. We had just returned from a couple of weeks in Washington state, doing a little poetry teaching at Fort Worden State Park in Port Townsend, and taking the boys on their first overnight backpack trip; this one in the Olympics. Coming home, we drove over Snoqualmie Pass and stayed a night with a man named Bill Weiss, who runs a commercial apple orchard in the arid upper Columbia River country; irrigation from the Grand Coulee;[†] living in the house that his grandfather built. Long hairy farmer-house scholar. Then drove south along the east side lava-flows and pine forests of the Cascades crossing the Columbia, to Madras, Oregon; where we spent a night visiting with Jarold Ramsey,[†] who is a poet and who teaches English in the winters at Rochester University, New York; and who in the summers works the family ranch in eastern Oregon. At Jarold Ramsey's we were joined by William Stafford[†] and Dell Hymes. You know Stafford, but perhaps not Hymes. Hymes is an old Oregonian, fellow-student of mine at Reed, now Dean of the School of Education at the University of Pennsylvania. His real field is American Indian linguistics, and the techniques and stylistics of oral literature. He and his wife are working on Sahaptin grammar for use in the schools on the Warm Springs Indian Reservation.[†]

And on south home. Working all fall on my book on Asia and nature,[†] I have been thinking about your book *Clearing*, and the finished edition of *The Unsettling of America*.

I think your points are clear and well-taken. The question I ask myself is, what next? My ignorance of the dynamics of economics troubles my sleep. I must keep working on that. Because, (as my study of China is showing more and more) the best intentions in the world will not stop the inertia of a heavy civilization that is rolling on its way. As poets, our politics mostly stand back from that flow of topical events; and the place we do our real work is in the unconscious, or myth-consciousness of the culture; a place where people decide (without knowing it) to change their values. Certainly that's the value of your work; in spite of the intensely local and personal focus of it, you keep the poems above the level that would cause people to simply say, "Hell, that's not my life, those aren't my problems." Or "Well, we can't all go live on the farm." Just as we hear, "You can't all go live in the Sierra Nevada." Meanwhile, week after week, we watch Jerry Brown struggle with responding to what seems to be the main questions that come at him from all sides, and they mostly have to do with business and employment. The question of growth has become in the last year a public debate, and a major issue in our own county. Our circle of friends helped spark that; but it actually has come about through the intense dynamics of the scene. Is there a device that will somehow cause the farmer to get a better break? Like those oldtime radical farmers in the midwest keep writing about. "Well, what the hell is parity anyway?" (I don't know). What you and I are really talking about, is reviving the value system and integrity and authenticity that belongs to the neolithic. The neolithic mind-set has been struggling to retain itself—in terms of what is called "folk-culture"—against the taxing powers of governments ever since.

At any rate the Chinese emperor, in spring went out with his top ministers and ceremoniously plowed some furrows. In the fall he harvested what had been grown there, himself, and offered it as his own personal sacrifice at the top of the earth-altar, and the altar to heaven. In the Chinese legal system, there were no executions in spring, because that would run counter to the natural energy of growing life. Capital punishment was carried out in the fall when everything else was ready to die. Such elegant parallels between nature and government run throughout the Chinese system; but it is in fact in turn a formalization of the Chinese neolithic.

I am just thinking out loud. I'll send you some pages from my work in progress, in a few months, that you may enjoy reading and have some comments. Around the fourth of March, I will be done with a three-week residency at Washington University in St. Louis. I have a reading to give at Bowling Green, Kentucky on the 7th. If it works out, I'd like to come over and visit your way the 5th and 6th. Let me know how this might be.

Steve Sanfield went up to Washington with us. I haven't seen much of him since we came back—right now he is doing an artist-in-the-schools thing, storytelling to children; with a California Arts Council grant. I certainly appreciated your kind words about the *East-West* interview (and Steve told me how you two laughed over all those wimpy ads). Whatever it is, let's keep doing it.

Faithfully, and to Tanya

Gary

GS: egb†

Enclosure: my last best poem—†

PS just gave a talk explicating and weaving around your poem *A Vision* in Michigan (just back. 9.XI)

WENDELL BERRY [PORT ROYAL, KY]
TO GARY SNYDER [NEVADA CITY, CA]

Port Royal, Ky.
January 14, 1978

Dear Gary,

About 5" of snow on the ground here. The last few nights it has only been down to about 20°, but we have had several nights when it went below zero.

I sure like your poem about the coons ["True Night"]. I like its immediacy, its news that you are alive there in your own life, its humor too. It's the immediacy that I feel always on the verge of losing in my own work as I get lured into tasks of principle and argument. And the closer I come to losing it, the more I value it. There's nothing without it, not even consciousness. I do see that, in the poem, you stand for us all—naked in the dark with your stick —but the universality comes as part of the shock of the immediate.

Well, good luck to you and the coons both!

I think you're right about the neolithic. We may have had a few chances since to recover that integrity and authenticity on somewhat different terms, but each time we blundered—maybe, each time, by failing to see which way technological innovation would take us, hence *never* limiting that. And so we must go to the neolithic for examples. Of course, innovation was slow then and they didn't have to deal with it. For dealing with it we have to consider the Amish, not so much for anything they have achieved but for their uncanny instinct about limits, about the connection between the spirit and tools. Where did they get it? I wish I understood. I'm sure the Bible can get you to where the Amish are, but why didn't it get the rest of us there? There's something else to be accounted for. Maybe some strand of neolithic conservation going way back.

I'm reading Steve [Sanfield's] copy of *Ishi*.[†] The description of the values and character of the California tribes (pp. 22-23) sounds like Lao Tzu.[†] It also sounds something like a minor strand of my own provincial inheritance that I reckon has become dominant in my own consciousness. Awful to consider what we got in light of what we want. It's why some of us, as Maury Telleen[†] says, will have to accept the duty of becoming contrary old son-of-a-bitches.

The main thing I have done in the way of news since I last wrote was to quit the university—as of Dec. 31. It's a relief. I get disillusioned at a pace just short of geological, but I finally saw undeniably that, aside from my "reputation," the university had no use for me, and that, aside from the library and two or three people, I had no use for it. It and I are going in perfectly opposite directions —which means we're bound to meet again, doesn't it?

So now I'm working "full time" for Rodale Press[†]—which I hope will leave me time for farming and at least some of my own writing. One thing this will do is make it possible for me to travel to see some of the survivals of tribal and peasant farming. Next summer I hope to spend 2-3 weeks in Peru with Stephen Brush,[†] looking at the little Andean farms he has studied and written about. I also hope to see the little horse-powered farms in Belgium, and, if possible, something of the Hopi farming.

Speaking of Rodale Press, I've been asked to tell you that they'd like very much to have you send something for *Organic Gardening*— prose or poetry. I don't know how certain publication is, but they seem eager to have something from you.

Steve [Sanfield] sent some haikus[†] about the rain, which I thought—both poems and rain—were very good. When you see that valuable man, tell him to cheer up, and tell him I intend to write him soon.

Larry Korn[†] sent me a Xerox copy of your essay on the Banyan Ashram.[†] I read it in the book when it came out, but I read it again on Larry's Xerox. I liked it both times. Wonderful passage about fishing.

March 5 and 6 are your days. I've marked them on the calendar. We'll be looking forward to it.

Tell Masa and the boys we think of them.

Your friend,
Wendell

◇◇◇◇◇

EDITOR'S NOTE: Gary Snyder wrote this letter after visiting Wendell and Tanya Berry at Lanes Landing Farm between a schedule of readings and teaching engagements in Missouri, Kentucky, and Texas.

GARY SNYDER [NEVADA CITY, CA]
TO WENDELL BERRY [PORT ROYAL, KY]

March 28, 1978

Dear Wendell, and Tanya!

Out of the Greyhound station, and southwestward across Kentucky, the snow got thinner till by Bowling Green had totally disappeared.

Everything went smoothly and the Bowling Green people were extremely receptive to the lecture based on the poem. Next day in El Paso, hot, getting informed on what's happening in Chicano literature by the sharp young New Mexico poet Leroy Quintana.† Back home safe, finally, all's well, and Masa went off to San Francisco to dance with her company, while I spent time with the boys. Driving back now myself from San Francisco, Arts Council business, and a big benefit reading† that Michael McClure, Lewis McAdams, Dale Pendell, Joanna McClure, and I did to raise money for the Greenpeace Foundation. Full house; we raised a lot of money. Saw McClure's brand new play, "Minnie Mouse and the Tap-Dancing Buddha."† Marvelously funny. Also, some delightful ways of presenting sophisticated Buddhist conceptions in the guise of comic operetta.

I hope the snow is off the ground at your place, and you are able to get your garden started. Our fruit trees are beginning to flower now, and I have six new ones in the ground and a large new fenced area for gardening. Oak leaves, as the Maidu† say, "the size of a squirrel's ear." Thank you for the good visit, and I regret that the rush and the snow at the end caused you extra trouble. We look forward to a visit from you and Tanya here. Masa sends her love, and Kai and Gen say hello to Den.

Yours,

Gary

GS: egb

WENDELL BERRY [PORT ROYAL, KY]
TO GARY SNYDER [NEVADA CITY, CA]

4/22/78 (Saturday) [*April 22, 1978*]

Dear Gary and Masa,

Work was delayed so long by the late winter that when spring finally did come it seemed that *everything* had to be done at the same time. We got a lot done by going pretty hard and fast until Tuesday when the weather turned wet. We needed the rain badly, and so the consequent leisure was free-minded and good.

When I've had time I've been reading and making notes in preparation for my trip to Peru. The excitement of that is slowly growing—the thought of seeing an *ancient* American agriculture!

Our early garden is mostly up. We have been eating fresh rhubarb; ought to have asparagus soon.

[...] Living at peace is a difficult, deceptive concept. Same for not resisting evil. You can struggle, embattle yourself, resist evil until you become evil—as anti-communism becomes totalitarian. I have no doubt of that. But I don't feel the least bit of an inclination to lie down and be a rug, either, and I now begin to ask myself if I can live at peace only by being reconciled to battle. (Stonewall Jackson, a kind of ferocious saint, said he felt "as safe in battle [as] in bed" —is that *satori*?)[†]

I am, I believe, a "non-violent" fighter. But I am a fighter. And I see with considerable sorrow that I am not going to get done fighting and live at peace in anything like the simple way I once thought I would. So how to keep from becoming evil?

Maybe the answer is to fight always *for* what you particularly love, not for abstractions and not *against* anything: don't fight against even the devil, and don't fight "to save the world."

You're in the same fix. How do you think about these things? I'd really like to know.

I send a poem.[†] Love to you all.

Wendell

May 9, 1978

Dear Gary,

I enclose a translation† of some lines (1584) of [Pierre de] Ronsard that I thought might interest you. I have an idea that these pockets of ecological sense and feeling are to be found in a good many places in western poetry. Our reading has just become too academic and specialized to keep us aware of them. The poem begins with an invective or curse that is maybe of equal interest, but I have never been able to make it sound authentic in English. These lines, after several years, may be getting at least readable.

So far, we have had a wet, cold, slow spring.

Our love to you all,
Wendell

August 1, 1978

Dear Wendell—

How was the trip to Peru? I still owe you a response to a letter earlier this spring, on the question of bad land use, the nature of evil,† and how one fights evil. I don't have a clearcut answer to all that, but I would say that I try to reserve the term "evil" for the very highest quality of bad; not for just plain out stupidity. Most of the negative things that happen in the world are a function of ignorance, stupidity, narrow views, simple-minded egotism. Evil is probably a by-product of intelligent, complicated-minded egotism. What I think you are dealing with, near your own place, is not high-quality genuine evil, but the lower quality stuff. In which case, I would say use any honorable tactics that come your way in opposing and fighting such things, with no fear of becoming stained by "evil" because that's not really what you're up against. And of course true warriors have a code: never to draw a sword until all other possible avenues of resolution of conflict have been explored, and upon using a sword to use it with full effectiveness, but no more. At least that's the Japanese teaching. As for whether there really is, or is not, a substantial metaphysical evil in the universe, my own hunch and received teachings have been that even the scariest and worst looking perversions or possibilities—satanic and luciferian—are ultimately enclosed within the totality of the organic process, and can be both understood and overcome.

Thank you for the Ronsard translation. We had a final editorial meeting† on the *Journal for the Protection of All Beings* yesterday in San Francisco; I'm dictating this while driving back home right now. David Meltzer, Lawrence Ferlinghetti, Michael McClure and myself. Everyone was delighted with the poem instantly, and we are very grateful to you for it. It adds, as Michael said, a touch of class to the somewhat heavy going of a lot of biological-oriented environmental writing. The issue is going to include an essay on Buddhist theories of enlightenment for plants and trees,† some of my own Asia book workings,† a marvelous poem by Peter Blue Cloud,† Peter Warshall's bird watching journals in the Farallone Islands,† and a lot of really interesting other things.

Peter Barry Chowka mentioned in his last letter that you were too busy to be interviewed by him. I certainly can understand that, but let me say, if you ever feel like being interviewed, that he is the best person I've ever worked with—totally unobtrusive, intelligent, sympathetic, extremely careful and polite, and a person I ended up feeling to be a new friend.

Masa is doing dance with her teacher in North Carolina; Steve Sanfield and Dale Pendell are down in New Mexico teaching some poetry seminars at Jemez Hot Springs Zen Center (a branch of Sasaki-roshi's Los Angeles based rinzai-zen school). I'm about to go for six days into Yosemite high country backpacking with some comrades, and looking forward to taking the boys out on another backpacking trip this month and otherwise be here at the place working away. Fencing for horses project gave way to building a solar hot water operated laundry house and shower house out back that seems to be called for with increasingly big boys and increasingly large laundries to do. So I don't see an immediate prospect of taking up Den's offer of coming out and showing us how to use a team. Hello to Den and to Tanya and to you. Keep me up.

Fraternally,

Gary

GS:egb

WENDELL BERRY [PORT ROYAL, KY]
TO GARY SNYDER [NEVADA CITY, CA]

August 7, 1978

Dear Gary,

It looks like the hit-or-miss way I conduct the writing part of my life in the summer time has caused a bad mixup. When I sent that Ronsard translation to you I didn't mean to be submitting it to the *Journal*—and, obviously, I should have said so. The trouble is that I did submit it at about the same time to *Hudson Review*, which accepted it, and I think will publish it next summer.

I will do whatever I can to make this right.

Since I assume your issue will be out before the poem can possibly appear in *Hudson*, I will phone *Hudson* today to see if by any chance they will agree to just let the poem appear both places.†

In case that fails, I'm enclosing a number of poems from which maybe you can choose something to take the place of the translation. I'll call before I mail this.

Several days ago I sent an account of my Peru trip† to Maury

34

Telleen with a stamped envelope addressed to you. I assume he'll send it on when he has read it—if he hasn't already. No need for you to return it. It needs cutting, I think, and will no doubt be changed in other ways, but I thought you might like to see it in first draft for sake of its information.

Mary was home for the summer but has now returned to Lexington to get settled and find a job before classes start. Den and I are trying to build some fence, but are being interfered with by wet weather.

The colts I was starting when you were here are broke now, and one has been returned home. I'll keep the other until my wood is in and the other fall work is done. Now I have two young ones of my own that Den and I will soon start breaking.

Thank you for your note about evil. I see it, I think, pretty much your way. If you *don't* see how much badness comes from stupidity, ignorance, confusion, etc.—if you don't see how much badness is done by good, likeable people; if you don't love, or don't know you love, people whose actions you deplore—then I guess you go too far into outrage, acquire diseased motives, quit having any fun, and get bad yourself.

What I'm beginning to see as the highgrade badness that is evil is the assumption that there is no value or order that precedes or outranks the human—that there is no mystery, no occasion for awe or deference. In practice, this seems to manifest itself in the willingness to decide for other people, usually by way of technological feats: depletions of nature, production of lethal substances such as atomic wastes, genetic and reproductive "engineering," etc. It is technological despotism.

Like you, I assume that in the long run nature includes what is done to it as well as what it does. I'm sure that human disorder and the extinction of humanity will be caught up in larger cycles and directed to more distant ends. At the same time, I'm biased in favor of the human species and of human good, and what seems to

me a technological power and even willingness to change the definition of both so troubles and frightens me that evil seems the only
word that will serve.

Will you be coming this way any time soon?

It was good to have your news. I was sorry to miss hearing you
at Lindisfarne.

Your friend,
Wendell

P.S. 8/8/78— I called David Meltzer and he very graciously agreed to
cancel publication of the poem, and asked me to send other work,
which I will do today. I'm sorry for all this. Obviously, if I had sent
other poems to you for the *Journal*, as I intended but neglected to
do, everything would have been ok.

GARY SNYDER [NEVADA CITY, CA]
TO WENDELL BERRY [PORT ROYAL, KY]

January 5, 1979

Dear Wendell,

The last time I saw you you were going out the door, so to speak,
for Peru. Thanks for sending me a copy of your account of that
trip. Very interesting—one gets the sense that agriculture has been
pushed there beyond its reasonable limits; that people are living
in places where human habitat shouldn't be pushed so hard. Like
potatoes as a crop have allowed the Sherpa tribe of Nepal to grow in
population, and in doing so they are now faced with severe firewood
shortages. A marginal question perhaps; but to one point: Whatever
it is that unleashes a growth dynamic, leads to a dead end. Peruvian
mountain agriculture a dead end? I don't know.

I had a good three week tour this fall; New Hampshire and
the Midwest; spent a weekend with John Todd and part of a day
with Leander Poisson.† Leander Poisson is in New Hampshire,

and designing very interesting solar house, solar greenhouse-type cover for outside intensive garden beds; a brilliant semi-architect man who is thinking along lines similar to New Alchemy,† but disdains such high-tech. John Todd seems to be turning away from the higher tech himself. I gave a reading in the big greenhouse while I was there. At New Alchemy they seemed to divide up the work though—that is, John and Nancy don't seem to be getting their hands in the dirt, there was the very pleasant woman from Germany who really does all the gardening. Hilda.

Our step forward, in regard to farming, this fall was the excavation of a much larger pond. It is three or four times larger than it was, and has a pipe in it now that will run out to grade with a valve. It hasn't filled up yet, but we can expect that it will be full before too much longer because certainly rains are coming. Once full it will provide enough water to grow a sizable vegetable garden, and enlarge the number of fruit and nut trees planted around our place. It might even enable us to do some late spring pasture irrigation, which I think would make a big difference in the economics of keeping a couple horses. The washhouse is almost finished too, with its solar collector and fifty gallon water storage tank. It's designed for taking showers, and doing laundry. A separate building. The temperature in winter is adequate for laundry, but a little cool for showers right now. We apparently burned the motor out on a second-hand washing machine the second time we tried it, with a generator I got, which leads me to think that I must study the relationship of generators to electric motors more carefully. Since other neighbors have managed to do their laundry with generators, I think we'll be able to do it too.

Also this fall saw an intensification of Zen practice here—we have been having *sesshins* three times in the winter and three times in the summer the last few years around. A *sesshin* means for us a five day or seven day period when there's two or three hours of meditation every night and an hour and a half or two hours of very early morning meditation before the children have to be aroused. In October Robert Aitken,† a Zen master from Hawaii, came and sat with us and gave instruction in *koans*,† which was really a quantum leap. Meditating together with the people that you work together with is, if anything, as good as dancing and drinking with them.

Your question about right occupation: right occupation is one of the eight things on the noble eightfold path, along with right meditation, right trance, right views, right effort, etc. I don't seem to have the literature here to research out the history of it all, but I do know from memory that in early Buddhism right occupation was clearly thought to be any order of occupation which was not exploitative of other human beings, did not lead to violence, did not take life. Thus, clearly proscribed livelihoods included being a soldier, dealing in weapons, and the like. Also, clearly spoken against was fortune telling, and astrology. Later Buddhism softened its view, and one curious and somewhat negative by-product of the ideas about occupation resulted in butchers and leather workers becoming low class (almost outcast) ultimately in Japan. At any rate, right occupation in Buddhist cultures has meant essentially what you and I would think it ought to mean. I believe at one time the Buddhists went so far as to condemn money lending as well. Amongst my neighbors, questions of right livelihood come into peoples' minds when they ask themselves about whether or not growing dope, or dabbling a little in real estate are ok employments. It's hard to come to answers when it gets that close to home.

I did some further good work on the Asia book over the summer and into early fall; but then going out to earn money and catching up after that has kept me from any further writing for two months. Perhaps the next month and a half will get me through another couple chapters. I have probably only another hundred pages to go, and I'll be done with China. I'm planning to leave it at that; and bring the book out as an outline of the environmental history of China. Perhaps some future date—after the boys are older and more fruit trees are in the ground—I'll go on and try to do something with

Japan and with the modern Hokkaido;† but the realization of how time-consuming this project has been led me to put it aside for a while so that other priorities would get a chance. One charming thing—Masa and I are going together to Alaska† in the first week in February for several days to try a poetry reading with Indian dance combination. Some of the Indian dances she does are derived from folkdance, bird-hunting for example, and may well be of interest and delight to the Eskimo audience in Barrow.

My next truly realistic task around here is to put in some kind of a place to work on engines and motors, with a proper set of tools. I don't see how you can live in the country much longer (with the price of mechanics) without some kind of a shop, a machine shop. That's what I call biting the bullet; I have always been a woodworker rather than a metal worker myself.

I'll be in Nashville and Louisiana sometime in February and if dates work out at all I'll hope to swing your way for a day or so. Now that I have my very own credit card, I can rent me a car and not trouble you with transportation to and from the airport. Hello to Den, Mary, Tanya, and all the other sentient beings that receive nurture within your fences.

Your friend,
Gary
GS: egb

Port Royal, Ky. 40058
January 24, 1979

Dear Gary,

If you can get close enough to us for a visit, please come. Remember that transporting you to and from the airport can never be worse than half bad, for we get to talk with you for half the trip.

When T. [Tanya] and I both go along, we talk to each other the other half, which makes it not bad at all. So come ahead, anyhow, with a free heart.

I'm glad to hear of your visit with John and Nancy Todd. I hope to visit them some time myself. I keep promising myself a real talk with them. John's theory of architecture is fascinating to me, and I think very suggestive of a theory of poetry. I have found a teacher[†] here who is helping me to learn something of Systems Theory and the Theories of Hierarchies and Values. John derives his theory of architecture from those theories, if I understand it correctly. It is apparently now possible to learn how to join one's work *properly* to the universe. Symbiosis becomes the ideal or standard, which applies to any kind of human product—a house, a factory, a farm, a poem. And if one undertakes to join one's work properly to the universe, then one has immediately at hand a critical standard. Abusable, like any standard—for some jerk is bound to assume that what's wanted is symbiotic *propaganda*. The corrective, I assume, would be a propriety of another sort—a fit sense of the complexity of the universe and its relationships, so great as to have to be acknowledged ultimately as mystery.

I have crossed paths a couple of times with Lea Poisson, and his lovely wife Gretchen too. I respect Lea greatly for his work, which I know mainly from his talk, and also for being a genuinely enjoyable man, capable of laughing and carrying on.

Thanks for your note on right occupation. Did I tell you what I wanted it for? I'm to speak in April at Southern Baptist Theological Seminary[†] in Louisville, and I'm going to argue that a *Christian* doctrine of right occupation is implicit in the Bible—that, in fact, it is almost *explicit* there, in passages that I have been quite a while locating and connecting. My argument will begin with the conditions surrounding the gift of the Promised Land in the Pentateuch and wind up with a passage in Romans where Paul says that not just mankind but all creation awaits a resurrection by which it will be delivered from corruption and glorified. If I can make it all stick together, it will be an argument against the otherworldly values that have caused or allowed so much Christian abuse of "nature."

Our newest farm developments are: 1). Terrible river bank erosion after the December flood, including a slip of almost an acre, coming within about 20' of the little building beside the old store; 2). 23.06 acres of new land finally officially bought from my uncle. The part of the new land that is not in forest is in a mess of bushes and briars. No light work there. I will hope for a chance soon to show you all my new projects and talk with you about them.

I forgot to say in my first paragraph that I'll be gone from home Feb. 12-14. Going to give a poetry reading and attend a horse sale in Ohio. If possible at a decent price, I may buy a yearling stallion, but I doubt it will be possible. There will be a sale at Indianapolis on Feb. 28. If you are here then, we will skip the sale or take you with us.

I hope you will have a fine trip to Alaska. All of us here send our best to all of you.

Your friend,
Wendell

WENDELL BERRY [PORT ROYAL, KY]
TO GARY SNYDER [NEVADA CITY, CA]

April 12, 1979

Dear Gary,

I've mailed you, book rate, a book by David Ehrenfeld, *The Arrogance of Humanism,*† which seems to me to strike at the root of the trouble.

I just got back last night from Arizona, where I went to look at Indian—and incidentally, white American—agriculture. A good, informative trip, four days of driving and looking with Gary Nabhan,† but scary. The Indians are losing, and I'm afraid are going to lose, their agriculture because it's hard to argue that young people should learn a difficult way of farming when they can get "jobs" or welfare and buy food. And white folks' farming is doomed on its own terms: use of fossil fuel to use up fossil water to irrigate cotton in a state that imports most of its food.

We'd love to see you. Come when you can.

Wendell

◇◇◇◇◇

EDITOR'S NOTE: In September of 1979, Gary Snyder and Wendell Berry took part in a conference in Topeka, Kansas, sponsored by the Menninger Foundation. It was titled "Size and Shape in Mental Health" and was organized by Gregory Bateson and Bradford Kenney. Its participants included Mary Catherine Bateson, Wendell Berry, John Perry, Richard Rabkin, Gary Snyder, and Lyman Wynne.

GARY SNYDER [NEVADA CITY, CA]
TO WENDELL BERRY [PORT ROYAL, KY]

June 29, 1979

Dear Wendell and Tanya,

Aha, I'm going to get to see you, Wendell (and Tanya?) in Topeka! For better or for worse, this little health undertaking conference is getting me to read the works of Gregory Bateson,† interesting and a trial at the same time. The people in Kansas will send you, I think, a copy of a paper† I just mailed in to them, "Poetry, Community and Climax," which I did over the winter and sums up my present state of mind on the art.

Quick report from Kitkitdizze: The water pond which was enlarged by backhoe last fall has gratifyingly filled, and now serves (with the line and gate valve coming through the berm) excellently to water the new lower orchard area, and future enlarged vegetable garden. All the fruit trees are doing well this year and the Gravenstein has set a number of apples for the first time since it was planted in seven years. The nectarine[s], planted only two years, have also set a bit of fruit. The Japanese persimmons, although alive, don't seem to be thriving. But then it is a hardwood (ebony family) and notoriously slow-growing. These are the ones that are soft and very sweet when ripe. Also put in a new apricot just this year to see how it will do. With the additional watering capacity from the pond the small vegetable garden has been doing much better too—so we are looking for the first time at real food production, or the edge of it. I've about come to realize that I don't have to put in heavy-duty fence through my gallery-forest, for horses, but can do it with battery operated electric fence. Some of my neighbors are doing that now. It blends into the landscape quite nicely and allows for certain flexibility. What's your experience with electric fence and horses? I remember that you were using it back of the barn. I hadn't realized that they could be run on a battery and that the battery had quite a good life on it. I'm going to figure out ways to wire it so that one large area which is marshy and not really suitable for winter, can be opened up in late spring when it dries out and is full of rich grass and closed off again when necessary. Cross-fencing is what I'm talking about, I guess. I remember you used just single strand electrified wire to serve as a gate.

I have been enjoying the *New Farmer* [*sic: New Farm*]. Somehow I never could read *Organic Gardening*, but articles in the *New Farmer* have new information in them, for me at least.

Here is a little book† for you, precursor of things to come (or is it harbinger?)—and, tell me sometime if you think you're interested in comparative myth and folklore studies; if so, I'll send you a copy of my recently published B.A. thesis†—of all things—which is on that field.

Weather here, as usual, crashingly good every day. We are actually off to Hawaii for ten days. Masa will be doing a dance performance with me at the University of Hawaii[†]—and then we're going to Robert Aitken's center on Maui, to see how his Zen students are behaved. W. S. Merwin and I will be doing a benefit reading together for Aitken's Hawaii Zen group in Honolulu—which is a novelty, I have never even heard Merwin read—and then we'll be back here for the rest of the summer. I intend to stay home Fall and possibly next Spring both to finish the book on China.

I hope things have gone well for you this spring—I heard reports of very heavy rains and ongoing high water. How is the health of the horses? Not to mention the children and the family. Masa and I think often of the fireflies and the tall night grasses of Kentucky. See you.

Best,
Gary

GARY SNYDER [NEVADA CITY, CA]
TO WENDELL BERRY [PORT ROYAL, KY]

18: VIII [August 18, 1979]

Dear Wendell—

Much thanks for all the useful information on electric fence,[†] and the Snell system! They even have the solar-cell charger to put right with your battery. I'm getting closer to it all the time—(tho the work on China book still goes glacial-slow.)

I'll bring a copy of my thesis to Topeka for you. And, if you feel like it, bring some of the new poems[†] you mentioned—rhymed; on Biblical themes. I'm very curious to see how they're working—I have faith in the power of rhyme, as well as the re-surfacing of basic cultural traditions.

Two weeks of Pacific air-mass over Calif. have kept temperatures down to 50° at night; today's high was 65°! Amazing. Kai wants to raise racing homing pigeons right now (he has a friend who . . .). Masa says hello—and Kai and Gen—

See you in a jiffy!

Gary

Port Royal, Ky. 40058
August 26, 1979

Dear Gary,

[...] I don't care how slow your China book goes—just so it goes. The pages in the Fall '78 *CoEvolution Quarterly* are wonderful.† Useful. The passage on Oxhead Mountain particularly. That connection between enlightenment and householding, I realized, reading your sentences, is the interest we have in common. It forces us onto rougher ground than that of the smooth purists—but it gives us traction.

That connection is much needed in both Buddhism and Christianity if the right work is to get done. (I don't mean Buddhism. I mean Buddhism as another American fashion of feckless spirituality.) Without it (that connection), it's all just getting high and "crashing" (no thought of proper landing) and getting on with destruction. Fossil energy pimps running off to meditate or pray.

I *will* bring the new poems, untested though they are. They are, among other things, an attempt on the problem of connecting enlightenment and householding (woods and fields).

Another rainy spell started here last Sunday night—with a really destructive downpour of 3-4 inches that put the creek breast high through my corn—and it's still going.

I look forward to seeing you. Hope we'll find time to talk.

Wendell

September 13, 1979

Dear Wendell,

Returning home [from the Menninger Foundation conference] —lightning flashes in the clouds over Utah, and reading a brand-new novel by the anthropologist Michael Harner[†] called *Cannibal*. It gave me an irony and a shiver to note in his story that the great Aztec sacrifice system was defended or explained in part as a necessary method of maintaining the cycles of fertility! I'm going to work on that riddle more, later. What I wanted to say was, that I'm feeling a little bad about having dismissed [Masanobu] Fukuoka so apparently lightly. What I neglected to say, when we were speaking of him, is that his root philosophy is in no way eccentric to Japanese and Chinese culture—he is working from a really clear, and well-understood, Taoist base. There are clear Zen elements in his life and teaching, too. His devotion, and single-mindedness, and obvious way of having run counter to his immediate neighbors most of his life, is what made me say that he was an "eccentric." The farming ideas, too, obviously bear trying out in certain cases. He did not understand what the California eco-system was about—but who does at first? Hardly anyone who lives and farms here now is trying to understand what summer-dry Mediterranean-type farming systems might be. There are some really tempting ideas in the book, too—like pelletizing seeds with clay to keep them safe from the birds. I have several little Fukuoka-type projects I am going to do this fall, including doing Chinese radishes amongst the fruit trees. So, you and Rodale have every reason to be proud of your role in bringing Fukuoka's work[†] to the attention of the American public, and it just helps to deepen our understanding of what can be done. I do think too—something in English should be written on the richness of the Chinese and Japanese vegetable garden system, in its more conventional form, because there's a lot to be learned from that. Especially on the Pacific coast.

I hope you got your Amish buggy home safely—I can hardly wait to see it. Thanks for the ride to the airport, and all the good conversations—to you and Tanya both—

Gary

◇◇◇◇◇

EDITOR'S NOTE: Here Wendell Berry lists a provisional account of Amish social principles that he had acquired up through 1979. In future years, he would revise and further develop these ideas by addressing matters of technological choice, economic scale, and education.

GARY SNYDER [NEVADA CITY, CA]
TO WENDELL BERRY [PORT ROYAL, KY]

Port Royal, Ky. 40058
September 25, 1979

Dear Gary,

What you said about Fukuoka didn't sound as indiscriminate or unjust as you fear. And it didn't surprise me. All due credit being given, the old man *is* something of a bigot. Editing the book [...] was largely a matter of toning Fukuoka down into the reach of credibility. Larry [Korn] says egregious overstatement is a norm of Japanese discourse, but it didn't seem especially exotic to me.

We spent all day Monday with the Amishman and his family, waiting for our cart to be finished. It was, in spite of the wait, a good day. Randy Wittman and his wife are converts, and so I had a rare opportunity to talk about Amish life with someone who has seen it from both inside and outside.

I now have a list of Amish social principles, which I want to give you:

1). No institutions except family and church. The church is the community.

2). The one community institution—the church—is not an organization: no building, no building fund, etc.

3). The only chosen leaders are church leaders, and those are chosen by lot.

4). They don't have specialization in the pure, modern sense. Their craftsmen, ministers, etc. are also farmers. Agriculture is a norm, like binocular vision.

5). They all work with their hands.

6). They force the issue of community dependence; won't buy insurance or accept government help.

7). They vote on technological changes. For adoption, the vote must be unanimous.

This last rule I learned from Randy Wittman. If there is even one dissenter, he says, they assume the Devil is with the majority. This would make "progress" very slow—but, I think, probably fast enough. It might, in spite of community pressure, give undue power to an individual at times. But it also gives the community the use of every mind in it. Every mind (or, anyhow, every *man's* mind) has to bear the burden of the possibility that, in any such vote, it may come directly to power.

What impresses me is that, though the community is seen as a positive good, most of these principles are negative in intent or bearing. Unlike modern American government which is snarled in many rules prescribing what to do, Amish government consists of a few rules saying what *not* to do.

I suppose I don't want a federal government patterned on the Amish, though. Their government is tolerable only as long as there is somewhere to escape to if you don't like it. The best way would be to have many community governments, and *no* "national" government. A good rule for a federal system?

It was grand to see you in Kansas, and we missed you sorely after we left you at the airport.

The cart, by the way, is a dilly.

Wendell

P.S.—I thought I would send along the enclosed essay.[†] It's going to be in *Sierra Club Bulletin* in (I think) December. It has been edited both by them and by me, so you'll have to pardon the mess.

WENDELL BERRY [PORT ROYAL, KY]
TO GARY SNYDER [NEVADA CITY, CA]

Port Royal, Ky. 40058
October 17, 1979

Dear Gary,

When I was in Emmaus [Pennsylvania] a while back I spoke with Larry Stains[†] about the proposed article by you for *New Shelter*. I told him he shouldn't have put you under a deadline, and should have made you a decent offer of pay.

Here is what he said: He will pay you $500–600 for a piece on your house; he would like the piece to be 2500–3000 words. He will be glad to have it *when you are ready*.

I suggest that if you do want to write such an article you should have an understanding as to whether payment will be on receipt of MS or on acceptance.

I enclose a bibliographical note that I ran across up there. It looked possibly useful to your book.

These days I am hurried past sense. I would quit something if I could. But what?

A marvelous trip to W. Ky. last weekend with an agronomist and a botanist[†] to look at the fugitive remnants of tall grass prairie (virtually the whole plant community we saw on the Kansas prairie) once native to Ky. "barrens" and meadows, apparently all across the state. You would have liked our expedition—educational and gleeful.

My love to you all.

Wendell

GARY SNYDER [NEVADA CITY, CA]
TO WENDELL BERRY [PORT ROYAL, KY]

30. XI. 79 [*November, 30 1979*]

Dear Wendell,

Encl. a quick answer to Judy Hurley.† I do regret missing a chance to see and speak with you again, but I don't so much missing *this* chance. Judy (whom I've known for years) is a bit over-energetic, and I do think trying to get you and me and a symposium together to lean on the university with (for 13 students) is a bit of overkill.

And this gives me a push to write you. I just saw the "Gift of Good Land" piece in *Sierra Club Journal*. I didn't know when I read it where it was to be published. An excellent place. I found the article very useful, re-opened my thinking—jumping over and beyond Genesis—(too bad Jehovah seemed to overlook the fact that people were already there living in the promised land, though—)

Thank you for the information on Amish social organization. Or non-organization. It makes excellent sense, really, and some of us have been tempted to at least try the "no fire insurance" relationship. It would work if a reasonable number of households agreed to it—maybe 12 or more. This is within possibility for our community.

Also for the further note on an article for *Shelter*.† I could be happy to work on it if I had no immediate deadline; at the moment —after months' lapse—back at work on China and Environment which I will call *The Great Clod* after a favorite phrase of Chuang-tzu;† I know what you mean, busy past sense.

Are you participating in any of these nation-wide Department of Agriculture public dialogues? Ours will be at Fresno, and I've not heard, so far, of anyone being involved that I know.

Wendell I don't think I can do the proposed five days or week teaching/seminaring/with you and M.C. Bateson†—suggested by Bill Thompson—either; at least not in July or August. I'm writing Bill and saying that after Labor Day is a possibility for me, but not before. Late July is just when we have our local *sangha*† mountain-walking week; and August is what I try and save for the boys and their trips to the mountains.

And: here is a copy of the *Mountains and Rivers Sutra*† for you. Truly elevated text.

Masa's in town for the day and I'm almost cotched [*sic*: caught] up on mail—love to all of you—

Gary

WENDELL BERRY [PORT ROYAL, KY]
TO GARY SNYDER [NEVADA CITY, CA]

December 17, 1979

Dear Gary,

I couldn't accept Judy Hurley's invitation either. I have been traveling all fall—every couple of weeks from our Kansas adventure until early December I went somewhere for something. And so I am newly determined (again) to keep traveling to a minimum. Besides, when people say that I am urgently needed to make a speech some-place, my deepening impulse is to believe that they are badly mistaken. Do you think it could be a general rule that the only place one is urgently needed is at home?

Thank you for the *Mountains and Rivers Sutra*; also for *He Who Hunted Birds* and *Back Then Tomorrow*. I haven't had time to read them yet, but hope to do so soon.

By that, anyhow, you'll know that I cannot mean the enclosed† to be a burden to you, in the sense that you should read it soon, or late, or that you even need to respond. I send it just by way of communication of what has been a good deal on my mind.

My brother† has been elected majority leader in the state senate for the session beginning the first of the year and lasting until April. He has been a maverick and critic until now. And so he is coming to the test. Given the place and the interests involved, I'm afraid it will be a severe one. I am going to feed his cattle for him while he is in Frankfort—which about exactly suits my taste for political involvement.

Whether or not I do the teaching work for Bill Thompson in Colorado, I am thinking of attending the fellows meeting at Green Gulch.† I want to see S.F. again for the sake of a novel† I have begun planning. If possible, I would like to see you all in your place again as well.

However that may turn out, don't forget that you have a welcome here anytime it is possible for you to come.

Our love to your household.

Wendell

GARY SNYDER [NEVADA CITY, CA]
TO WENDELL BERRY [PORT ROYAL, KY]

[*February 20, 1980*]

I've told Sim [Van der Ryn] that if his 3-day meet in *lieu* of fellows meet takes place (June 9-10-11), I'll come. Hoping you might too. And if you do, plan to come visit here too. I'll not be able to stop in Ky. this spring—as sort of hoped. (Economics won out—a profitable couple of readings.)

more later
Gary

Port Royal, Ky. 40058
2/26/80 [February 26, 1980]

Dear Gary,

I told Sim [Van der Ryn] I couldn't make the conference, but since then it has begun to look more like I may come to the Bay Area either then or at another time. If I can see you then, that certainly increases the likelihood that I will come then. The longer I go without seeing you, the more things I think up to ask you and tell you. You'll never hear the half of it.

If I come to the meeting and we see each other there, then I may not be able to come up to Kitkitdizze. I've got business with Jack [Shoemaker] and his partner, Tanya and I will have to visit with her kinfolks, and I want to "research" a little bit over in the city. If that leaves time for a trip to your place, I want very much to come. But June's not the best time for me to be gone from here.

We had a blizzard last night—hard wind, little snow. Today there has been just a little feeling of the possibility of spring. Actually, I could use another month of winter to read and write in, but I reckon we have to take spring when we can get it.

Love to you all.
Wendell

P.S.—Talking with some students the other night, I noticed that their thinking did not start with definition of a problem, but with vague personal concepts (?): their "space," their "thing," their "life," etc. Have you experienced this? It never hit me so forcibly until then that, starting where they start, they *can't* think. And the schools apparently aren't encouraging them to start any place else.†

[*March 14, 1980*]

Dear Wendell—

Well if you can't make it [in] June it'll work out some other time. But I wanted to let you know I planned to be there. Thanks for *Heraclitean Fire*† and *The Arrogance of Humanism*! (I had the latter, so Jack S. is taking it back.) The Chargaff book is totally new to me. Marvelous! Nothing on "Sabbaths" yet worth sharing.

Wet winter—looks like spring now—

    best,

    Gary

◇◇◇◇

EDITOR'S NOTE: Gary Snyder's comments on Wendell Berry's draft of the Sabbath poems of 1979 opened up an ongoing and rigorous dialogue concerning questions of history, anthropology, belief, and right occupation in regard to expressions of Zen Buddhism, Christianity, and what Snyder called the Old Ways.

GARY SNYDER [NEVADA CITY, CA]
TO WENDELL BERRY [PORT ROYAL, KY]

3 IV [April 3, 1980]

Dear Wendell—

April 3—Japanese flowering cherry at "popcorn" stage and the Nectarine past bloom. Apples and cherries still bud. Apricot half-open. 7" new snow on Donner summit; still good skiing (total 14 feet!) And planting the summer garden now. Hardier seeds; we cd still get frost til 10 May.

I'm between a trip to U. of Tx and NW Louisiana State U. Reading *Sabbaths*. I can enjoy the poems, but not the theology—I am truly

convinced both from study of theory and personal practice that
there is no one central informing and organizing "Lord" to invoke
(and that the "center" is everywhere, simultaneously) and, also, that
Human and non-human are not qualitatively removed—that it is
not a unique characteristic of the human to have free-will and be
in a position of challenge to the "Lord's command."

All this at poem #I. No need to go on. But the skeltonics are a
delight! And the *poetic enterprise* the poems represent is praiseworthy!

#II— "generative slime" is rather tired;

  #IV is remarkable—and well beyond any "theology." personal,
    actual.

   #V leaves that new thing, "pain" hanging: as you intended no
     doubt. And raises questions.

    VI "the fox cub trots his almost pathless path"

    GREAT LINE!

    And the last line too. But "a joy without defect" rings false
    —like a goopy line from a hymn—against the solidness.

    IX hymnbook language almost, and for me, a "forced joy"
     —the almost heretical expectation of *perfection*. No other
     world but here.

    XI. yes. and XII. yes. XIII. yes. XIV. I think so; XV ? those
    leaves.

My superficial comments. (And beware of hymnal language-tone
—tho I know you are deliberately skirting that tone, to your credit
—take care!)

Greetings to all. Maybe you come in June? Seems Bill [Thompson] is tooling up to have a [Lindisfarne] Fellows meet after all. I
must go now and hook up new submatic drip irrigation system.
Hope it don't clog.

Yr old Buddhist Buddy

Gary

Port Royal Ky. 40058
April 13, 1980

Dear Gary,

I imposed that long MS of poems [Sabbaths] on you because I didn't want you to be unaware what I was trying—hating, all the same, to ask you to spend time on something I know to be very imperfect. Maybe you will guess from that how grateful I am for your response.

I wonder if it might not be possible to define a Western theology, sufficiently responsive to Biblical tradition, that would not alienate a Buddhist such as yourself. The question may be merely naive, yet I think Thomas Merton[†] had it much in mind. I don't think of this question because of any competence in theology of any kind, but because sectarianism has always troubled me. People more knowing and experienced than I have testified that all religions are one. I suspect so, but perhaps only because I would so like to find that they are.

I too believe that "the center is everywhere simultaneously." But I also believe there must be "holy places" such as those venerated by the Indians or those where, as Eliot says, "prayer has been valid."[†] And I don't think that this is a contradiction or a weak attempt to have it both ways. You can find good Biblical support for an argument—for instance—that God is at once transcendent and immanent. The question of the innocence of non-human creation, which I do pretty much believe in, may be more difficult. I hope you will say more about it next time we meet. But Biblical concepts such as "sabbath," "incarnation," and "resurrection" seem to me just particular names for general principles. That's misleading. They do have their particular meanings. What I think the churches have done is use the particular meanings to obscure general ones. Though the terms of my poems are pretty literally Biblical, I tried to use them so as to keep them from being too specially understood. Your letter helps greatly to define the difficulty.

These poems are the result, partly, of a whole pattern of dissatisfactions: with my time and history, with my work, with my grasp of problems, with such solutions as I have found, with the traditions both of poetry and religion that the poems attempt to use and serve. That last dissatisfaction is the cause of all the immediate difficulties. There the traditions are, inextricably braided together, very beautiful in certain manifestations, but broken off, cheapened, weakened, encrusted, with hateful growths—yet so rich, so full of the suggestion of usefulness and beauty, that I finally can't resist the impulse to try to lay hold of them.

Your particular comments are also very useful. I will probably have to delete #2—a sort of translation of one of Spenser's stanzas that never really decides between his language and mine.

So far, we have had a cold, late, wet spring—not a handful of days yet that you could call workdays. Pasture is coming late and slow, we've planted no garden, worked no crop ground. We have 4 calves, 7 lambs—one ewe still to lamb. One mare is due to foal today, one next month.

Our girl, Mary, is planning to get married next January—after she finishes school—to a young farmer here in the county. It's a bad time for marriage, looks like, but we're pleased. And surprised too, some, for Mary has not always appeared to be headed in any such direction.

I hope you all are well.

Your friend,
Wendell (buddhist)

June 5, 1980

Dear Wendell,

There is much that should be said by sitting down together. I
found myself on the verge of writing a long essay on the history
of religion right now—and then realized that that isn't really what
I want to do. So I'll look forward to when we can meet and talk.
But for now I'd like to respond to your letter of April 13 with just
a few comments. People have indeed testified that all religions of
the world are one. That is probably true, on one level. But the religions of the world (two categories—"world religions" and natural
religions, or ethnic religions); the "world religions" at least, and
probably others as well—operate on two levels. A word about the
natural religions: Whereas "world religions" tend to have great charismatic human leader-founders, the natural religions, the old ways,
take their teachings direct from the human mind, the collective
unconscious, the ground of being. Rather than theology, they have
mythology and visionary practice. The shaman as key figure in the
Old Ways, rarely becomes a teacher-figure; but is a medium, a vehi-
cle for powers of nature and the mind. I said a little bit about this
in the preface to my thesis, *He Who Hunted Birds in His Father's Village.* (By preference I would be a follower of the Old Ways: which in
Buddhism is referred to in quick language as "the ancient Buddha"
—but the considerably more literate and sophisticated Zen teachings are more accessible. The old "red hat" sect of Tibetan Buddhism is called the sect of the "old timer".—Its connections with
paleolithic shamanism are quite clear.) The two levels, of course,
are (1) acting as social glue and intensifying the bonds of the culture and the coherence of it; the other is liberating and transcendent, of freeing one from the bonds of ego and conditioning. It's
fascinating to see the dialectic of these two roles as they work out in

different times and places. Some traditions within great traditions tend toward total mysticism, others ground themselves entirely in secular affairs. All religions are one at the point where life is given to the spirit, and real breakthrough is achieved. I doubt that any of the world religions ever have or could achieve a fusion of the two levels; I like to believe that some ancient religions—Old Ways—did achieve it: like perhaps the Hopi. The thing is, "world religions" are always a bad deal: they are evoked by the contradictions and problems of civilization, and they make compromises from the beginning to be allowed to live. The Great Fact of the last 8,000 years is civilization; the power of which has been and remains greater than the power of any religion within that time span.

Christianity and Buddhism both, as "world religions," are products of that compromise. My problems with Christianity are two: One is basically theological, the place in the Bible where the Lord says the living creatures of the earth are "meat" for our use;† and the distinction from the beginning which is hardened into dogma by the Church, between creator and creation. It is heretical for a Christian to aspire to be completely one with the maker. That this did not trouble some mystics—notably Meister Eckhart†—is testimony to the truth of the truth that people will crack through dogma. Secondly, historical: The church inherited the mantle of the Roman empire and set out to spiritually colonize the world. I think it is still trying to do that. In following this course, it has taken preexisting theology and intensified it. A hierarchical and authoritative model of the universe. Most of Christianity becomes a centralist teaching; which objection I raised in my comments to you—whereas those who seem to have transcended somewhat (Christians or otherwise) testify, as you and I have already agreed—that the center of being is everywhere.

Well, I could get along with Christianity. My mother, being raised in a strict southern town, gave me more than my share of atheist hostility, I know, and my Marxist leanings of my twenties reinforced it. My own Zen teacher, Robert Aitken, is by example softening me. He has been in quite a dialogue with Christian Zen people in recent years—leading some intensive meditation weeks for groups of Catholic Workers† and Trappist Monks† up in Seattle; and in touch with the Christian Zen people in Japan and in the Philippines. Witness the little piece I have enclosed.† Zen, as the arm of Buddhism most given to the life of the spirit, really doesn't care about theology or dogma; it takes people where the spirit leads, and has a complete authenticity of its own, one must adjust this authenticity to whatever received teachings one started from on one's own. The Christian Zen priests believe that they can help bring spiritual life back into Christianity by these practices—meditation and the use of *koan.* And I have long studied some of the early heresies, and am following along as best I can on gnostic discoveries, so can see that there is a real core of teaching and practice in the early Christian church; and that Christ himself was a true teacher. True teachers are called into being by the contradictions generated by civilization, as I said above. And I guess we need them.

And I myself am not comfortable with unnecessary exotic Far Eastern baggage in my secular and spiritual life here on Turtle Island.† Trappings of the ancient Judeo-Roman world, or Greek Hellenistics, also strike me as exotic. Where to draw a style of our own from? The plain style of plain folks is truly attractive—and also the free use of found feathers and beads, and the beautification of daily life with the things at hand that the Indians did so well. Oh boy: We sit in my barn doing Japanese Zen meditation, using those alien texts, but in the dialogue with the teacher, nothing is exotic —it is really the depth of the natural heart. But the work that lies ahead, of creatively making a coherent style that fits our daily life, as well as our inner needs, is a big one; it could be a whole work in itself, even if there wasn't a planet about to crumble around us.

And so, I'll leave that where it is. I have another sort of question to ask you—is there some validity in the thought that one could use a tractor to get his place where it would grow enough grass to keep horses, and use horses from there? I have a friend who argues that, and is doing it, and with the price of hay around here, I see some possible sense in it. Also, what is the role of the rototiller? I remember you had one. We are on the verge of thinking we really should get one (I'm looking at the "Mainline")—but are also wondering if what we can do with a good heavy-duty rototiller is hold the line between horses and a tractor for a while and make it do until we can enlarge our grass growing capacities without a tractor. Not that I can afford a tractor. I guess what I am asking is can a somewhat larger, sturdier rototiller do useful work around the place beyond just small gardens?

New Directions is about to send out my new book,[†] selected interviews and talks of the last fifteen years. With your strictures on interviews in mind. But I think my interviews for the most part pass muster—since they are almost all substantive and very little about opinions or even literature for that matter. I hope. Hello to all and I really did like your Sabbath poems. Yes, Sabbath, Resurrection, Incarnation, are general principles. They are all found in various ways in the Old Ways.

[PS] I hope this doesn't sound too much like a lecture—hastily—but with feeling—

yours,
Gary

WENDELL BERRY [PORT ROYAL, KY]
TO GARY SNYDER [NEVADA CITY, CA]

Port Royal, Ky. 40058
June 26, 1980

Dear Gary,

Tanya and I will be at Bill Thompson's place in Colorado July 27–Aug. 2. Then we're coming to S.F. and will be with Jack [Shoemaker], Aug. 2–4. Then to Mill Valley. I have a reservation to fly home on Aug. 6.

What I *wish* I could do is stay an extra day or two and come up to see you at your place. There is some *little* chance I may be able to do that—but impossible to tell yet, and the trip is already long, Den will be here by himself, etc.

I do want to see you, and will be very sorry if I don't.

So tell me—will you be home, say, Aug. 4–7? And is there any chance you'll be in the Bay Area Aug. 2–5? There would be room for you at T's [Tanya's] aunt's and uncle's place in Mill Valley, we think. We're busy as well.

Our love to you all.

Wendell

WENDELL BERRY [PORT ROYAL, KY]
TO GARY SNYDER [NEVADA CITY, CA]

Port Royal, Ky. 40058
June 29, 1980

Dear Gary,

I'll answer your June 5 letter from the hind end forwards, working from confident response downward.

First, most confidently, I wish you would not think of what I said about interviews in connection with yourself at all. I *do* continue to regret the popularity of that genre. Most poet-interviews I see strike me as glib, shallow, self-exhibiting, worthless, embarrassing, and irresponsible. But I have read some that I thought were valuable—yours preeminently among them. You have important things to say, you have schooled yourself to say them well, and you can think and talk at the same time. Any one of the above would make you rare. I assume the book will contain interviews that I have already been grateful for, and I expect to continue grateful.

On the tractor question, I think you *must* do what seems to make most sense in your particular circumstances. I regret tractors, I guess, at least as much as I regret interviews. Both, however, can be well used. See preceding paragraph, and remember that I'm dependent on a tractor myself to get my hay baled, and occasionally for some other purpose. I don't expect it to be immediately clear how to get altogether free of these dependences. If you see a way to improve your land by use of a machine, I say use it! I'd say the same thing to anyone wondering about using chemical nitrogen to start a grass cover on a starved or strip-mined hillside. I can "grow" my own nitrogen, using legumes. To get "organic" phosphate and pot-ash I'd have to order a carload to get a little. So later this summer I'll top dress some alfalfa fields with chemical P and K. It's a trap I hope to work my way out of but it'll take a while.

That's compromising with the enemy, dragging our skirts in the mire, etc. But how are we going to escape that and *do* much of anything? The tough thing about compromises, once we see that's what they are, is that we're pretty much alone with them and with the practical/ethical questions that come up next: How much, exactly, must we compromise? How, once we've made a compro-mise, do we work our way out of it instead of deeper into it? Etc. All right, I think, to look on compromise as a necessity; dangerous to make it a virtue.

I don't know the Mainline tiller. Have heard many good reports of the Troybilt. Would it be possible, I wonder, to get a used 8N Ford tractor for what a new Troybilt would cost?

What are the chances that your community could support a tractor-man or woman and/or sooner or later a teamster, who would do the custom work for everybody?

End of the least bit of confidence. Now I'll get on down to the-ology. First a couple of—not objections, maybe—at least differences.

I don't have a very good concordance, but I can't find the Bibli-cal passage you allude to ("where the Lord says the living creatures of the earth [all?]† are 'meat' for our use"). But that's certainly not all the Bible says on this question. The book of Job is a ferocious indictment of the assumption that the world is man's meat. The creation is not subject to our understanding much less our use. "Canst thou bind the unicorn with his band in the furrow?" (39:10). There's no way, I guess, to keep somebody from answering that the unicorn (the wild ox) *can* be put in harness. But the point is that some things were not created subject to use. Beyond that, I think you can argue, from the Bible, that nothing was created *entirely* for use, though use of some things is allowable within limits.

And though I am probably ineligible to hold such an opinion, I think you are wrong in your statement that "It is heretical for a Christian to aspire to be completely one with the maker." To be at one—"atoned"—with the maker is, as I understand it, a Christian's aim.† I believe it is understood as the replacement of one's own will by God's will: "Thy will be done ...";"... not as I will, but as thou wilt." And this is possible, as Dante says, only by grace and preceding merit. I don't know what is heretical, but what is dangerous about this is its inversion: the assumption that your will is God's.

Which raises what is for me the worst problem of religion: that of authority.

Your distinction between world religions and natural religions is useful, and I feel it is true—though I feel extremely hesitant and uneasy in the presence of terms like "collective unconscious." The distinction serves well enough to define my own critical attitude toward the Bible, particularly the Old Testament.

July 1

I was about to say: I read the Bible, can't help reading it, as the outcropping of something timeless, unhuman, and true—all encrusted with shards, artifacts, and fossils of what you call "civilization." I feel that this sort of civilization is possible work. Aside from that, I read the Bible pretty literally, not seeking "explanations" for wonders. I believe wonders have happened because I see that they happen.

July 4

I suppose I know what you mean by "atheist hostility"— though my own hostility was against only the *institutions* of religion as I knew them. From early childhood I disliked churches and their functions, and this was maybe the main issue of my "adolescent rebellion," which lasted too long. I now see that rebellion as tragic, though probably inescapable. Alienation from one's community, for whatever reason, by whoever's fault, is seriously damaging. And for me probably permanently so, for I still see no church that I could be at home in. I am a solitary Christian—a most paradoxical creature.

And though I keep my old distrust of institutional authority, reinforced by experience, experience has also required me to mistrust the authority of the individual conscience, or "inner light," or what you call "teachings direct from the human mind." Or inspiration or revelation or vision. That is, I don't unreservedly trust "the human mind," which I think is infinitely subject to error, bad motives, etc., and infinitely subject to correction. This is what I meant by the problem of authority—or, as I probably should say, the problem of spiritual authority.

This problem is painfully bewildering to me. I guess it has been a problem for individuals from the human beginnings, and has been a public issue for English speakers at least since Cromwell. It has come about by a disintegration that must be far more calamitous than Eliot's "dissociation of sensibility,"† though it includes that. I have begun to think, myself, that it was a sort of explosion of the human definition, so that all action began to be conditioned merely by possibility (technical possibility?) rather than by cultural or religious moral limits.

I see your distinction between kinds of religion as also a distinction between kinds of spiritual authority: social-institutional/personal-communal. (Are those terms right?) As a sort of beginning of work on the authority problem, I suggest that both kinds of authority, in this world, have to live and validate themselves on the ground of practical experience: the collective consciousness, the collective or communal or common or shared (*not* "public" or institutional or governmental) knowledge of what works to keep body and soul, creature and creation together. I think we can say that moral law is either the beginning or (as Lao-tsu said) the fossil (and maybe potentially again the beginning) of that kind of knowledge. I agree with the strictures Lao-tsu and Jesus put on the idea of law; it's clear that if we love our parents we need no legal prompting to "honor" them. Law can't take you the whole way, but at least at our stage of growth I think we have to acknowledge the possibility that practical experience can be condensed to good purpose into moral law: Do not let the topsoil wash away. That does not have to be stated as a moral law. It's a "universal." It could also be stated: "God has forbidden us to let the topsoil wash away" or "Grandpop said don't plow that hillside." The point is that if such a limit has no lively existence in the community, then the hillside is not safe from authority—charismatic reformer, visionary leader, progressive institute or whatever—that may say to plow it. Or, without that kind of law, how are people going to tell the difference between a person of authentic spiritual authority and some charismatic son of a bitch who wants the hillside to produce a taxable income or a "surplus" to improve the balance of trade?

So, granting the limits of moral law, I would still disbelieve the authority of any spiritual teacher who encouraged or condoned or ignored the waste of topsoil, or the corruption of community or family life. I think such a teacher would have to meet that kind of test.

What I'm feeling more and more inclined to argue, in other words, is that there's no "high culture" without low culture. No use talking about getting enlightened or saving your soul if you can't keep the topsoil from washing away. No use expecting excellent art if there's no excellent farming and carpentry. This is hard (and instructive) to deal with because, of course, it means that I'm in the wrong lifetime to expect Port Royal to produce an excellent poet. I'm in the wrong lifetime to even get a good glimpse of what the excellence of an excellent Port Royal poet might be.

That is so hard for me to think because I came along under the specialist system in the arts, which proposed among other things that diseased society could be ransacked for the "subject matter" of "great poetry"— a notion full of silliness and despair. I think, now, that our work must settle for being, at best, a fragment of a glimpse of a better possibility. Speaking for myself, I'm pleased with that conclusion. I see a lot more hope and satisfaction in that than in the possibility of making an "artistic triumph" out of the ruin of the world.

July 5

All that has a coherence that may seem to contradict my assertion that I couldn't speak with confidence. But I don't feel I have spoken confidently. Even unconfident speech has to cohere, and one may be driven to act on such a provisional coherence. I think I have only traced out a possible little path through a lot of confusion. And more ignorance, both of books and of the meaning of my own experience.

But I'm looking at a part of your letter now—the part where you say you're "not comfortable with unnecessary exotic Far Eastern baggage ... here on Turtle Island"—that I feel a little surer about. I think that until we can reassemble the pattern that can hold body and soul, creature and creation together, all the parts are bound to be more or less uncomfortable. All our foreign baggage is going to be a little alien. But so—so, at least for me—is American Indian baggage. Something can, and must, be learned from it and put to use. But I didn't get any of it unconsciously, as I'm convinced the real inheritance must come—as our real language *does* come. Hard to winnow out exactly what I have in my head that is truly indigenous, native to this place. I learned unconsciously some stuff that may be. I know a lot of foreign stuff, some little of which I may have made to fit here. What doesn't fit is all probably a burden.

Still, I think it's wrong to think of anything that's at hand as exotic—not if it's available to your life and your doings. It's [not] possible to truck a bunch of foreign stuff into your poetry and make it at home there when it remains alien in your life. But if I understand you correctly, you are not putting it into your poetry until it is available in your life. That makes all the difference in the world. Your life *includes* poetry, along with much else. If Japanese Zen can help you to settle and live there in your place, then I think it belongs there with you, and you have as much right to use it as the plains Indians had to use horses. If the Japanese (or Greek or Jewish) wisdom can help us, then it's, by that fact, not alien. We can't help what's in our heads, and we're not to blame for it. If we don't use what's in 'em for good, we're to blame. And we're to blame if we're dilettantes and learn a lot and do nothing—if we collect "spiritual" experiences and objects of "high culture" and fail to nurture the young and take care of the soil.

Well, this letter is both incomplete and too long. And it sounds even more like a lecture than yours, so don't worry.

Yours most effusively,
Wendell

WENDELL BERRY [PORT ROYAL, KY]
TO GARY SNYDER [NEVADA CITY, CA]

3.VII [*July 3, 1980*]

Dear Wendell,

Alas, your timing cuts right across mine. Aug. 6 night is when I return from a week backpacking in the central high Sierra. And then Masa returns from her 6 week study in Connecticut (her dance teacher will be at Wesleyan this summer) on the 8 or 9, and then we're off again on a little family mountain hike.

Well, let's stay tuned and something will work out sooner or later.

My friend the seedman David Padwa[†] was here and spoke at fascinating length on molecular biology, recombinant plant gene work, and seed research. He says work is underway to make cereals capable of fixing nitrogen like legumes do, saving 17 billion dollars a year in fertilizer worldwide. Out of playful curiosity he telephoned the Archbishop of New Mexico for an opinion on the Supreme Court living cells/patent decision. The Padre told him "My son, the Church does distinguish between Animal, Vegetable, and Mineral. As long as it's vegetable you're working with, it's alright."

I'm hoping to get some progress on the China essay this summer, so apart from the mountain trips will be in seclusion. Did I mention—at the Lindisfarne conference, the Teilhard[†] evolutionists began to show their true colors—mind/matter dualists, eager to shuck off matter for pure spirit, whenever the chance comes. (Conversations with assorted folks after my talk on China, where they—some did—tried to play down the seriousness of species extinction.)

Onward,

Gary

WENDELL BERRY [PORT ROYAL, KY]
TO GARY SNYDER [NEVADA CITY, CA]

Port Royal, Ky. 40058
July 11, 1980

Dear Gary,

Alas indeed. I'm pretty much resigned to the several privations attendant upon my choice of life. Am even pretty much resigned to seeing people I don't want to see. But I would like to see you and talk a while.

You didn't mention the "mind/matter dualists" who came out of the closet at the Lindisfarne meeting, but I am not surprised. I've heard among them several murmurings of the wish to be freed by technology, etc. for pursuit of higher things. It's a cheap out—getting shed of bodily demands and disciplines in order to specialize in thinking or meditating or praying or whatever the hell it is they do.

Is it even possible? And where does it come from? Is it traditional, or just a rare faction of the contempt for material things implicit in the "materialism" of the industrial revolution? [...]

And I guess I hold the science of genetic manipulation in about the same suspicion. I can see very readily the advantages of nitrogen-fixing cereals. In a good kind of farming they could be beneficent. In a bad kind—the kind they are most likely to be used in —they will be used to prolong the industrial practice of continuous cropping. And to increase the wealth of industrial plutocrats. We already have good plants that, in general, we are using very poorly.

I now see that I have written you a grumpy letter. Forgive me. None of the grumpiness here is directed at you. I speak my mind to you as to an ally—the nearest, probably, that I have. The real cause of my grumpiness, I think, is the sense of having too much to do that comes over me with a kind of panic at times and that kept me awake some last night.

It'll pass. I *am* getting work done that there is some sense in. So are you.

Yes! Let's carry on.

Onward!

Wendell

WENDELL BERRY [PORT ROYAL, KY]
TO GARY SNYDER [NEVADA CITY, CA]

Port Royal, Ky. 40058
7/22/80 [*July 22, 1980*]

Dear Gary,

I have finished reading *The Real Work*, and want to give you my opinion of it. It is conversation—is of the genre of conversation— and has the limitations and the virtue of that genre. That is, one sometimes wishes for a more studied elaboration; at the same time, the excitement of conversation is obviously turning up insights and connections that greater deliberation would reach much more slowly, if at all. And it is conversation extraordinarily abundant, precise, and generous—teaching of the best kind.

It is by being the best kind of teaching conversation that the book escapes the genre of the literary interview and the characteristic weakness of that genre: shallowness, incoherence, self-display, etc. The editor's [Scott McLean's] mention of the *Life of Johnson* is suggestive, and I wish more had been made of it. In all of Boswell's talks with him, Johnson is always a conversationalist, never an interviewee. He always speaks consideringly and well—even when he speaks capriciously—and his speech is always under the influence of his practice as a writer. He doesn't babble, but always speaks *as he has prepared himself* to speak—which is manifestly true of you.

That's my "critical" opinion. If you can make use of any of it in promoting the book, I hope you will.

Speaking just for myself and to you, I will add that I read this book with a delight and gratitude that I rarely feel for the work of a contemporary. Given our obvious differences of geographic origin, experience, etc., it is uncanny how much I feel myself spoken for by this book—and, when not spoken for, spoken *to*, instructed. It is a feeling I have only got elsewhere from hearing my brother speak in "environmental" controversies—the realization and joyful relief of hearing someone speak well out of deeply held beliefs that I share. And this always involves a pleasant quieting of my own often too insistent impulse to speak.

We have been having very uncomfortable weather—hot, humid, and dry. But rain came last night and is continuing this morning—a better liberation than most. Today it's *easy* to think about the fields.

Our main work lately has been fencing—literally an uphill, rocky proposition here. By fall I hope to have a new sheep-tight pasture of about 8 acres, reasonably safe from dogs.

And Tanya and I are leaving Sunday for the West. I'll be gone 10 days, Tanya 2 weeks. For me there's always craziness in these departures, worse in the growing season, but I can't help looking forward to the mountains, the Bay, the Shoemakers, etc.

Our love to you all.

Wendell

July 25, 1980

Dear Wendell,

By the time you get this, I guess you'll have been to the west coast and back home again; I might as well send it to your home though because it might miss you if I mailed it to Berkeley. Ninety-six degree weather here now, apple tree loaded with apples, and a heavy grass cover wherever it's open. I haven't been able to do anything new, though, really focused on trying to finish writing about China. Tractors! There's no tractor alive on the west coast that would come as cheap as Troy or any other big rototiller. They are expensive! Two or three thousand dollars, at a minimum for a used one. But, I'm still playing with the idea.

Not to go on too long, but I wished to respond to both your letters briefly.

The passage I alluded to is Genesis 9.2: "And the fear of you and the dread of you shall be upon every beast of the earth and upon every fowl of the air and upon all that moveth upon the earth, and upon all the fishes of the sea; into your hand are they delivered. 3. Every moving thing that liveth shall be meat for you; even as the green herb have I given you all things." That's King James; it might be different in the revised. Next point, as for being "completely at one with the maker" that is the interest and goal of some schools of Hinduism, and mystics of all religions; although some would very early in the game point out that "maker" is a term that has to be rephrased. But everything I have read on Christianity (and I am less eligible than you to have such opinions ultimately) says to me that creature and creator are not one. Creature is indeed to replace his will with the will of God, but that is not the same as oneness! The mystics' oneness with God is one in which there is no God's will or his will, but just one will. That may be a subtle point; in some cases not so subtle. Atonement, in my dictionary, refers to the acts a man must do to restore his relationship with God when he has failed to act in accordance with God's will. Atonement, and repentance, restores that relationship—requiring, of course, personal sincerity; and vicarious prayer or sacrificing will not achieve it.*

> *v Roethke*
> *"In a Dark Time"*

It is quite correct though that the assumption that "one's own will is gods" is a great devil. Zen master Dōgen says the same thing in his own way: He says that "when the ten thousand things come forward and verify you, that is enlightenment but when you go forward and verify the ten thousand things, that is delusion."

What you read the Bible as—the outcropping as something timeless, unhuman and true—I guess I read the world mythology and folklore as. Not going so far as Jungian "collective unconscious", etc. But—my Bible is the archaic universal world body of folk lore and folk mythology. Encrusted indeed; but somehow, for me, wondrous. And, of course, for me, the Bible is part of that Bible.

> *v*

When I said "teachings direct from the human mind" I was really being sloppy. What I meant was from the deepest non-human levels of the human mind:—or Buddha mind—or the vivid reality that is within all things. Interestingly, in Buddhism there is no "authority" except in the credence one gives Buddhas and Dharma. If there were no living human beings one could measure oneself

---

*Snyder inserted a comment about his doubts concerning the etiology of "at one" in relationship to "atone." However, after consulting the *Oxford English Dictionary*, he crossed out the sentence and confirmed that the "Etymology *is* from 'at one'!"

against and come away feeling one had learned something, Buddhism would be dead. But they are not presented as either perfect, or exactly as authorities; but as reliable critics, good spiritual friends, guides in tight places. There need be no ultimate authority; the power is throughout the organism itself. And, of course, no single human will could grasp or control the totality of the organism.

Now with your point about social institutional, personal communal sorts of authority for religion, I would suggest another way of looking at it: more anthropological perhaps, but a functional viewpoint. Every religion that works has I think three simultaneously functioning levels: On one level it functions to give meaning, harmony, daily life values, stability, legitimacy to daily life and justify the stupidity of secular authority, often. On another level, antithetically, it tends to take at least some individuals and totally pluck them out of the comfortable social nexus and make them view the terrifying nakedness. And on a third level, an even smaller number of individuals are enabled to return from that spiritual extreme and social alienation to a higher harmonized sacramentalizing view of a social and human life. In institutions like the Catholic Church, you can see the three levels at work in history, quite independent of each other, and sometimes at odds. Often at odds. I'm not sure if it has to be this way. But when the last level is at work in a society, *then* you don't have to pass laws about letting the topsoil wash away; people know how to do it because grandpa said so, because they know it's right, because it's in their bones.

Amen: No high culture without low culture. There is just low quality culture, and high quality culture—and low quality means monoculture, spectator, commercialized culture. Anyhow, when you get the book *Real Work*, maybe you can look at that last essay I did,† which is really also about how a culture can come out of a place and out of a community.

To respond to your other letter a little, of July 11, I feel compelled to look into Teilhard de Chardin and find out what he really is up to: Since some of these people keep invoking him, and I have not really read him. It's clear, though, that dualism is as much if not more from outside of religious circles these days than in; a part of the culture really, going back to Newton and Descartes and now common habit of mind; mind is one thing, body is another, matter is an artifact. I guess I knew this years ago when I was in college, but it comes back on me with renewed freshness when I see such assumptions at work in the language of very intelligent people.

I am all alone here. Masa is in Connecticut and the boys are up in the Sierra camping. I just came back from the mountains doing a workshop in poetics at an outdoor camping scene; for three days I led an intensive workshop on oral narrative poetry, actually teaching mostly from and about the "secret history of the Mongols."† Very refreshing, to work with a poetry that no one writes in our culture (i.e. long narrative) and—heroics—which also no one thinks of in our poetry now. For three days we studied the way the Bards sang and wrote on the rise of Genghis Khan, and the formation of his character. (One author says of the Mongols' destruction of the sedentary towns of northeast Persia, "apparently the foreign policy of the Mongols was simply to replace agriculture and cities with grasslands.")

Enough. More later.

Faithfully,

Gary

Port Royal, Ky. 40058
September 15, 1980

Dear Gary,

The passage in Genesis 9 seems a fairly representative Biblical problem. (I'll tell you how I think about it—for what it's worth; I'm *not* more eligible than you in this matter.) What seems most misleading about the Bible is the use of a single verse or two alone. I suppose this must be true of most texts, but it is why "the Devil quotes scripture." Taken alone, the verses you quote sound horrible. But they come at the end of the story of how God made Noah and his family the means of preserving all the species of living things. And they are followed immediately by the statement that God's covenant is established not only with humans but "with every living creature that is with you."†

I think the verses you quote, have at least two functions. First, they give the humans permission to use other creatures as food. Because God has just demonstrated his great concern that the species should survive—and that they should survive an evil that was specifically human—one imagines that such a permission was necessary. Second, it is a statement of the fact that humans are the dominant species; they *do* have fearful power over the rest of creation.

Some of the trouble you have may come from the connotations of "meat" and "deliver into your hand." We can use "meat" as a term of contempt. But I think the King James translation meant by it simply "food"—as in the sentence "They sat down to meat"—and the Revised Standard reading is "food."

We are apt to read "into your hand they are delivered" as an absolute grant of power. But even if that language was not strongly qualified by the immediate establishment of the covenant with all creatures, one would still have to reflect that nowhere in the Bible is absolute power ever granted to humans. And if I read it right, the Bible understands human power as more conditional upon good use, the farther its human history develops. The "plot" is the granting and the abuse of power. The human species is dominant, and its dominance is disastrous without responsibility. Dominance and responsibility—the two together—account for the human place in the Chain of Being, which Milton and Pope understood pretty much as an ecological structure, the part dependent on the whole. There is ecology in Blake. Shelley wanted to set the parts free from the "tyranny" of the whole.

September 16

As for "oneness with God," I have long been, and am more and more, suspicious of it as a "religious experience." I have sometimes a kind of grudging envy of "mystical experience." But I'm suspicious of it too. The sort of "oneness" I am really interested in requires solutions to a lot of practical problems, and I think the possibility of it may be two or three generations away. Anyhow, I'm not interested in spirituality that is dependent on cheap fossil fuel, soil erosion, and air pollution. I take it that you're speaking partly against this sort of dependence in your discussion of spiritual economics —when you say there can be too much sitting meditation.

I'm far from thinking that the timeless, unhuman, and true is all confined to the Bible. What you say about lore and mythology is pretty much acceptable to me. And I would add that the timeless, unhuman, and true continues to turn up here and there—and not just in the work of "trained minds." But it seems to me it characteristically, if not always, turns up encrusted or mixed. The critical problem implied in that is the same as the problem of authority.

My own problems with the Bible go back to childhood. In a society even nominally Christian, the Bible is bound to be a source of cheap religious thrills and of a false and abusive authority. It also becomes a kind of "parent" against which the rebellious will rebel. My own disgust and rebellion lasted longer than I wish it had.

October 16

What I was about to say is that I now think or hope there is a kind of critical love that can make our inheritance from the past usable and useful. The Bible is no more escapable than any other body of teaching; there is too much truth in it for it to be escapable. One has to read it critically for what it says, and critically for what it is tending toward that it does not say. Same for the English poetic inheritance. To dismiss it all by quoting a few passages out of context [...] is a bad waste and damage.

I like the reviews by Bill Devall,[†] good exercises of good judgement.

But I can't tell about George Sessions.† He knows a lot, has his heart in the right place, but I finally get tired of his cataloging, and long to hear him say something critical and practical.

What impresses me increasingly about the New Agers and Aquarian Conspirators is their lack of interest in what I can only call virtue. They seem unable to come up to the realization that for things to get better a lot of people individually will have to do good acts, do them right, and do them probably at some cost to their "selves."

I've been just terribly busy since I last wrote at this letter: doing fall chores, sawing wood, fencing, etc. Now I'm getting ready to leave tomorrow for a week's trip to Detroit, Ames, and Rock Island.

In the midst of all this work and hurry I realize—sometimes with sorrow, sometimes with rage—that I wish my life were far more quiet, contemplative, and studious. My fate, it seems, is to learn primarily from work, but I never quite succeed in reconciling myself to that.

Thanks for the lovely poem—and for the phone call, which Tanya reported to me.

And I hope my responses make clear how grateful I am for your letters.

I must end this. Come to see us when you can. Our love to you all.

Wendell

GARY SNYDER [NEVADA CITY, CA]
TO WENDELL BERRY [PORT ROYAL, KY]

21: XII: 80 [December 21, 1980]

Dear Wendell,

I certainly don't want to try (further)—to make points by quotes —esp. Bible quotes—(I'm responding to yours of 15 Sept.-Oct. 16) and am content to let the matter rest. There are no people anywhere who don't act hastily and with less than adequate gratitude—most of the time—East or West—and I'm too well along on my studies of environmental problems in Asia to think E/W dichotomies teach us much—rather, I keep thinking we need to understand better what civilization itself is.

Here it is day of the solstice (and full moon too—) a full quarter since you wrote me. I got back from E. coast and midwest well worn out and went right to work on a foreword I'd promised (I'm about to quit promising any more of those—) and then got the firewood in before rains came. Somehow took 6 weeks to do those 2 things. I'm about to radically change my life—finally—by cutting down on excess projects and efforts and promises. I begin to see it as a kind of very culpable spiritual pride that I keep thinking I can do so much. The effort becomes graceless after while.

The return to Zen study with a teacher the past two years is helping me get a perspective on this. The first thing, I think, that will go is my insane notion to be a scholar of the sort that is proper in graduate school. I'm paring down and simplifying my China work [*The Great Clod* project] in light of this realization—who am I trying to please?—anyway—as you are well aware I know, about our time in life it's ripe to clarify realistic possibilities. I'm actually enjoying looking at things anew this way.

Did fruit tree pruning and dormant spray yesterday—and went in half-owner on a hydraulic wood-splitter. I'm seeing cutting and selling a little firewood as a skill to start teaching the boys—by the time they're in mid-teens they could always make themselves some money that way. More than enough dead and down wood through these hills.

Masa and I are staying home through the solstice holidays and feeling about (for the nonce) "caught up." We wish you and Tanya and Mary and Den a fine Christmas and winter—have you noticed Jupiter and Saturn together in the East in early morning?

Faithfully,
Gary

Port Royal, Ky. 40058
December 29, 1980

Dear Gary,

My own fall has been a real frenzy of work, writing jobs, travel by air and road, etc., etc. I'm tired, cross, still overloaded, and have a foot high stack of mail that I've neglected ever since March. So I know what you mean by graceless effort, the need "to clarify realistic possibilities," etc. And I take heart from your determination to clear your life of excessive work. If you can, I'll be thinking, maybe I can.

I'm even hypothetically willing to hear you say you're going to revise your "insane notion to be a scholar of the sort that is proper in graduate school." To the extent that that notion *is* insane I can only concur, of course. But since I've never seen the insanity of it myself, I have to say I'm a little uneasy over your proposed cure.

There is, I know, a kind of niggling, pointless, even destructive scholarship to be found in graduate schools. But I have never seen it in your work so far, and I have not even suspected it in what I have seen or heard of your China work. So I hope you won't let an exuberance of simplification cause you to undervalue your scholarship. This is meant in praise. You know how ignorant I am of much that you are learned in, and you must correct me if I am wrong, but it has been my belief that the soundness and authority of your work comes in considerable measure from your competent, careful scholarship. *The Real Work* is so excellent because it is informed by a competence that is *both* practical and scholarly. That, I think, is why your Buddhism has none of the taint of the feckless, dainty, bodiless, brainless spirituality that goes with most U.S. religion, Eastern and Western.

I know that is uninvited and probably unnecessary, and you

will probably have to overlook or pardon it. Maybe I'm writing mostly out of the growing awareness of my own lack of adequate scholarship.

What you say about the uselessness of East/West dichotomies seems to me much to the point. Just to keep rushing from one side of the boat to the other is foolish and dangerous. What we badly need is reliable, knowledgeable criticism of both traditions, expecting both to be humanly good and bad. By that we could escape fads of thought and start to think. [...]

Teilhard de Chardin distresses me too. I've finally got around to reading some in *The Future of Man*. In light of his own tradition, it seems to me, he is a monster or a devil. You suspected him, I think, of being the source of the technological determinism-and-optimism of some of the Lindisfarnians. I hope not, but I'm afraid the tune is familiar. The essay on the atom bomb† is vulgar, foolish, repulsive, and frightening as anything I have ever read. It is almost thrilling to find the enemy's argument so concisely stated (in such overweening rhetoric), but my innards quake reading it. "Not only could matter be expressed in terms of mathematics, it could be subjugated by mathematics .... [Man] had discovered ... another secret pointing the way to his omnipotence." Some Christian!

T. de C. talks like the serpent in Genesis, like Satan in the N.T. Temptations, like R. Buckminster Fuller,† like Weston in C. S. Lewis's trilogy,† like the Chief in Ed Abbey's new novel, *Good News*.†

Here, we're en route from Christmas to Mary's wedding on Jan. 10. After the middle of Jan. I hope to be ready to settle down to two or three months of work on my *own* writing.

Well, as Thoreau said, Simplify! But, as I hasten to add, Not too much!

Your friend,
Wendell

Port Royal, Ky. 40058
December 30, 1980

Dear Gary,

I've been meaning to send you these poems, but forgot when I wrote you yesterday. They are the 1979 Sabbath poems, much revised, with some new ones from 1980. The stanzas from Dunbar are extra.[†] This is not meant to add to your burdens of reading and letter writing. I'm just sending copies to a few friends, which is the only form of publication I intend for these probably for a long time. I don't know either how long this work may last, or what the final order of it will be.

And this morning I happened again upon a quotation to put beside the quotation from Teilhard de Chardin in yesterday's letter:

What was fruitful in the thought of the new scientists
was the bold use of mathematics in the construction of
hypotheses, tested not by observation simply but by controlled observation of phenomena that could be precisely measured. On the practical side it was this that
delivered Nature into our hands. . . . By reducing Nature
to her mathematical elements it substituted a mechanical for a genial or animistic conception of the universe.
The world was emptied, first of her indwelling spirits,
then of her occult sympathies and antipathies, finally of
her colours, smells, and tastes. . . .The result was dualism
rather than materialism. The mind, on whose ideal con-
structions the whole method depended, stood over against
its object in ever sharper dissimilarity. Man with his new
powers became rich like Midas but all that he touched had
gone dead and cold. This process, slowly working, ensured
during the next century the loss of the old mythical

imagination: the conceit, and later the personified abstraction, takes its place. Later still, as a desperate attempt to bridge a gulf which begins to be found intolerable, we have the Nature poetry of the Romantics.

> —C. S. Lewis, *English Literature in the Sixteenth Century*,
> Oxford, 1954, pp.3-4

Lewis, I think, is speaking as a Christian, also out of what he called the Old Western culture (*Selected Literary Essays*, pp.1-14). T. de C. [Teilhard de Chardin] is speaking as a Shelleyan or Promethean romantic (and like a strip miner).

Wes Jackson[†] says that what Prometheus needs is a bridle and reins.

I paid a visit to Dana and Wes Jackson just before Christmas to write an article about them.[†] I like them very much.

Wendell

◇◇◇◇◇

EDITOR'S NOTE: Satish Kumar, editor of the British magazine *Resurgence*, as well as founder and then chairman of the Schumacher Society in England, had contacted Gary Snyder and Wendell Berry to speak at the annual Schumacher Society Lectures in Bristol (1982). Letters leading up to October 1982, include occasional discussions of travel arrangements, plans for visits with friends, and thoughts on speaking engagements.

GARY SNYDER [NEVADA CITY, CA]
TO WENDELL BERRY [PORT ROYAL, KY]

14 I 81 [January 14, 1981]

Dear Wendell,

Thank you for your words on scholarship—I need clarification, I guess I need to distinguish the standards and styles of academics from a more relaxed but highly informative prose (such as your *Unsettling* presents.) (Speaking of which, I thought it passing odd that you weren't mentioned in a recent *Time* article[†] on "Agrarianism" in literature. They stayed mostly w/ the old Tennessee boys.) [...]

Satish Kumar of *Resurgence* says October 1982 in England; and speaks as though you have agreed to that too. It's a good time for me; I hope it works out.

I'm asking for a little permission here[†]—card to return enclosed. Trust there's no problem.

I really appreciate, to go back, your warm defense of (my) scholarship. Back to the fields! To work.

Just bought half interest in a hydraulic wood-splitter—8 hp. w/ 25,000 lbs. pressure. It works! Old twisty oak rounds fall in two. Part of the idea—beside to ease our own wood-supply—is that in 3 or 4 years Kai and Gen could become wood cutters and make a lot of money while being their own boss. We have all the other tools. With vast public lands virtually at our door, and the rising price of cordwood, it makes good sense.

Thanks for T. de C. [Teilhard de Chardin] tips too. The book I read is *The Phenomenon of Man*. Biological/theological w/ a boundless-progress message. Two sharp put-down reviews of Teilhard from biologists (Gaylord Simpson and P. B. Medawar) are reprinted in Philip Appleman (ed.) *Darwin* (Norton pb, '79).[†] Medawar is particularly wicked to Teilhard! A perverse delight to read. I'll xerox and send you. Enough for now.

Your friend,
Gary

Port Royal, Ky. 40058
January 22, 1981

Dear Gary,

I've already signed and sent back the permission card.

I did hear from Satish Kumar, but haven't answered. Have you? He told me that *you* had already agreed. I don't like it that he told you that I had, but am pretty much willing to go in Oct. of 82 if everything can be worked out satisfactorily. I would like Tanya to be able to go, would like to know exactly what he wants, don't want it to be too much, etc.

It would be a good idea, I think, if you and I could talk about this by phone. Why don't you call me next time you get to a phone? Call collect—I'd like to pay for the call but can't call you. I'm usually at the house after 6:30 or 7:00, also around noon. I'll tell Tanya to refuse the call if I'm not home.

Excuse my haste. Jack Shoemaker has me surrounded by deadlines. The man is a slave driver.

We're dry here.

Your friend,
Wendell

3 II 81 [February 3, 1981]

Dear Wendell—

A great pleasure to speak with you Sunday, and on the way back from cross-country skiing at that—so was still full of crisp new snow and blue sky.

Here is the review of T. de C.'s *Phenomenon of Man*. As well as

Promethean Romantic he may well be old-style Gnostic (Dualist) heretic, which is why the church would never give him the *imprimatur* (and thus *not* because he was a "scientist") —

The point of the C. S. Lewis quote from *English Literature* ... is also on dualism. Dualism either goes excessively spiritual or excessively materialist. ("Dialectic materialism" an interesting, if unsuccessful, attempt to rectify extreme materialism...)

On "Mind" and "Reality"

Yün-men (862–949 AD)

Talking to the group, held up his staff. He said—the ordinary person takes this as "something real."

The Hinayana Buddhists would say it is "nothingness"; the Hindus would say it is "illusory existence" and the Mahayana Buddhist philosophers would say that "its reality is in its nothingness"—

But I say, "It is just a staff. Movement is movement, sitting is sitting; but don't wobble!"

Which is the Zen way to deal w/it—backed by actualization, experience.

Nobody with half a brain would say "reality is in my mind"—or the reverse—because nobody knows the meanings of the terms—either "reality" *or* "mind." They are just words.

Whatever one wishes to call it, we are in it together—(all in "the same Mind" or, "the same System" or "the same Void") and in a process of mutual reflection. Solidity or absence of same is not a real problem. ("Ouch! My toe hurts!") (so does mine, says the legless man—)

Anyhow—

More later—

I'm off to read poems in Oregon at the crack of dawn tomorrow.

Snow melting now

Gary

Port Royal, Ky. 40058
February 7, 1981

Dear Gary,

Thanks for the comment on mind-reality and the Yün-men text. That's useful. We'll have to talk more of this. There's a chickadee eating suet outside the window now. I call him "real," if by nothing else, by courtesy. But I think it is more than courtesy. I could be wrong about his reality (and importance). And I could be wrong about him in such a way that he could no longer live here. If I refuse to let him in my mind on the assumption that he is "out there" on his own standing, then I may get him out of my mind by getting him out of the world. But I want to extend myself the courtesy of being out of my own mind. Bad to be stuck inside your mind, worse to be stuck in somebody else's—both are possible

Thanks also for the articles by Medawar and [Russell] Means.[†] Medawar seems to me to be right on the mark. Means, though I think I agree with him, obscures his argument by a very uncritical choice of terms. He is cutting his meat with a mop. That line he draws from Newton to Marx is *not* "European culture." Plenty of Europeans have understood that that line is the antithesis of European culture or any other kind of culture. But I doubt that much can be meant by "European"—or, for that matter, by "American Indian." [...] I think it is necessary to be more critical. Otherwise you wind up with performances, personality exhibits. In Means's statement I don't hear a Lakota speaking, but an Indian version of a 1960s radical making a very general 1960s radical speech to the effect that "we" are better than "you." And the whole baggage of "personality" comes pushing out ahead of thought.

I don't feel comfortable saying that. It doesn't seem a very mannerly way to respond. But I wanted to tell you how I felt. Forgive me as much as necessary. And tell me if you think I'm wrong.

I wrote Satish Kumar that I agree "in principle" to his proposal, but I don't want to be overloaded.

We got rain enough on Sunday to put water in our well.

I've been busy trying to correct some of my old work (writing).[†] Am feeling rather humble about my infallibility.

Wendell

GARY SNYDER [NEVADA CITY, CA]
TO WENDELL BERRY [PORT ROYAL, KY]

10 III 81 [March 10, 1981]

Dear Wendell,

Frogs in the pond, sand-hill cranes flying north over. Didn't hear the cranes til the frogs stopped suddenly. Similar sounds. Those cries. (No difference between reality "in the mind" and "out there" —a seamless continuum—*especially* if one can accept the fact that his own "consciousness" is not personal, private, special, or unique but just another sort of air and water).

—Ha— @ Means' article, boy, was I coming to it from another direction. I was impressed by it because it is such an *improvement* on what Indian activists have been saying—so gentle and open! by comparison. Heartening in that sense. I *do* like his use of "European thought" to implicitly mean Imperium or Metropole thought. Which of course does not speak for Breton thought, or Basque, Manx, Welsh, Lapp, Friesian, Walloon, Bavarian, Northumbrian, Irish, Tuscan, etc. thought. There's the difference.

Of course Means isn't a Lakota. He's a 20th century brown person with a big FBI file on him like you and I would never have, because he's brown, talks tough, and resists exploitation (uranium I think) of his inherited (Lakota) territory. Those guys have sure taken their knocks from the Feds lately—like Leonard Peltier,[†] who probably won't get out of prison alive.

Mmm. Nectarines blossoming, apricot about too, spring's about here, here. But 33% short on annual rain.

More later—

your friend GS

Port Royal, Ky. 40058
March 14, 1981

Dear Gary,

To me, very interesting and difficult questions rise around the Means article. I understand your point—am *almost* embarrassed that my response was unsympathetic. I would be sympathetic to him himself, I think. But the rhetoric of us—them I usually find frightening.

I accept the tragedy that we must take sides. But there is nothing I distrust and fear more than side-taking, especially when one's argument becomes an apology for one's side. What I liked about M. L. King was that though he chose a side and spoke for black people, the *sense* he made belonged to everybody. In other words, I think you have to take a side, but you have to serve the truth. The idea that truth is all on your side is the worst danger to your side. If Yeats had dissolved all his disagreements with Irishmen in a righteous fury at "British colonialism" he would be worthless and forgotten by now. So I would respect an attack on "European thought" that took due notice of the flaws in Irish thought, etc.

I *am* sympathetic to what you say about the "seamless continuum" between consciousness and the world. But now you will have to instruct me. Is that continuum an ideal or goal, or does it always exist? It has always seemed to me that in your criticism of our abuses of nature your assumption has been the same as mine: that minds can be wrong about the world; that to correct themselves they will have to learn more about it; that the possibility that it can be learned about implies that it has an objective "standing"

89

as reality or truth. If I am wrong in thinking that we agree about that, then tell me, for goodness' sake. And then I hope you will also tell me, if what is "out there" is to be granted no objective standing, what do you see to be the difference in validity between the ecological household and the household of industrial economics?

Spring is coming on here. Hard frost last night; bright sun and birdsong this morning. Lambs are coming, the first mare to foal the 25th. I've been working all winter against Jack Shoemaker's deadlines, and believe I will make it. But I have done no new work to speak of—except for notes—and I'm sorry for that.

I enclose copies of an exchange of letters with Bill Thompson.[†]

Plans seem to be going forward with Satish Kumar. I have a letter from him in which he commits himself to "three public gatherings" and "a relaxed tour." David Ehrenfeld says we must make them be very precise about their plans—otherwise, he says, they will weaken us with vegetarian meals and take advantage of us. I will write back before long and say that I want to see a proposed schedule in detail well in advance. Tanya, I am determined, will go.

Love to you all.

Wendell

GARY SNYDER [KOBE, JAPAN]
TO WENDELL AND TANYA BERRY [PORT ROYAL, KY]

9 VI 81 [June 9, 1981][†]

Dear Wendell and Tanya,

Visiting Masa's father's side—all Okinawans—farmers—with at least 300 years family history (big tomb)—very hard working and prosperous. Staying at the house of a dairyman—26 Holsteins. Reads the Japanese Holstein dairyman journal. I was sorry to miss Lindisfarne this year, but these travels in Japan are worth it and more. Kai and Gen love it, and Masa is instructed by her (formerly *poor*) family's prosperity.

Good summer days to you—

Gary

24 VII 81 [*July 24, 1981*]

Dear Wendell and Tanya—

Nobody in Japan who farms, w/ few exceptions—can live by that alone. They all moonlight! Gov't price support of rice (and *tons* of SW rice in storage) keeps it going. But they still keep at it. My wife's sister's husband is in the cattle-feed import business—fascinating man from rural background—he and I have talked a lot. He might want to advertise in *Small Farm* [*sic: New Farm*]† if he gets a Japanese small-agricultural-machine-export business going (he hadn't heard of Rodale etc.) (but is most interested—went to see Amish farms in Peru twice, on his own,) == so could you drop a postcard to Rodale people to send a bundle of samples of *Organic* and *Small Farm* to him—as they would to potential advertiser/customer w/ other info.? [...] He's fine in English.

Masa's Okinawan relatives are a village based network who *do* live entirely by agriculture—near the big Naha city markets, with *bitter-melon* as a speciality crop which they send as far as Tokyo.

Japan is so delighted with being a success that the rapidly building confusion and contradiction hasn't hit yet. They do excellent work, they're *nice*, and I find my own eyes beginning to accept vast earthmoving projects because they *seem* to know what they're doing. Buddhism is coming back to life, as a strong critic (low key) of the excessive-growth direction. Education is superb! I'll tell you more when I have it sorted out (and likely see you in April, w/ J. Shoemaker's help—). Masa says greetings—Kai and Gen want to go home now (1 more week).

Yrz.

Gary

Port Royal, Ky. 40058
December 12, 1981

Dear Gary,

I owe you several letters, I think, but don't know what to do about the debt except just despair of it.

Most of the outdoor work and most of my travels, anyhow, are over for several weeks, and I'm hoping to get some writing done. I have a few winter projects for the afternoons, mainly clearing some new pasture, that ought to help clear my mind. Too much flying, too much talk, too many strangers have smudged it up, I think.

Jack [Shoemaker] gave me a copy of Aitken Roshi's MS, *Taking the Path of Zen*. I have read it with great interest and pleasure. He has an unusually straight forward and lucid mind.

No grandchild yet. Nothing in sight to worry about, and yet of course we worry.

I enclose a check that I hope will cover my half of the calling that has been and probably will be done about the business with Satish. If my part comes to more than this, let me know. If it comes to less, then call me up sometime just to visit.

Real winter here now—14° last night. We're settling into the routine of feeding.

We're well, and hope all of you are.

Your friend,
Wendell

21 Jan. '82 [January 21, 1982]

Dear Wendell—

Good grief I still have this honest but excessive and unnecessary check which I'll return—lord knows I'll get it back from you other simpler ways—

16" snow here, but not cold. You folks been having some winter! I hope the horses can get their feed.

Came back from a quick visit w/ Shoemaker yesterday (and 84-yr old stepmother's birthday). I'm glad you like Bob Aitken's MS.

Waiting for Satish [Kumar] to come back from India to respond.

Yrz.

Gary

WENDELL BERRY [PORT ROYAL, KY]
TO GARY SNYDER [NEVADA CITY, CA]

Port Royal, Ky. 40058
January 26, 1982

Dear Gary,

Well, then, I hope you'll call me collect the next few times. I hate for all the burden of these necessary and pleasurable calls to fall on you.

We *have* had some cold weather here −20° below zero, the coldest, wind chill of −50°. But we have not had much snow, nothing like yours. I like to feed stock in winter, and be intellectual and literary regular every morning, and look forward to spring.

Tanya and I have a granddaughter now, and so have been promoted.

We're well here and hope all of you are.

Wendell

P.S. Thanks for the book mark, which has done me no end of good.

Port Royal, Ky. 40058
February 19, 1982

Dear Gary,

I have a copy of Satish Kumar's Feb. 9 letter to you, accepting our terms. Aside from the practical difficulties of leaving here, I am very pleased with the prospect both of a trip to England and a trip with you.

If possible, I would like to go a couple of weeks before the lecture week. My private purpose of the trip will be to see what I can of survivals and relics of the traditional farming. At present, I have no idea how to go about this, and will need time to ask questions, make contacts, etc. I will keep you informed of what develops, and I hope you will let me know about your own intentions, plans, etc.

I have been very busy with a long essay,[†] begun two winters ago, resumed after Christmas, and just finished this morning. And just in time too, I think, for I have some trips ahead of me now, and spring work is close. Our lambs should begin to come on Feb. 25, then calves and foals.

Love to you all,
Wendell

17 March 1982 [*March 17, 1982*]

Dear Wendell,

After a little flurry of apricots and peach starting to blossom, we've got an inch of snow and a bit of a freeze today. Snow down throughout the Sierra Nevada. It's good to hold the fruit trees down awhile longer. They were showing signs of blooming too soon.

I responded to Satish [Kumar] along the same lines you did saying ok. As it turns out, my Swedish publisher [Reidar Ekner] has enticed me to spend ten days or so in Sweden before going to England, and that's what I'll do. I might also stay a little longer on in England and go on from there to Lindisfarne in Colorado.† As you, I don't have it all worked out, and will let you know more what I am thinking when I have it clear in mind.

It would be nice if we could travel just a little together while there, away from the lecture tour format.

Hard-working and busy indeed, this year. We have this *Zendo* building project† mounting up on us now. One of these days a chance to speak with more ease.

Yours,
Gary

WENDELL BERRY [PORT ROYAL, KY]
TO GARY SNYDER [NEVADA CITY, CA]

Port Royal, Ky. 40058
July 5, 1982

Dear Gary,

This is mainly to say hello. I hoped to see you at Jack's place in May, and was very sorry when I didn't.

Lots going on here, as usual. Den was with the Jacksons [Wes and Dana] at The Land Institute from Jan. to the end of May. He's home now, mainly working for Mary and her husband who have bought a 180 acre farm. Serious business, buying a farm in the midst of an agricultural depression in the midst of inflation and usury. It is troubling to see what a tight situation young farmers have to learn in. No room in this economy for the usual shifting for a right fit between mind and place, no room for *experience*, no room for the second chances the young always need.

So the concerns spread out. It is clear that life does not get simpler. I learn it over and over, always with the same reluctance and regret. The notion that life could somehow be simplified has been powerful with me. I still yearn toward it.

If you were here, I'd get you to give me the Buddhist way of dealing with this problem.

We haven't yet got the pieces of our English trip together. But by now there have turned out to be pieces, which do look like they can finally be put together. The strongest likelihood now seems to be that we will go to Ireland on about the 7th or 8th of Oct., then to the N. of England, then S. to Wales, Devon, etc. ahead of our lectures of Bristol. I'd like a free day or two in London at the end of the trip, for museums, etc.; maybe to meet Kathleen Raine.† Then home a few days before the Lindisfarne meeting.

If you'd like to come here to rest on your way from England to Colorado, we'd be glad. Then you and I could fly to Colorado together.

Your friend,
Wendell

GARY SNYDER [NEVADA CITY, CA]
TO WENDELL BERRY [PORT ROYAL, KY]

28:VII:82 [*July 28, 1982*]

Dear Wendell,

Really good to hear from you. Thanks for keeping in touch. Our *Zendo* is more or less constructed and finished, though there is lots of landscaping to do—heaps of raw earth here and there—but it is in use, and beginning to settle into its function. So, you'll be going to Ireland. I'll be in Sweden from around the 10th of October until the 22nd when I fly to London and I'm not sure at what point our paths will connect but it will be right in there. I'm working on a talk that will be a slight variant on your theme; I may even title it "The Gift of Wild Land." Touching on the nature of wilderness and the nature of the sacred. Also, exploring our attitudes towards worthless or non-productive parts of the globe, which are often de facto wilderness. And some extensions of that into human nature.

The Old Ways was recently translated into Swedish, so that is what brings me up there, the publisher wants me to travel around a bit and give some readings. As for return, I am thinking of staying on a little longer—to do some of what you mentioned, seeing the museums in London, and also I have an invitation to Cambridge; so I'm planning to leave November 4th and fly directly to Lindisfarne. I am gambling that I can do it without a rest or a wait as well as trying to catch up. Also, going from East to West is much less jet-lag problem than the reverse.

What's this about a simplified life? I tell people who are interested in that, that they should be single and get a rented furnished room somewhere south of Market Street in San Francisco above a twenty-four hour cafeteria. There's a lot of old retired railroad men and divorcees down in there who are having a good simple life. I guess the answer to complexity, seriously, is organization: and the acceptance of the necessity of maintenance. I always liked the quote, "Energy flowing through a system tends to organize that system."[†]

Kai's working for a neighbor, carpentry, riding to work and back on his motorcycle. You can hardly keep up with the way things leap ahead. See you this fall.

Staunchly,
Gary

Port Royal, Ky. 40058
August 6, 1982

Dear Gary,

My talk in England, written last fall for the Schumacher Society meeting in Amherst, Mass., has so far been titled "People, Land, and Community."† It is about the possibility of harmonious connections. My assumption always is that the land, as "given," is wild, and that it is the character of good farming (or other use) to keep a certain wildness in and around it. There is, for instance, a wildness in the soil that we call "fertility." Our talks, I imagine, will approach wildness from opposite directions, and so complement and balance each other. Would you like to see a copy of my paper? I would like sooner or later to see a copy of yours. I want to revise mine anyhow, and if a way occurred to me I would like to make it as good a companion piece as I can.

Yes, when I get fed up with complications, I have been known to say, "Let's go live on the 5th floor of an apartment house."

And Tanya says, "Who're you kidding?"

Well, *some* flowing energy will organize a system. But some human energy—some humans' energy—scrambles any system it flows through.

Hard to imagine Kai motorcycling off to work. But I'm a grandfather now, and ought to be getting used to unimaginables. I ain't.

Wendell

[*August, 1982*]

Dear Wendell

I'll be in the Bay Area in a few days and will call you, but, yes—I would like to see your Schumacher talk if it's written up. And I'll send you a copy of mine when I get it in order (some revisions). Are you interested at all in the Findhorn "Onearth" invitation.[†] Well, I'll call you. Got back from a great 5-day hike with Kai in the Sierra. Big apple crop coming.

Yrz.

GS

Port Royal, Ky. 40058
August 21, 1982

Dear Gary,

I have your card, and will look forward to your call.

I enclose a letter and invitation that includes you. I wrote Mr. Young[†] that our plans have already been made for us by the Schumacher Soc. His article on [Robert] Lowell assures me that I will be found wanting. I hope so.

The person I would like to meet on the Colchester jaunt is Michael Hamburger.[†] He lives not far NE at Saxmundham. I'll write to him that we'll be at Colchester.

Your friend,
Wendell

August 26 [1982]

Dear Gary,

I'm sorry for the badness of this copy [of "People, Land, and Community"]. If you can't read it, say. Everything possible is going on here. I'm off for Knoxville for a speech. Have had no response to my affirmative reply to Findhorn.

Your friend,
W.

Port Royal, Ky. 40058
September 21, 1982

Dear Gary,

Now it seems that I'm to speak at Findhorn on the 17th, you on the 20th. We (Tanya and I) will need to leave Findhorn the morning of the 18th and head south, looking at sheep farms and whatever of agricultural interest may present itself.

We will get to Edinburgh sometime on the 21st to lecture to the Soil Assoc. that night, and then leave by train for Bristol the next morning.

We are to stay the night of the 21st with a member of the Soil Assoc.—which organization, I believe will put you up that night as well. But they say they need to know if you will be in Edinburgh that night. Best way, I think, is for you to work all this out with R. Doudna,† who will inform the Soil Assoc.

Whew! Such a lot of planning! And we have a lot of irons in the fire here. I'm hurrying and gritting my teeth, but I do believe we may be ready when the time comes.

Wendell

3 X [October 3, 1982]

Dear Wendell,

It works out as I will be travelling to Findhorn the 19th and join-
ing you in Edinburgh the 21st. I have reservations on the same (9
AM) train to Bristol the 22nd. I leave this Friday (8th) for Sweden.
So will be out of touch. [...]

My paper's finished,† will have a copy for you when we meet.
"Good, Wild, and Sacred Land"

Yrz.

GS

◇◇◇◇

EDITOR'S NOTE: Wendell Berry's letter was written shortly after
returning from the United Kingdom, where he traveled some with
Gary Snyder. The two writers spoke at the Schumacher Lectures
in Bristol.

Port Royal, Ky. 40058
November 26, 1982

Dear Gary,

Thanks very much for the ballad† and for Jerry Martien's† good
poem.

I too am getting back into stride—and reading and writing, have
cut some firewood for next year, am getting started on a new shed
on the little barn by the house. Though I do still feel a little the
effects of the long interruption.

But it *was* a valuable interruption. I would like to go back again before too many years and see the West of Ireland, the Scottish islands, Yorkshire and Cumbria, more London.

I'm trying to find out about the possibility of getting some Shetland sheep—John Moses seemed to admire them most of all the rare breeds—but no luck so far.

Our best to you all.

Wendell

◇◇◇◇◇

EDITOR'S NOTE: In this letter Wendell Berry enclosed an article by Dean Rotbart titled "Colorado Town of 60 Is All the Rage with Some Tibetans," *The Wall Street Journal* (November 19, 1982). The article concerns Maurice Strong, a millionaire and land developer, who controlled 120,000 acres of land near Crestone, Colorado. Strong was giving away plots of land to select spiritual and philosophical groups, which created an influx of people moving into the rural area. Since 1979, Crestone had been home to the Lindisfarne Association, which was established through Strong's invitation and mentioned unfavorably in the article.

WENDELL BERRY [PORT ROYAL, KY]
TO GARY SNYDER [NEVADA CITY, CA]

Port Royal, Ky. 40058
December 6, 1982

Dear Gary,

Wes [Jackson] sent me the enclosed article. I think I know about exactly what is wrong with the attitude of the 60 year old Crestonians —"We don't need no outsiders," etc.—but I have some sympathy with them, none at all with Mr. Strong's multimillionaire game of "social science," "throwing diverse groups together." The real name for this game, of course, is "colonialism" and the parallels with the settlement of the eastern seaboard are striking—a rich landlord planting villages of weirdos on the territory of a population of locals who don't need outsiders, for the purpose of increasing the commercial value of said territory, etc.

It makes me sick. I feel like maybe I should say something about it, at least to Bill Thompson. What do you think? Take care of the clipping, or return it to me, please.

I've been loafing through the Haskins book. The chapter on the industrial revolution is full of industrial revelations. Very suggestive and useful. I'm trying to write about our trip. Slow work. Trip too fast. Love to you all.

Wendell

P.S. The situation at Crestone would be different, I think, if it were not for Maurice Strong and his grants of land.

◇◇◇◇◇

EDITOR'S NOTE: In this letter Gary Snyder enclosed three poems by Dennis Hansen, a farmer from Emmetsburg, Iowa. He also sent pages from *Planet Drum* (February 1980), including a poem by Reidar Ekner titled "Unbroken Chain" and a corresponding article by Snyder titled "Letter from Sweden."

GARY SNYDER [NEVADA CITY, CA]
TO WENDELL BERRY [PORT ROYAL, KY]

[January 18, 1983]

This gent [Dennis Hansen] is trying hard to really farm and is very lonely. If you know anybody living near him it would be nice to put him in touch.

Port Royal, Ky. 40058
January 21, 1983

Dear Gary,

Thanks for your letter from Sweden and Reidar Ekner's poem. A fine poem, I think. And a good, swift letter too.

What kind of company do you think Dennis Hansen needs? I don't know any literary company in his area; am somewhat acquainted with a couple of farmers worth knowing.

Do you know Hansen? After my extravagantly wrong first opinion of Satish [Kumar], I should give up being suspicious—but those two farmers out there are important to me and I want to be careful who I send to them.

I'll be lecturing and reading at Grinnell College on Feb. 21 (lecture at 7:30) and 22 (afternoon reading). Maybe you could tell him —though it would be a pretty long drive for him.

I've been staying swamped with work of various kinds, but have got a good deal done. Have built a new shed on the little barn since about Thanksgiving. Am breaking 3 two-year-olds. And so forth.

Wendell

2 II 83 [February 2, 1983]

Dear Wendell—

Quick reply: I don't know much about Dennis Hansen, I met his brother who teaches at University of the Pacific Stockton—and got those poems. His brother said Dennis really needed some contacts.

I'll drop him a card about the Grinnell reading. Peter Coyote went to Grinnell—so did my neighbor Jerry Tecklin.

See you in April it seems possibly. Trying to arrange readings for 11th and 12th (Mon–Tues.) and be arriving in the area around 9–10—rent a car and come to Port Royal if that's ok. Greet Tanya!

Fraternally

Gary

WENDELL BERRY [GRINNELL, IA & PORT ROYAL, KY]
TO GARY SNYDER [NEVADA CITY, CA]

As from Port Royal, Ky. 40058
2/22/1983 [February 22, 1983]

Dear Gary,

Excuse me for sending you a stranger's letter† so complimentary to myself, but it is such a good letter it seems a shame not to pass it on.

Week before last I was in western N.Y., came home sick with flu and pneumonia, got back on my feet in time to leave again on Sunday. I'm in Grinnell, Iowa, now, lecturing and reading and recuperating. To Oberlin tomorrow night, home Friday.

Then I got to really get to work—winter jobs to finish up, spring jobs to start, lambs and foals will be coming, got to try to finish writing up British agricultural travels, etc.†

It is good to look forward to seeing you in April.

2/26/83 [February 26, 1983]

I'm home again now. Got back last night. No more trips till April 23, so I'm celebrating. Ewes are bred to start lambing today. I don't think they will, but looks like they'll start soon.

Masa, thank you ever so much for doing the ideogram† for my book. Jack [Shoemaker] sent us a copy. We are very pleased with it, and have it propped up on the mantel where we can admire it. Tanya and I would be happy if you would come to see us with Gary when he comes to Kentucky in the spring.

We hope all is well with both of you and your boys.

Your friend,
Wendell

WENDELL BERRY [PORT ROYAL, KY]
TO GARY SNYDER [NEVADA CITY, CA]

Port Royal, Ky. 40058
March 11, 1983

Dear Gary,

North Point is going to publish my book *Standing By Words* in the fall. I have been thinking a long time about dedicating it to you, but it's clearly not something you should be surprised with, for it may be an "honor" you'd rather do without.

It has seemed appropriate to me to dedicate this book to you because I have benefitted so much from your effort to bring your knowledge of Oriental and American Indian cultures *to bear* on present, local, practical problems. And in this book one of my efforts is to do the same thing with a strain of Western and English culture.

(That, of course, is not my only debt to you, by far.)

My *worry* about the dedication is that it might make the book an embarrassment to you. There are places in it, for one thing, where I'm afraid my reading may be insufficient and I run the risk of error. For another thing, the book takes issue with things said about poetry by a number of contemporary poets. I don't believe that this is done meanly, but I know that one of the essays has already caused some hard feelings.

Also, because we have a good deal in common, our differences are instructive and clarifying and useful to me. Sometimes my awareness of where you are standing gives me a sort of binocular vision. Because, for instance, my point of view is pretty much that of a Christian—a forest Christian—it seems likely that you will want or need to disagree to some extent with my book. If by dedicating the book to you, I made you feel that you should not disagree, I would look on that as a deprivation.

I am very much in earnest in wanting to know exactly how you feel about this, and am not at all in dread of any possible answer you may give me. My book quotes you or refers to your work at several crucial places, which you may think a sufficient acknowledgement, or a sufficient embarrassment, even without the dedication.

Our lambs have started coming. We have four so far. The first foal is due the 24th. Exciting times.

We have had an extraordinarily mild winter—lots of firewood left over for next year—though today is damp and cold and gray with a blustery north wind.

We're looking forward to your visit.

Your friend,
Wendell

GARY SNYDER [NEVADA CITY, CA]
TO WENDELL BERRY [PORT ROYAL, KY]

16:III:83 [*March 16, 1983*]

Dear Wendell,

Good grief, I'd be delighted and honored to have such a book dedicated to me. I never thought we would have to agree about everything anyway—clearly you are pro-agrarian, and I am pro-hunting and gathering, which only shows I am even less credible, in the 20th century, than you are. Some other differences, we should talk about some time. But yes, please do.

And I'll be seeing you: my flight from Pittsburgh arrives in Cincinnati by U.S. Air (formerly Allegheny) Flight 95 on Saturday 9th April 10:25 am. Is that ok? Can I be met? Don't bother to write an answer, I'll be travelling from here in a couple of days, and I'll check in with you or Tanya by phone some time in the next week or two.

Seventy inches of rain, and warm temperatures. The blossoms are out early, and now clear nights are frosting them. We may lose the nectarines and the apricots at least.

See you,
Gary

◇◇◇◇

EDITOR'S NOTE: On April 11, 1983, Gary Snyder read poetry with Drummond Hadley† at the University of Kentucky. On that occasion, Wendell Berry introduced Snyder to those in attendance with the following speech:

> It is generally understood that Gary Snyder belongs prominently among those workers who have made Oriental and American Indian cultures available, not just to our minds but to our hands as well. I believe that it will *come* to be understood that in his working out of the applications of these cultures—since he writes in this country, in English—he has renewed certain questions vital to *Western* culture: How did we *get* where we are? How do we *know* where we are? And once we have got where we are, and know it, how should we *act*? These questions are Jewish and Greek. They are English questions also, and are native to English literary tradition; they are central to the work of Spenser, Shakespeare, Milton, and Pope. And now in the work of a number of writers, the work of Gary Snyder preeminent among them, they are at last becoming American questions—questions, that is, that are being asked, not too soon, by the white people of Turtle Island.
>
> To ask how we got here, and where we are, and how we should act—as the older poets I have mentioned all knew

—is to ask about the proper use of unearned gifts—spiritual or natural. The dominant question of the American conservation movement so far has been whether some particular natural gift should be used or spared: *Should we, for instance, log or mine this watershed or make it a "wilderness sanctuary"?* That is a valid question, of course, and a necessary one. But the question of *how* to use—which is the question Mr. Snyder's work carries us to directly—is *more* necessary, and it is more difficult and more interesting. *Shall we spare this tree or cut it?* is a question that, even after it is answered, remains somewhat theoretical. But *How shall we cut this tree? How shall we use it? What returns or compensations must we make for its use?* are questions that must be answered practically, by practice. They involve our lives.

Because Mr. Snyder has allied his life to a place that has been logged and mined by people who asked no such questions, he knows that they must be asked. And he knows the futility of asking them if they are not answered correctly. If some answers are correct, then some are incorrect, and the proof is in the practice. If some tools and acts and ideas are proper, then some are improper. And so by the measure of our dwelling places in the world and of our own lives in them, we are brought back again to the possibility of intelligent self-judgment, are made eligible to do what this poet has called "the real work," and are given a sound curriculum at last for *home* economics. Nobody has spoken and written of that curriculum with more careful preparation or more precise intelligence or better humor than Gary Snyder.

It is a pleasure to me to welcome Gary to Kentucky again, for I know that he is a bringer of gifts.

◇◇◇◇◇

EDITOR'S NOTE: Wendell Berry's letter was written shortly after Gary Snyder and Drummond Hadley departed after giving readings at the University of Kentucky and the University of Louisville. Snyder had left Berry a draft of his essay, "Good, Wild, Sacred," which renewed their ongoing dialogue on Christianity and Zen Buddhism, as well as differences between hunting-gathering and agrarian cultures.

WENDELL BERRY [PORT ROYAL, KY]
TO GARY SNYDER [NEVADA CITY, CA]

Port Royal, Ky. 40058
April 13, 1983

Dear Gary,

You and Drum were no sooner gone than we had one perfect April day. Today it's rainy again, and the radio speaks of rain for the rest of the week.

I sat down in the woods yesterday morning and read your essay. It is excellent, I think, and I wonder if you would let me recommend it for inclusion in the book† that Wes [Jackson] and Bruce Colman and I are working on. I'll try to call you today to talk about this.

I have made a good many small suggestions, the reasons for which will be clear to you, whether you agree or not. But I see three small problems that are more important than the rest, and I'll discuss them a little here:

On page 1, "potentially sacred" is unclear. Pages 15 and 20–21 suggest that what you really mean is that you, the present inhabitants, have the potential to recognize that the land *is* sacred. The danger of the phrase, left unexplained for so long, is that it seems to imply that you have the power to *confer* sanctity on it.

On page 17, I partially note an objection to "Jehovah or a victorious king," but would like to say a little more. The land itself is not given by Jehovah, but only the right to inhabit and (within strict conditions) to use. One of the conditions (Leviticus 25:23) is that "the land shall not be sold forever." In the Biblical understanding of this, which is worked out at length, with great care, there is no resemblance to the division of spoils or to a Spanish land grant. From an Old Testament perspective, the Spanish in America must be seen as repeating the arrogant self-crediting of the bad kings of Israel.

Moreover, though Jehovah is called a king, it is very carefully understood that this is not a metaphor to be worked backwards: a king is not Jehovah.

On the top of page 18 the problem is that if the word "monoculture" is applied to *all* agriculture, then we are left without a term for the huge single-crop plantings of modern agriculture—and so are less able to talk about differences in kinds of agriculture. I see that my note on the manuscript ignores your insertion of the adjective "civilized," and I'm aware that there was a tendency toward one-crop agriculture in some places from the beginning, and yet monoculture, as I understand it, is an *extreme* possibility and a modern one, pretty much dependent on petroleum and agri-industrial chemicals.

What I'm suggesting, I guess, is that you should think more about this problem. My own notion is that monoculture is the *result* of the wrong path of civilized agriculture, not the wrong path itself. Gene Logsdon[†] has been insisting for years that the name of the wrong path is profit. But both profit and monoculture, it seems to me, only *stand for* the civilized depreciation of sacredness and the consequent willingness to desecrate.

Pardon my meddling, as much as [may be] necessary.

It was *good* to have you here. Come back soon.

Your friend,
Wendell

P.S. (4/14)—Gary, I thought I had your phone number, but I don't.

So I'll just have to use this letter for my request about using your essay in our agriculture book. I don't think there is any *big* hurry, so just write me a note to say whether or not I can suggest to Wes and Bruce that we should use it. If you agree, I will send this copy you left with me to Wes, who will Xerox it and send it on to you.

Mary and Den appreciated and liked your readings. I liked what you said at Lexington about beginning 2500 years of work to make our poetry sensitive to our land. Mary did too. She said that gave her hope.

W.

WENDELL BERRY [PORT ROYAL, KY]
TO GARY SNYDER [NEVADA CITY, CA]

Port Royal, Ky. 40058
April 16, 1983

Dear Gary,

I believe this is your map. I know you are a map man, and don't want you to be deprived.

Old Peggy is still holding on to her colt—she's 12 days overdue today. The old yellow Jersey had a fine heifer night before last.

A pretty morning now, but it got down to 23° last night.

Yours for expeditious deliveries,
Wendell

GARY SNYDER [HONOLULU, HI]
TO WENDELL BERRY [PORT ROYAL, KY]

Honolulu 6: V: 83 [May 6, 1983]

Dear Wendell,

Much thanks to you and Tanya for your wonderful hospitality to Drummond and me, I hope that adding another person to the party was not too much extra trouble. It was very good for Drum to come along. And thanks for getting us to Lexington and your fine introduction.

Your thoughts on my paper (as per the letter of April 13). Your comment on my use of the term monoculture is to the point I realized instantly: there are many scales and degrees and it's not fair to speak of sensitive small-scale traditional garden plots in the same breath with agribusiness. Yet, to H & G peoples (hunting & gathering) I suppose *any* little garden seems impious. In some cases, anyway. I'll have to refine that part.

About land and Jehovah. For the purposes of my discussion I'm speaking as a cultural historian, which is to say I assume that Jehovah is a projection, not a real personage. In this analysis, what people did is more important to look at than what they said they were supposed to do (though that's a study, too). So I'll say, human kings preceded the idea of an all-powerful God. The centralization of power in fewer and fewer chiefs has an analog in the reduction of many gods and goddesses to one. The North Star, around which all the other stars revolve, became one of the natural images invoked for the "Divine King"—the Chinese "Son of Heaven" and many others. I'm not well educated on the history and prehistory of Yahveh amongst the Jews, but I sure do feel that the "promised land" (which was somebody else's land) was like a land-grant. But actually they justified their invasion after the fact with the mythology of a promised land, which is not unlike the "manifest destiny" doctrine in the western hemisphere. The Mormons and their mythology is really instructive.

(I must confess that, picking and choosing among mythologies to live by I am much more drawn to the polytheistic, pagan, fertility goddess world or the ancient near east, than that of the old testament.)

But in Buddhism we finally give up trying to find mythologies to live by anyhow, and see what can be seen of what's right here.

I'll straighten out "potentially sacred" too—

David Orr[†] is such a nice man. And Tom and Ginny Marsh, too.[†]

I had a good talk with Den in Louisville, he seemed interested in possibly visiting [Drum] Hadley's Arizona ranch. I'm sure it could be arranged and he'd be welcome. Saw Drum again in Berkeley this May 3 and 4, he's been re-entering the study of the literary world after many years lapse by quietly attending some of the various poetry-readings in the Bay Area.

This little typewriter, an elderly Royal super-tiny portable, is pretty cranky, or I'm not used to it yet. Many a birdsong to be heard, right here in residential tropical Honolulu.

your friend,

Gary

[PS] Wendell—Dear me, I hope you take this letter as just a scholar's blunt way of talking and nothing personal—G.

GARY SNYDER [HONOLULU, HI]
TO WENDELL BERRY [PORT ROYAL, KY]

Hawaii
6 IV [sic V] 83 [May 6, 1983]

Dear Wendell

I also wanted to re-affirm my pleasure at the dedication for *Standing by Words*, I am honored indeed. Saw it in proto-format at North Point several days ago.

Recently figured out the nature and importance of ritual Shinto dances as incorporated into *Nō* plays:[†] A dance by a maiden goddess becomes the "signature" for the totality of a *biome*/watershed.

More later

Gary

P.S.
The Hawaii bird stamp,[†] I swear, came up by luck of the grab. Amazing!

Port Royal, Ky. 40058
May 7, 1983

Dear Gary,

My uncle was stationed in Hawaii during the war, so it has always been a mythical place to me. He sent me a book about the birds there, which particularized my feeling that it was exotic and far off. Yours was the first live voice I ever heard coming from there.

Here is the essay ["Good, Wild, Sacred"], with a good many little suggestions and comments. But the *real* comments are in my letter.

I can't remember if I mentioned the titles of the 2 David Jones poems I'm so eager for you to read. They are "The Tribune's Visitation" and "The Tutelar of the Place"— both in *The Sleeping Lord*.[†] David Jones, in his prose, makes pretty much the same distinction you do between culture and civilization.

Well, I'll be thinking of you way off out there. Maybe you have grown used to it, but to such an inlander as I am the *idea* of an island is utterly elsewhere and charming.

Wendell

Honolulu
12 V [May 12, 1983]

Dear Wendell

Now I'm getting down to doing my work properly, finally, and—thanking you!—for the time and thought put into my "wild, sacred" MS [and] want to respond with more finesse to some of the questions you put me in yr. letter of 13 IV [April 13, 1983]. Leaving the Jehovah question go —I've dropped his name from the passage and altered it—

I'm talking about Wes Jackson and "monoculture." As I understand Wes' book,[†] the very point he makes from the beginning is that criticize agri-business as we will, validly all, he wants to go farther back, and sees the roots of our agricultural condition in the very beginnings of the tradition. There are, as I understand it, exceptions to what Wes is aiming at—primarily monoculture of annuals —and in particular, cereals—but they are few. From an ecological standpoint virtually *all* horticulture and agriculture is "arresting succession, establishing monoculture"—even a Taro patch or a maize garden. Natural plant communities are mosaics. The "wildness" of soil is its fungal and bacterial mosaic. So agri-business is the industrialization of monoculture. Now it's perfectly true that contemporary practices are no longer to be trusted as sustainable, but in the past they were not always so good either. Wes makes this point. Sahlins' *Stone Age Economics*[†] makes it another way. As I read Wes, he is looking at some very rare, tiny examples as models of what would be a total revolution in the very cultivars employed in world farming. [Richard] Felger and [Gary] Nabhan [are] doing that work and research as botanists. Felger says 20% of the wild plants in *any* biome are edible and potentially expandable, but only a tiny tiny percentage of the plant's flora have ever been drawn into cultivation.

So it seems to me Wes is saying it's *all* been the wrong path. (Seems there's a strong effort on the part of some Hawaiians and new settlers here to revive traditional Taro growing. All part of cultural renaissance throughout Polynesia, and there's a semi-secret pan-Polynesian (incl. Hawaii) independence movement.

Onward!

Gary

[PS] Dear Wendell, if you haven't mailed it back yet could you mail the copy of the MS I left w/ you. [...] Thank you.

Port Royal, Ky. 40058
May 20, 1983

Dear Gary,

By now you should have the copy of your ["Good, Wild, Sacred"] essay that you left with me.

Nothing in your long letter of May 6 offended me. "A scholar's blunt way of talking" is welcome to me for the time it saves—so long as it's not unfriendly, and I just *assume* your friendliness.

About Jehovah, I guess I would say that you should be more charitably slow in making up your mind—if, for no other reason, to make it possible for you to speak with Jewish allies like David Ehrenfeld. In the title essay of *The Gift of Good Land*, I say exactly what your letter says about the taking of the promised land, about the resemblance to our taking of the west. But even that story is bewilderingly mixed, for the *terms* of that grant are not at all the terms of our "manifest destiny," but are formidably ecological, as better scholars than I have pointed out. He (Jehovah) may at moments appear as a "projection" of the selfish wishes of the Israelites, but more often, and throughout the O.T., he speaks on behalf of an order that has nothing whatever to do with their selfish wishes. I don't think "projection" comprehends that kind of speaking.

So far as I can see, the possibility of intelligence about Biblical religion depends on seeing that it has manifested itself in many kinds and degrees. Sometimes, for instance, Christianity has been aloofly spiritual, puritanical, contemptuous of "the world"; sometimes it has seen the Incarnation as virtually the same as creation, sanctifying *all* creaturely *life*. Sometimes it has seen God as wholly transcendent, sometimes as immanent as well. Sometimes it saw paganism as devilry, sometimes it made one fabric with it.

The pagan deities have survived fairly blithely and usefully right through English Christian literary tradition, for instance—a late and very moving instance of this being the reappearance of the classical gods as angels at the end of C. S. Lewis's fine novel, *That Hideous Strength*. It could be very satisfactorily argued that the best Christian poets in English have all been half pagan, and not necessarily for unchristian reasons.

About agriculture too, I would insist on the necessary recognition of a range of degrees and kinds between the no-farming of hunters and gatherers and the large cash-grain industrial monocultures of the present. I think it is wrong to think or talk as if we have no choices between the eroding industrial annual grain fields and Wes's perennial grain-bearing polycultures. Ultimately, if industrial agriculture continues and if Wes succeeds, we may have that choice to make. But as I see it, my job with respect to Wes, and often in conversation with him, has been to point out that we *now have* a better (larger) repertory of ways than that—which Wes knows, of course.

What I'm saying, I guess, is that confusions both historical and human are in both religion and agriculture, and that to escape various damages of either-or, criticism has to discriminate very alertly among kinds and instances.

If this sounds like I think you need me to tell you such stuff, I apologize. I mean to be just talking along on my side of the conversation.

The river's up again (falling slightly, finally, this morning) for the 2nd time in 3 weeks. Almost nothing in the garden yet because of so much rain. And it has stayed cooler than usual too—the trees aren't fully leafed yet. The weather is probably smiling on you out there. I hope it is.

Your friend,
Wendell

Port Royal, Ky. 40058
May 21, 1983

Dear Gary,

In letters like mine of yesterday, I am trusting you to know how uneasy an apologist for Western tradition I am. A good deal of the history of the West is a thorn in my flesh. But what I am perforce dealing with more and more is that insofar as I am a cultural product, I am a product of Western tradition. I should say, I guess, a *country* and Western product, for in my most intimate makings I am not much a city product. I do think there is good in Western tradition; I *find* good in it. But so much unconsciousness and so much resentment is involved in my Westernness that there is much difficulty and strain in the threshing out. When I speak in defense of the Bible to you, I am inevitably talking partly to myself. I hear you speaking as if out of my own discomfort with it, and I then reply out of my own repeated finding that it is, for me, not only inescapable, but indispensable.

I mentioned yesterday that Christianity was sometimes grafted directly onto the local pagan religions that it supposedly superseded. My awareness of that had just been refreshed by H. J. Massingham's *The Tree of Life*,† a very useful history of the relation of Christianity and nature in Britain. And this morning I found a wonderful instance of it in Frank O'Connor's short story, "The Old Faith."† Read it if you can find it. It is short, very funny, and will speak to you anthropologically.

Yours ever so rainily,

Wendell

26 V 83 [*May 26, 1983*]

Dear Wendell,

Just out of a five-day retreat with Bob Aitken and all. Lots of pre-dawn meditating has given me a real sense of what the birds say early, which one each, and when. Good birds here, especially Bulbuls.

Your letter w/ my MS ["Good, Wild, Sacred"] arrived before the *sesshin* and I am *most* grateful for the care with which you went through it. I incorporated virtually every little suggestion you made into the MS—did some further re-writing—and then had it all re-typed. It's finally shaping up. I think, from the difficulties I've had with that, the lesson is learned: working from transcripts of a talk and transforming that into a *paper* is not always easy or possible. It would have been faster and better if I'd done this piece as *written* from the start.

Your gentle and illuminating rejoinders to my cranky comments on Judaeo-Christian matters points up for me the depth of my old irrational resistances to the whole tradition. Clearly I *know* virtually nothing about it. I should start with further study. Very interesting to see your point as to how the Christian tradition has held varying views. (Some of my thought was shaped by Robert Graves —*The White Goddess, King Jesus, Nazarene Gospel Restored*; the rest by my Mother's lifelong revulsion to her Texas Methodist upbringing.)

Obviously, if the O.T. is an ethnic, mythology, it's a fascinating one, in that its main figure Yahveh is constantly castigating his people. Good question: how would (or why would) a culture "project" this on themselves. Hmm.

Just talked to Masa on the phone—out California way it's gone straight from winter to summer, and things are now happening too fast, after no chance to plant. Arrgh.

Kai is going to Drum's ranch from mid-June til July. Get his ass kicked by a horse—

I'll write later on the Hawaiians I've met and especially some who are trying to keep up some aspects of traditional farming. If I wrote something on this where might it be publishable? I gather Rodale's no good anymore.

Love to all. And I hope the new Jersey feels at home now, and that Peggy's colt is getting unbent.

Yrz/Gary

WENDELL BERRY [PORT ROYAL, KY]
TO GARY SNYDER [NEVADA CITY, CA]

Port Royal, Ky. 40058
August 27, 1983

Dear Gary,

I want you to see this ["Two Economies"], since you are mentioned in it.[†] It may be that on p. 10 instead of Gary Snyder I should say simply, "a Buddhist." But I still would like to keep your name and Wes's at the end, because the essay is so much an effort to define the terms of a kind of practice that you and he exemplify preeminently.

This is a first draft. Please let me have any suggestions that occur to you. I'm a little worried by the maneuver on p. 6. This sort of relinquishment of special cultural terms, after use, seems a necessary courtesy to me, but have I done it right?

I am speaking from the depths here, not because I am profound, but because I am, as usual, in over my head.

Your letter of May 26, though I have not answered it, has been much on my mind. I should at least have responded to your question about where to publish. I can't really answer it, because I'm able to answer it for myself only one essay at a time. There are two questions, in fact, that I can't answer satisfactorily: 1 – How does one reach the audience of one's allies. 2 – How does one reach the general public? It almost looks as though we need two magazines that we don't have. We must talk some about this. Bob Rodale is a special problem for me because I feel personally at odds with him.

If you write something on the Hawaiian traditional farmers, will you show it to me?

I surely am looking forward to being at your place again.

Our love to you all.

Wendell

◇◇◇◇◇

EDITOR'S NOTE: The following letter from Gary Snyder was sent after Wendell and Tanya Berry visited Kitkitdizze in September of 1983. During that visit, Snyder and Berry read together at Grimblefinger Bookstore in Nevada City, California.

GARY SNYDER [NEVADA CITY, CA]
TO WENDELL BERRY [PORT ROYAL, KY]

7 XI [*November 7, 1983*]

Dear Wendell,

We certainly enjoyed having Tanya and you with us here—plan to loop this way more often when you're out to the west coast. My trip went well. The huge wheat farms around Moscow-Pullman (Idaho-Wash.) have to be seen. Biggest tractors.

Here are the little notes I took on "Two Economies"—I send them to you to remind you of our conversation on it. Maybe of some small use—

Now some weeks at home to get things working again!

Faithfully

Gary

大同 *Datung* "Great Society" = "Great Togetherness"

The Kingdom of God:

the pure land, the *Dharmadhatu*

the essential realm; no increase : no decrease

p. 6–7—all this time to establish the use of the term, "Kingdom of God" then leaving it behind—either *keep* it, or get on with the "Great Economy" language earlier.

p. 18—all sorts of excess pre-date industry.

industry	*endo*	within	L. *Industria*
	+	to pile up, to	"diligence"
	stru	construct	"activity"

Q. to Wendell: Where does he think the problem starts?

—How does all this differ from a basic presentation of ecology?

—Try and sell this to the public

p. 27—of course little wheels turning against nature is all part of nature

p. 31—a little forced?

Basic error: To try to escape death.

WENDELL BERRY [PORT ROYAL, KY]
TO GARY SNYDER [NEVADA CITY, CA]

Port Royal, Ky. 40058
November 15, 1983

Dear Gary,

Thanks for your note and for the useful notes on "Two Economies."

Yes. The basic error is to try to escape death. One of the many clarifications I'm indebted to you for was your statement at Cincinnati that there are worse things than extinction.

I know that the excesses—or some of them—that we're talking

about started before industrialism. Basically the issue is the old one about pride and greed. But the metaphor that now rules and justifies pride and greed—treating things and beings as machines —seems pretty new.

A couple of years ago I saw those wheatlands around Moscow [Idaho]. The scale was apparently huge there from the beginning— 40 horse teams on the combines, etc. Severe erosion rates—20 bu. soil per 1 bu. wheat—"justified" by deep soil.

Our visit with you and Masa was a joy. We will, of course, hope to come again.

Your friend,
Wendell

P.S.—A great Morris Graves retrospective,[†] now at the Whitney, will come west in spring. Oakland, Jan. 18–March 25. Seattle April 19–July 8. San Diego, July 24–Sept. 4. See it if you can.

GARY SNYDER [NEVADA CITY, CA]
TO WENDELL BERRY [PORT ROYAL, KY]

8: II: 84 [February 8, 1984]

Dear Wendell,

Early spring greetings to you and Tanya. Our California weather continues unpredictable and oscillating, this year with a six-week dry spell that we are into now, of no particular import at this time because we had so much rain earlier in the season. But it begins to force the buds out on the fruit trees.

I finally read Karl Polanyi, *The Great Transformation*.[†] A very instructive book, in which he argues that the utopian idea of a "free market economy" rather than industrialism itself is what has created such a difficult and social landscape the last century. Although written in 1944, he is aware of the potential environmental damage flowing from a market set of values that has no checks on continuing exploitation. This is the book that lies apparently behind much of Ivan Illich's inspiration, as well as Murray Bookchin's. A kind of non-Marxist, or neo-Marxist socialism, is implied.

Saw Wes Jackson briefly in Berkeley last week at Jack's while down there to look after my stepmother's health. He's in great style. I'm enclosing here a xerox[†] from a little Sacramento newspaper, on page 2 you'll note a reference to Sharon Dubiago and you appearing together. I thought you'd like to see how she speaks there. To my recollection, I was never invited to debate her at Wisconsin, and obviously I couldn't have declined. Who is the contact person there for your visit? I'd like to make sure about this.

Just planted some grapevines and one more Hachiya persimmon alongside some persimmons that haven't done so well the past six years, to see if I got some poor cultivars, or it's a soil and nutrition problem. We're in fine shape—Masa is going to Hawaii for three weeks of Zen and hula study in March and I'm working for the Alaska Humanities Forum[†] as a consultant and researcher for Alaska for the whole month of April. May the grip of cold release you soon—

Gary

WENDELL BERRY [PORT ROYAL, KY]
TO GARY SNYDER [NEVADA CITY, CA]

Port Royal, Ky. 40058
February 13, 1984

Dear Gary,

Warm and pouring rain here this afternoon. A little green beginning to show on the hillside. That's *very* premature. Cold is still to come, and plenty of it, I expect.

I'm writing, feeding stock, etc.—the winter routine—but already I feel the spring work pressing toward me.

Thank you for sending on the [Sharon] Dubiago article. I had heard from Jim Cheney [at University of Wisconsin], that you had been invited but couldn't accept, but the rest of what she says is news to me. No debate was ever mentioned. I sent Cheney her sentences about the alleged invitation to debate, and stated my displeasure at either of the two possible alternatives. [...] I'll let you know what I find out, and if you learn any more, please let me know. [...]

Our earliest bred ewe is due to lamb on the 22nd. We're expecting only one foal this year, but this is the spring to breed my good fillies. I have a trip in March, and four in April. After this year, I think, I'll arrange it so I do all my travelling in the fall. That I do go on spring trips does not make them less impossible.

We're all well here—except that we're having the front downstairs rooms painted. *That's* complex!

Don't forget us. Come to see us as soon as possible.

Wendell

WENDELL BERRY [PORT ROYAL, KY]
TO GARY SNYDER [NEVADA CITY, CA]

Port Royal
February 26, 1984

Dear Gary—

I have a copy of this [Dubiago article] of my own now. I thought I would return this copy to you, since it has your markings in it.

Jim Cheney wrote me that there was no mention to Sharon Dubiago of any "debate."

I have done about half my plowing for this year—ground to be resown to alfalfa and orchard grass. We have three lambs. So it starts around again.

Wendell

EDITOR'S NOTE: Dexter Roberts, a poet and founding member of the Wilderness Institute at the University of Montana, invited Gary Snyder and Wendell Berry to speak at a conference titled "On Common Ground: A National Conference on Agriculture and Wilderness" (1985). As participants, the two writers read poetry together and spoke on a panel titled "Wild Land—Good Land."

GARY SNYDER [NEVADA CITY, CA]
TO WENDELL BERRY [PORT ROYAL, KY]

20:VIII:84 [August 20, 1984]

Dear Wendell,

Greetings from the summer-dry west coast climate. I am growing a successful little crop of okra and sweet potatoes this year. Really learning what does well here. It seems like a long time since I've communicated with you; this must be brief because we are between two *sesshins* here and have plenty of details to handle.

Dexter Roberts of the University of Montana will be writing you asking you to participate in a conference to be held Fall of '85 —Montana—something on wilderness. I was in one of those conferences ten years ago;† this is the next step. [...] I certainly hope that you will be able to join in on this one. It would be great fun for both of us. Please give it your consideration.

How is your summer? And Tanya, and Mary and Den doing? We are back to the good long dry summers that are normal, after several summers with such shocking events as having an inch of rain in August. Hope to see you sometime in the coming year, before '85 that is.

Fraternally,

Gary

Port Royal, Ky. 40058
September 3, 1984

Dear Gary,

We've been summer-dry here too—seriously dry, for the second summer in a row. But today it's raining. I'm resting up from the tobacco-cutting and answering some mail.

Dexter Roberts and I have agreed, I think, on December 5-7. Is that going to be ok with you? I'm sorry it's so late, but I had already agreed to two two-week trips earlier, and was going west in Dec. anyhow. I *hope* it's all right for you, though I regret it's not earlier, on account of the weather.

I hope, too, that I'll see you before then.

We're all well here. Den has set himself up in lordly bachelor-hood in a before-empty house up in the river bottom. Mary will have a second baby in Feb. Tanya and I putter along in our grandparently way.

Tobacco cutting may be our version of a *sesshin*—a hard communal discipline that stops everything else, and always restores and instructs. An opinion that is worth very little, I know, for it is both uninformed and eccentric.

Wendell

Port Royal, Ky. 40058
August 1, 1985

Dear Gary,

I don't know whether or not I told you, when you called, that I'm to be at Nebraska Wesleyan University on May 2, 1986. If I could come on to Davis from there, that would be convenient. But in any event, I'm keeping the first two weeks of May (after the 2nd) open until I hear from you.

Also, I told you my fee would be $1000 and expenses assuming that you wouldn't need me to stay in Davis more than one night. When I have been asked to stay longer, I have been charging more. However, insofar as this involves you and me, my wage scale need not apply. I'll come and do what you want me to for whatever is available, whatever you pay other people, or whatever.

You're in Alaska, I hear—up there in the big woods having a fine time, I hope—and won't get this till you get home. There's no hurry, I just wanted to write you this while I had it on my mind.

Your friend,
Wendell

◇◇◇◇◇

EDITOR'S NOTE: Wendell Berry wrote the following letter concerning a correspondence with Patrick Murphy, then a doctoral student at the University of California, Davis. Murphy had completed a master's thesis on comparative differences between Snyder and Berry, and published some of the arguments in "Two Different Paths in the Quest for Place: Gary Snyder and Wendell Berry" (1984). Murphy was now working on a second article titled "Penance or Perception: Spirituality and Land in the Poetry of Gary Snyder and Wendell Berry," later published in *Sagetrieb* (1986) and reprinted in *Earthly Words: Essays on Contemporary Nature Writers* (1988). Murphy had sent Berry a draft of that article, which led to a brief and argumentative exchange of letters. Berry sent Snyder copies of his exchange with Murphy, refuting claims that the two friends are divided by irreconcilable religious and cultural differences, as well as assertions that Berry's work suffers from male chauvinism, patriarchal subordination of women, and an insufficient understanding of the economic consequences of holding private property.

Port Royal, Ky. 40058
August 3, 1985

Dear Gary,

I think that this fellow Patrick Murphy has badly misrepresented me and my work. Both his text and his bibliography suggest *that he has not read everything he should have read,* and has not read well what he did read. He evidently knows nothing of the work of Sir Albert Howard, which has been indispensable to my work and life for twenty years. I can't imagine what may be the standards, if any, of his teachers and editors. As I hope you will see, I am not troubled because he takes your side in the allegedly irreconcilable opposition between you and me, but because he is wrong about what I have said. I do think that the business about our irreconcilable differences is a piece of mischief.

Your friend,
Wendell

◇◇◇◇◇

EDITOR'S NOTE: Gary Snyder wrote this letter shortly after returning from Alaska, where he was teaching a course at Summit Lake and Chimney Lake in the central Brooks Range. The course was sponsored by the University of Alaska–Fairbanks and was titled "Nature Literature: Gates of the Arctic National Park."

28.VIII [August 28, 1985]

Dear Wendell,

I returned from Alaska last weekend. It's a shock to come back to the hard clear sunlight of California, the intense dryness, and the strict alteration of light and dark. I had just been getting adapted to 24 hour light, and the long mild shadows all day; a kind of mellow twilight, the moist mosses underfoot and always cool breezes.

I've gotten into my mail now, and have read your responses to Patrick Murphy—I'm embarrassed to say I glanced at the paper rather hastily and directly told Patrick he should send you a copy, thinking it couldn't be too bad and that you should see it; (which you should) but reading it carefully now, and following your responses to it, I can certainly see why it disturbed you. It would me too, and I hope you understand I didn't tell him to send it to you out of a spirit of mischief. I'm also embarrassed by west coast people with their own self-righteous sense of wilderness using me to beat you (or other people east of the Rockies, with different problems) with. I'm glad you make the point that I am doing experiments with farm and orchard and animals just the same as everybody else, and that's what is exciting. I made that point, to a degree, in "Good, Wild, Sacred," which Murphy may not have read.

I did say to Patrick, when I met him first in Davis in late May and had glanced at the lead page and title of the paper, that "Promised land" and "Garden" do represent two traditional, and differing, positions. I was thinking in terms of Christianity itself and the difference between mystical and immanent schools that stem from the Adamite heresy and see salvation as a return to the original condition of innocence and blessing, the "Garden of Eden", and those especially Protestant schools that see us working out salvation in history, moving ahead rather than back. I don't know a whole lot about it, but there's truth in saying that people have argued these points. But that's not what's between you and me, I'm not sure if anything is except distance and differing plant communities and climates. That's how it feels to me, anyhow.

So ... I guess we should say some theological enthusiasts might define the garden and the promised land as irreconcilable (and that would be their literalistic dualistic awful historical error) but there is nothing of that spirit or problem between you and me either in life *or* art.

Buddhism handles the same rough dichotomy in a handy way by saying they are different aspects of the same reality; from one side seen as historical and "in time" in the realm of cause and effect, a realm in which we can improve things (or ruin them) and do our training, practice, moral effort, work on our character, gradually become enlightened. The other side, the "eternal moment" is inherent, self-created, immanent and perfect, always there, so that when a person has finally "perfected" himself, they say, he might say "Oh, I was here all the time and didn't know it."

I wonder if that way of seeing things is analogous to the old Christian interior dialog. I don't really know. Anyway: painful though it might be, it's a good thing that Patrick Murphy got that feedback from you, is apparently re-thinking his position to a degree, and altering a lot of the paper. Forgive me for generating time-consuming trouble; but maybe better now than later.

I am alerted to the point that I must head off utopian misconceptions of how I lead my own life, also. I had a person express dismay and disillusion recently when I offhandedly said I owned a chainsaw. Wait til they hear I have three cars, one truck, and two motorcycles all registered to run!

Your earlier August letter mentioned May 2 in Nebraska. I see no reason why your visit to Davis couldn't be scheduled for April (28, 29) (30, 31)—earlier or later—depending on when you want to arrive at Nebraska Wesleyan. For example: if you want to get there Thursday evening or night, we could do something at Davis during the day Wednesday with a reading in the evening, breakfast with a friend on Thursday and fly out. If you had time and could come to the west coast Monday, I'd meet you in Sacramento and we could spend Monday night and most of Tuesday on the ridge (would you like to see what clearcuts look like?) and go down to Davis Tuesday night or early Wednesday. Tues. afternoon *might* be my class day at Davis, which would work out o.k. too. Or if you had business in the Bay Area you could come up to Davis Tuesday and meet me and we could both spend the night in Davis and proceed with Wednesday and Thursday's affairs. I have a budget for this now and can pay you $1200 plus all expenses for roughly that scenario. Is that OK? If you'd prefer to get to Nebraska mid-day Friday we can adjust everything slightly to be later in the week. All this will go on the condition that there isn't some awful conflict, which I doubt. I'll check it out.

I seem to have to work harder, travel more, and be gone more than I ever was before. I guess the two teen age boys account for some of that, and more auto insurance to pay. It has forced me to become more organized and "serious" about writing during the brief times I'm home, so I've made a big office for myself out of Allen Ginsberg's house. My little Ditch Hut was fine for poetry but not roomy enough to spread out the papers for several simultaneous prose projects. But less time for berry-picking and skin-tanning (not sun-tanning, "hides") and gardening. How to keep that in our lives, central to it. Look at Hawaiian luau food, Japanese special New Year's Day food, it's always old-time subsistence treats. Subsistence equals Sacrament.†

Enough for now—Hello to Tanya.

Yours for no religious wars!

Gary

WENDELL BERRY [PORT ROYAL, KY]
TO GARY SNYDER [NEVADA CITY, CA]

Port Royal, Ky. 40058
September 2, 1985

Dear Gary,

I'm happy to have your letter this morning, to know you're safe home from Alaska, and to have your wonderful sentence about Alaskan light.

And I'm relieved by your response to my exchanges with Patrick

Murphy. I didn't feel at all that any mischief was involved on your part, but it is nevertheless good to hear you talking across the proposed abyss.

What bothered me was Patrick Murphy's complacency about division, as if it is not deadly, but merely a matter of intellectual interest. I am more and more worried about divisions between people who ought to be together, defending a common ground. I have a publishing project, having to do with this worry, that I want to talk with you about. I'll call you up pretty soon.

I know what you mean about working harder and traveling more. We added 50 new acres last spring. Den is working with me in a kind of (a beginning of) a partnership, that will eventually need still some more land. This means that I have help, and more freedom to travel, but also more need to travel—to be able to pay Den a living wage, make improvements, etc. The idea is to have, eventually, a farming livelihood for Den that will be economically sound, and at the same time belong decently to the nature of this place. We are still very close to the bottom of that climb. [...]

Such events always renew the question of the relation between economics and nature. What kind of economy would cherish trees?† I guess it would be an economy that made wood products of excellent workmanship. And those products would have to be made close to the forest, so the dependency would always be clear: if you want good wood for a long time, then you have to have good forests for a long time. And it might be that that sort of economic cherishing of sources would suggest, in a fashion broadly cultural, the idea of leaving some woodlands entirely alone. The economy of Port Royal is not local enough. [...] Doesn't that virtually guarantee that the sources of production will be used carelessly?

And doesn't that set you to thinking about what a good local economy would be, and what its landscape would be?

My left knee has been lame ever since the middle of April. It isn't a serious injury, but I have re-hurt it probably a dozen times, and so prolonged the trouble. Aside from that, we're well here and doing fine.

I'll get to work on that date for my visit to Davis and let you know as soon as possible.

Your new poem† is a good one. Many thanks. I remember that you spoke of the country lanes in Devon as "mouse trails." Was that where the image started?

Our greetings to Masa and the boys.

Wendell

P.S. (Same day)—As it turned out, I spent most of the day on travel schedules. It looks like April 28 and 29 will have to be the days at Davis. Then I'll have to go down to the Bay for a talk on the evening of the 30th, and fly to Lincoln on the 1st.

If I could leave Davis on the 29th early enough to get to Berkeley by suppertime, that would give me a chance for a visit with the Shoemakers, which I would very much like.

Now I'm wondering if that schedule will rule out the possibility of a visit to the ridge, a look at clear cuts, etc., before we go to Davis. If that is still possible I would surely want to make the attempt. I do want to, need to, see what clear cutting looks like. And I would like to be in the *un*cut Sierra forest again, if only for an hour. I would love to sit beside one of those clear, fast streams and look at a dipper.

On the other hand, I *don't* want to be something extra for you to deal with at a too busy time. So tell me how all this looks to you.

W.

Port Royal, Ky. 40058
September 5, 1985

Dear Gary,

Liese Greensfelder has asked if I would speak at a farm conference at UC Davis on Feb. 15. I'm going to say that I'm interested in coming, and ask about the fee, which she didn't mention. But before I accept, I want to make sure that my coming in Feb. won't make useless anything you want me to do in May. Would you let me know?

Sincerely,
Wendell

12. IX [September 12, 1985]

Dear Wendell

Can you wait til about the 20th for an answer about your possible trip to Davis in Feb… I'll be speaking with the people who raised the money for your April/May visit in a few days and see how it looks. Maybe the two audiences are totally different. But I'd like to find out—

Here's a fine little piece on forestry. [Richard] Brothers† is a braided longhair with a PhD who lives in southern Oregon where he's known as Bobcat.

Yrz.

Gary

10: I: 86 [January 10, 1986]

Dear Wendell—

I see that after February you'll be in Berkeley again in March and then Davis again in April. Don't wear yourself away, my friend ...

Here are folders on the agricultural segment of the Davis library special collection. You could see it, if you wanted, while here in April.

Wendell I *would* like to see a copy of the paper ["Preserving Wildness"] you read in Missoula—when it's ready.

best

Gary

Port Royal, Ky. 40058
January 17, 1986

Dear Gary,

Thanks for the information about the agricultural library. And for your note.

I *am* traveling a lot, and am getting tired of it. The chairman of the English dept., U. of Ky., has asked me to teach there again, maybe one day a week, and I am thinking of doing it. It wouldn't put an end to travel, but it would permit me to do much less. I wish we could talk about this.

Two wilderness books I'd like to recommend to your students:

Wm. Bartram, *Travels*, Dover.
Theodora C. Stanwell-Fletcher, *Driftwood Valley*,[†] Little Brown (I think).

If we should indeed go to Alaska in fall of '87, how long will we be there, do you think?† And where?

I look forward to seeing you in April. My knee is much better. I can now walk 2–3 miles without tiring it too much. So by April I should be able to make a moderately strenuous hike.

And here's the essay.†

I hope you're all healthy and audacious.

Your friend,
Wendell

◇◇◇◇◇

EDITOR'S NOTE: The following letter includes Gary Snyder's critique of Wendell Berry's "Preserving Wildness," an essay presented alongside Snyder's work on wilderness at "On Common Ground: A National Conference on Agriculture and Wilderness," sponsored by the Wilderness Institute at the University of Montana the previous year. Snyder's letter is followed by a detailed response from Berry.

GARY SNYDER [NEVADA CITY, CA]
TO WENDELL BERRY [PORT ROYAL, KY]

10 : II : 40086 [February 10, 1986]

Dear Wendell,

Thank you for sending so promptly the two fat papers.† Jack had described them as dealing with "bioregionalism" rather than deep ecology and that is what I was interested in ... but it was useful to read Richard Sylvan's attack and Warwick Fox' defense. Fox does a good job of showing, I think, that Sylvan had not read or had not understood the material he was criticizing. In fact, Fox does what I take to be a meticulous rebuttal.

And now I have been reading your paper "Preserving Wildness" which confirms what I thought in Montana when I heard you deliver it [at the Wilderness Institute], namely that there is a lot there that I question to one degree or another. At least would use different language for. So I'll run through my thoughts.

§ Your first paragraph will be taken as though it were directed at deep ecology thinkers, plus maybe Earth First! radicals and a few others. As such it is simplistic and does not actually reflect what they say or think unless quoted very scantily and without context. I do not think the people you speak of as "nature extremists" standing aloof from human use, or literally believing that the universe is an "egalitarian system" actually exist. The choice of the word egalitarian—by Næss[†] I believe—was a poor one, but his qualifications of the intentions of that use clear it up. And of course, on one level it *can* be argued that all creatures are equal in value, but that is within a very sophisticated framework—such as Dogen's philosophy, which proposes that all things are equal *while* different, bigger and smaller, eating and being eaten, but on a very deep level, still equal. Deep ecology texts support subsistence hunting in the arctic, the integrity of jungle-dwelling cultures, the inhabitation of semi-wilderness or wilderness margins by traditional people—things Rod Nash[†] and the Sierra Club are usually against.

§ p. 2 Proposing that the universe is dangerous to us, and saying that it is going to kill us, is really murky. First of all it's a truism that we're all going to die. But what you're saying is blaming Mother for giving you birth when you're going to have to die. We *are* the universe, right? It's not dangerous to us, we're simply of the same fabric. It is going to die too. But the universe is not to blame for the "human condition" that some beings foist upon themselves.

§ Living in harmony with our native wilderness is not the forever unfinished lifework of our species, ("speak for yourself, white man") but the task of our particular history-based culture. Allowing as no harmony is perfect, there are millennia of reasonably decent human-natural interaction behind us and it would be a mistake to presume that the particular impasse that *western culture* seems to have come up to speaks some inevitable process and fate that the whole species is involved with. Such a statement is close to sounding as though we are assuming that 20th century occidental life is what all of human history has been tending toward, again garnering to ourselves all the glory, all the evil.

§ Your point 7 does not follow: to say that "there is no escape from the human use of nature" does not lead to the assertion that "human good cannot be synonymous with natural good." Nature does not—as you point out—mind being killed and used all that much—within reason. First you have not defined human good, a critical point. You *have* mentioned local practice, a step in the right direction, and what follows is local *culture* which is often quite capable of proposing and enforcing (culturally, religiously) "ecosystem ethics." Take a look at Richard Nelson's *Make Prayers to the Raven*† for an exact account of how one subarctic group alive and well at this very moment does do that.

§ page 4—an interesting thought that David Brower† I believe once brought up: We are *not* a domesticated species, we are a wild species. Nobody has ever controlled our breeding to produce certain desired characteristics. Our genetic program is typical of the wild. Not so.

§ Comments for page 6 same as earlier, to say that nature is not the perfect hostess, seems to me, to be saying nothing, or to be saying merely that "existence is unsatisfactory." And to create a false dichotomy between "our intentions" and "what happens." Maturity is a matter of learning how to deal with that. Nobody *asked* for comfort, what we get is reality. In fact, difficulty, danger, discomfort are precisely the delights that "nature" offers us. It is literally meaningless to say "nor do wild creatures always live comfortably or easily in nature"—they *are* it.

§ p. 7 It is true that humans require a long incubation in culture to arrive at maturity and independence. To say it is necessary because of "the dominance of humanity in the order of creatures" is a non sequitur. And also (following on the above point) it is also the case that there *are* no human beings stripped of the "restraints, disciplines, and ameliorations of culture"—they were all raised in *something*, there are pathological personalities who are truly monsters, but the rest move through culture. Like the highly cultured men of fine education that ran the Nazi machine. Monstrosity might well be a function of how *removed* a culture is from wildness, from nature. As Paul Shepard suggests in *Nature and Madness*.[†] [Ezra] Pound is an odd one to invoke as a model, since he was a monster, he betrayed poetry, and he was over-cultured.

§ So, (p. 9) I'm not sure that the reverse point, that we need nature to preserve culture, is clear enough in your argument. But more to the point: Nobody has ever *said* we can preserve wildness by making wilderness preserves. That's a dead horse. As refugia, habitat for Grizzlies or Black-footed ferret, they are of course essential. And pitifully small across the world. And those who fight for the preservation of these tiny refugia, or for a kind of management practice on BLM [Bureau of Land Management] land or Forest Service land that will not just be agro-forestry or subsidized grazing, have to be alert to economics and politics indeed. You will be pleased to know that the activists with the Wilderness Society, and related groups in Alaska, are politically very sophisticated (and cultured) people.

§ p. 10 Calling for an economy that rewards and enforces "good use" is like saying the world's problems will be solved if people would just be "good." We still have to nail down the specifics of the first steps of the cultural transformation that implies. "Love for local things, rising out of local knowledge and local allegiance" is a good start, I happen to think, out here we call it "bioregionalism."

§ p. 12—I'm not at all averse to the idea of a few closed wildernesses. I notice you crossed that out. It may take some areas closed like that in Yellowstone to preserve the Grizzly ... otherwise, bid farewell to the presence of Great Brown Bear in the lower forty-eight

and when the bear is gone
the mountains are lonely
incomplete, not all there,
the big one is missing
the edge of the weave is torn,
it begins to unravel from there.

Walking last summer in the Brooks Range in the *presence* of Ursus Arctos† taught me the difference. A living presence, all the time, that made us alert, respectful, alive, *delighted*, awed. In a sense, we are not the dominant ones. The Big Old Man is the dominant.

§ p. 15 The whole population discussion bears refining. I don't know anyone who seriously hates his species, but that does not mean we cannot responsibly take on the task of defining an *optimum* world population (about one tenth of the present) and think of the moves that would lead, over the decades, in that direction. We must create more wild *habitat*.

§ If the creatures who came onto the scene with us at the opening of the Holocene are to be lost, *that* would be what I would call immoral. The possibility of a biological holocaust is no trivial matter. It is *not* premature to say that there are too many people in the USA as of right now. The condition of the Grizzly Bear confirms that. A major culture shift (Buddhism for example) could perhaps produce a population as large as ours that could co-survive with Grizzlies, Bald Eagles, antelopes, Elk, mountain lions, and plenty of stands of Old Growth, but even so, it's not *necessary* to have so many human beings, in fact it's degrading. For people.

§ I of course agree with your comments on technological heroism.

Your highly diversified multi-purpose landscape is a temperate-zone agrarian scene with year-round rainfall. Millions of acres of desert, and hundreds of millions of acres of boreal forest, make up much of the planet. Millions of acres of tropical rainforest. I look forward to the horticultural sort of inhabitation in the tropics that

Edgar Anderson† suggests … and the return of much of the high plains to Bison herds. We could have both logging and lots of old growth. There is enough fine soil in the Sacramento valley to grow all the rice we need and still have millions of acres of tule marsh inhabited by migratory waterfowl. I'd like to see the old growth hardwoods in some quantity in the midwest. I do believe a smaller number of human beings would make this easier.

Well, this was fun to read and fun to write down some responses. It fires me along in the work I'm doing this week, i.e. cleaning up my notes on bioregionalism (I met a great bunch of people who take that name up in British Columbia this September.)

See you down the trail, Brah—

Gary

WENDELL BERRY [PORT ROYAL, KY]
TO GARY SNYDER [NEVADA CITY, CA]

Port Royal, Ky. 40058
February 24, 1986

Dear Gary,

Those two papers on deep ecology should be returned to Wes [Jackson] when you are done with them. He had not read them when he sent them to me, and there is no telling when I will ever have time to read them.

I wanted to respond, point by point, to your response to my essay on "Preserving Wildness":

1- My first paragraph has in mind the book *Deep Ecology* by Sessions and Devall.† I didn't mention it by name because they are critical of me in it, and I wanted to argue with the idea of "biocentric equality" without the appearance of quarreling in my own behalf.

I do think that book is irresponsible in its terminology, and not very clear or specific in its application. On page 67 it says: "…

all organisms and entities in the ecosphere ... are equal in intrinsic worth. Næss says that biocentric equality as an intuition is true in principle, although in the process of living, all species use each other as food, shelter, etc." I can understand the usefulness of a principle that cannot be fulfilled in practice, but I can't see the usefulness of a principle that must be *contradicted* in practice. Once use is allowed, which it obviously must be, then one's equality with what one uses just disappears as an issue; then the issues are the very particular and practical ones of how and how much to use, which I don't think can be resolved philosophically. What is called for almost immediately is the study of good local practice, with examples. I don't think *Deep Ecology* addresses itself very competently or directly to this problem, which is, in fact, the issue of work, which I think that you yourself have always dealt with responsibly—though you have not, of course, yet dealt with it fully. *Nobody*, I think, has yet dealt with it fully; we are all feeling our way in the dark.

Deep Ecology seems to me to be comfortable with the issue of preservation, uneasy with the issue of use. My impression is that this is generally true, so far, of the conservation or ecology or environmental movement. It shies off the issue of use because that is ultimately the issue of how you live, how you work.[†] I think that I am shying off that issue myself, much as it means to me, simply because of my bewilderment about it: how much of my involvement in what I don't like (internal combustion, air travel, etc.) is necessary, and how much is just inertia or self-indulgence?

But use is anyhow the issue, for me, and my impression is that the ecology movement is still not much interested in it. I know that the issue of preservation of farmland and farm people has drawn nothing like the attention that has been given to wilderness preservation. And I know how difficult it has been to draw attention to the agricultural issue.

My point in my essay is that these are not opposing issues, but ultimately the same.

2- I am not "blaming" the universe for anything. It does not seem to me wrong to note that it is a dangerous place to live. I don't understand your statement that "We *are* the universe …" It seems to me that we are parts of it.

3- When I wrote that living in harmony with nature is "the *forever* unfinished lifework of our species" I was not speaking for myself as a white man. (I don't hold myself answerable to that name, as you use it.) I understand "lifework" as the work of culture, which I see as changing necessarily in response to changing circumstances. I don't think that is in error. I am as aware as you of "the millennia of reasonably decent human-natural interaction behind us," but I am aware of no reasonably decent culture that was either perfect or static. A successful culture, it seems to me, would be always in process of being made in response to what has happened, and in that sense "forever unfinished." My statement has nothing to do with "western culture" or "20th century occidental life" at all, and I can't see in my text any reason for you to suppose that it does.

4- I understand something of the history of the development of industrial economics in the West, but it seems to me pretty much an anomaly as an artifact of "western culture." It is violently antithetical to the Bible and Biblical tradition. It owes a good deal, I guess, to the strand of individualism in the development of democracy, but in result it is violently anti-democratic.

But can this be called, at this stage a *western* impasse? Japan has by now probably taken it farther than we have. It seems to me a world-wide impasse that is not the result of culture but the contradiction of it. Our "multinationals" are all over the world, and other people's "multinationals" are here. It is the same economic imperialism or colonialism everywhere.

5- My point 7 (p. 3) seems perfectly clear and logical to me. If a man eats a fish he is opposing his good to the good of the fish.

6- I should have made it plainer in my essay that, as I understand it, every creature is domestic from its own point of view: every creature has its "house," its *domus,* and "makes itself at home." So we, who are domestic to ourselves, must be wild to the hawks, who must be wild to the robin on her nest. I wrote that at one point, but took it out because it didn't fit into the argument very well, and made it too long.

7- Our genetic program is not typical of the wild, any more than it is typical of domestic animal breeding. Our breeding seems to me, if anything, wilder (less controlled) than the wild. There is less natural selection among us all the time, because of medical science, etc.; and there seems to be less of "breeding to type," which occurs in nature as in domestic animal breeding. I don't see any choice but to regard the human breeding program as all right, but it is also unlike any other that I know.

8- I have now deleted my joke about Nature not being a "perfect hostess," but there certainly does seem to me to be a dichotomy between our intentions and "what happens." I *intend* to get my hay up dry, but that is not always what happens. So, I would think, the mother bird *intends* to raise her young, though what happens may be intended by a snake. I think we all do ask for comfort, humans and wild creatures alike. And there is no doubt in my mind that there are degrees of difficulty, danger, and discomfort that are not delightful. Suffering is real for all of us, surely, and I think that most of us are sorry for it.

9- Each creature, I think, would have to be considered a part of nature. But insofar as it was conscious, it would consider itself also to some extent separate from nature: obliged to fend for its *own* survival, etc.

10- When I was talking on page 7 about the length of time it takes for humans to become human, I was speaking of cultural maturation, not biological. The cultural part takes so long—maybe too long now—because it requires not just the knowledge to use power but also the knowledge to restrain and withhold power.

11- The men who ran the Nazi machine were not cultured in my sense of the word, but outside culture. It has been a long time since

I read Hannah Arendt's essays on the Eichmann trial, but one of the problems she dealt with, as I remember, was: How do you prepare young men raised on the Bible to do the daily labor of mass murder? Her answer, as I remember, was that you short-circuit their culture by tampering with their language—by giving them the language of slogans and propaganda, so that they need not tell themselves what they are doing. I think that's the longest lasting horror of it, maybe: that people can act altogether outside of culture. That some of them collected paintings and were "finely educated" only shows how decorative and frivolous culture becomes to people who are outside it.

12- Your anger at Pound surprises me. I don't think he was a monster. I think he was sometimes a great fool, and very wicked in some of his opinions; I don't doubt that he was crazy, at least some of the time. But he was also right some of the time: about usury, vanity, the worth of many poets and other people, etc. And sometimes he wrote with great artistry and beauty. I certainly don't agree with all his opinions, but I do acknowledge a large debt to him, and a troubled love for him and his work.

I *don't* invoke him as a "model" in the essay we're talking about, or anywhere else. He *is* an example of what I say he is an example of on page 8. And the lines I quote from him seem to me both appropriate and beautiful.

13- My sentence about the insufficiency of wilderness preserves is followed by a sentence that completes the point. I understand very well the need for wilderness preserves, the need for more of them. But I hold to the point that they are not safe, are not really "preserves," in our present economy. I am surprised that you disagree with this. It seems readily evident to me that if we can't save farmland, and small wildnesses and wildernesses of all kinds—can't farm and log and build and make properly—then there is no hope for the preserves. So I am indeed calling for a good economy, and I am calling for people to be good, or try to be. I don't see how this can be done except by understanding how our lives are now involved in waste and ruination.

14- I struck out the lines about closed wildernesses to shorten my talk. I like that idea.

15- If grizzly bears were dominant, it seems to me, they would be in no danger and would not need preserves.

16- Mark Twain called us "the damned human race." In this century, I think, many people have known in their hearts what he was talking about. I know that I do. I love a good many humans, and I find many of them easy to like. I love many human works. I don't think I am a misanthrope, and I have hope and faith. But I admit that I find the modern history of our species (culture) profoundly discouraging, and I don't think I am alone in this. I see a lot of what looks to me like evidence of outright misanthropy: in advertising, on TV, in modern weapons, in books and movies, in popular and scientific attitudes toward bodily life and sexuality. A lot of contempt for what Blake called "the human form divine."†

I think that a lot of that contempt is implicit in the propaganda and methodology of "birth control" and "population control," especially in the present eclipse of sexual discipline.† I know from reading, from acquaintance, and from my own experience that abortion and sterilization can cause great anguish, which is not enough acknowledged by advocates, and great loneliness *because* the anguish is not acknowledged. The health and sanity of many women has been damaged, and many have been killed, by the chemicals and devices of "birth control." By comparison, Laurens van der Post's account† of infanticide (in response to famine) among the Bushmen seems to me humane, because adequately prepared for culturally. The present campaign of "birth control" among us seems to me a sad combination of evangelism and industrial opportunism.

I don't see how anyone can responsibly determine and prescribe an optimum human population. That would be a job of enormous intricacy, and I think there would be an enormous risk of error. It is a *kind* of responsibility that I would not like to have, and would not like anyone to assume. A lot of monstrosity could be the result, and I unhesitatingly prefer extinction to monstrosity.

The idea that there are "too many" has been devastatingly consequential in our time. The idea that there were too many Jews resulted in the murder of 6 million of them. In our country the idea, dominant for the last forty years, that there are too many farmers has resulted in the dispossession and migration of perhaps 30 million farm people. I see no reason at all to trust human judgement in such matters.

I don't have an adequate answer to the "population problem," and I don't believe anybody else does. My belief is still that, now in the United States, the problem is secondary to those of use, consumption, and pattern. It seems questionable to me whether it is useful to argue about population from necessity. From nature's point of view, probably, no humans are necessary. From a utilitarian point of view, no human is necessary in particular; one is as good as another. From a human or humane point of view, all who are alive are necessary.

17- I am not so foolish, of course, to propose that you could have "a highly diversified, multi-purpose landscape" in a desert or in the tropics or the arctic. It would make good sense in the U.S. wherever there was enough arable land and either enough rainfall or the possibility of surface-water irrigation—some of the West and a lot of the East. The rest, ideally, I think should be native prairie or forest. The domestic landscape, ideally, would include sizeable patches of native prairie or forest. I mentioned such a landscape to place it in contrast with "monoculture," and because I think it promises indispensable help to the preservation effort. If the domestic landscape were adequately wild, then its inhabitants might not have to join the crowds trampling the national parks. For somebody like me, for instance, who has a stand or two of big trees next door, one trip to Yosemite might last a lifetime. In fact, just knowing about the great woodlands of the West and Northwest gave a charm to the woods here, before I ever went to a Western park.

It is necessary to talk about the kind of landscape that I described because it is possible in so many places, and because virtually everybody in the country now is living off "monoculture" and so ought to think about it.

But while we try to imagine how the country ought to be, I think we must be hesitant and careful about the political means. I know of instances in which both white people and Indians have been put off their land under the law of eminent domain for the sake of wilderness or wilderness recreation. I don't approve.

I got home yesterday from ten days of traveling, mainly speaking to "farm-problem" meetings. Sunday I'm to leave again for the Bay Area—to be mainly literary this time. This is a difficult way to discover what it means to be a homebody.

Your friend,
Wendell

P.S.—It occurs to me now that this letter may be unintelligible to you without a copy of yours. If you need one, write us and Tanya or I will make one. I have a copy of this.

WENDELL BERRY [PORT ROYAL, KY]
TO GARY SNYDER [NEVADA CITY, CA]

Port Royal, Ky. 40058
February 26, 1986

Dear Gary,

I've been thinking some more about Pound. When I wrote you before I said, I think, that he was crazy, a fool, wicked, and sometimes right, and sometimes a wonderful poet. I didn't mean to imply that I know how to untangle all that, except that it *seems* to me that when he is a wonderful poet (sometimes in an isolated line) he is not crazy, wicked, or foolish. Then I feel spoken for and grateful. In the terms of my previous letter, maybe, he can be seen as part of the time in culture, part of the time out. But of course I don't know enough not to be bewildered by him. How the hell *all* of that could have ever been stuck together in one man, I just don't know. I do read him pretty often—but about always on *my* terms, going back to my own little bunch of selections from the *Cantos*.

Wendell

WENDELL BERRY [PORT ROYAL, KY]
TO GARY SNYDER [NEVADA CITY, CA]

4/9/86 [*April 9, 1986*]

Dear Gary,

We'll be getting to Sacramento on April 26 at 12:15 p.m. on United 575 from Chicago.

After thinking over the Alaska invitation, I decided I couldn't accept. It wouldn't be fair to the others here to come home from a nine week absence and tear off again on another long trip. I'd love to see that country up there, but would prefer to do it when I'd be rested and ready.

We've been plowing. It has been a fine time for getting work done outdoors, but we're very dry now.

I look forward very much to our visit there.

Sincerely,
Wendell

GARY SNYDER [NEVADA CITY, CA]
TO WENDELL BERRY [PORT ROYAL, KY; FORWARDED TO
BUCKNELL UNIVERSITY, LEWISBURG, PA]

[January 10, 1987;
Forwarded to Bucknell University,
Lewisburg, PA, on January 14, 1987]

Dear Wendell,

Greetings for the new year. Maybe this won't get to you before you leave for Pennsylvania,[†] but then forwarding works. I realized I haven't written you since before your visit to Davis last spring, and also that I never responded to your long letter [February 24, 1986]. I didn't respond, I realize now, because I couldn't think of anything to say but to repeat what I'd said the first time. I respect and I think I understand your position, and I guess I'm more "mystical."

Had a spectacular time last summer first on the Tatshenshini River (with Gen) where we saw Griz Bears at least once a day, and got rained on for five days and nights, and the tent hardly leaked. Five-mile wide twenty mile long glaciers curving down to our river, 18,000' peaks above. The ice age still going, here. Then to northern Alaska, where Kai joined us, to explore the headwaters basin of the Noatak River and delight in much company of Dall sheep, caribou, arctic fox (walks right by your tent) 2 wolves one afternoon, 1 wolverine and more Griz. Big lake trout to catch. And snow flying on the 22 of Aug. Parent and calf caribou swimming the little river right in front of our canoes.

Now this fall just handling the mass of paperwork that is self-generated in this century, working more on my book on wild and cultured,[†] and very much enjoying conversations with Masa, now that the boys are both out of the house and we can actually *talk*.

Bob Aitken said how much he enjoyed his visit with you and Tanya.

Have a good stretch of writing and reading. See you down the trail,

Gary

◇◇◇◇◇

EDITOR'S NOTE: Wendell Berry's letter was sent on letterhead that reads: "Nothing takes the place of MILK!" with an image of a child stacking blocks inside a clear milk bottle.

WENDELL BERRY [PORT ROYAL, KY]
TO GARY SNYDER [NEVADA CITY, CA]

1/13/87 [January 13, 1987]

Dear Gary,

A friend of ours thought we needed this letterhead. Actually, we're not selling the milk. We're selling the bottles. This is our day care version. The night care bottle is black. Very safe because impossible to climb out of. With the lid on, they're virtually sound proof. Parents are thus set free to pursue the higher things of life.

I really appreciated your phone call. It was good to talk. Though I'm sure I should not be taking on new lectures and readings for a while, I'm still a little sorry we're not going to do that job together [in Alaska]. Our last visit out there [to California] was so fine a time. I still have a lot of it clearly in mind.

Too soon after our phone conversation Jack [Shoemaker] told me about Kai's accident, and then Masa told me more. I'm sorry you all had to go through the great anxiety and difficulty of that, and am sorry for the pain and trouble to Kai. I hope he's coming along all right and is not having too much discomfort.

We're all doing all right here. I have spent the whole holiday answering long-neglected mail and cleaning up messes that I left behind in my busyness and haste over the last year or so. I'm hoping that, by saying no a little more, I can have a little more leisure and order in my life. The problem, of course, is that I'm not altogether in charge of my life.

We've had almost no snow here yet, and far from enough rain. But the ground has been frozen for some time, and that makes it much cleaner around the barns. I'm enjoying feeding and the other winter work. And I have some projects ahead that I'm looking forward to.

Let us have some news, especially about Kai, when you have the time. And come to see us when you can.

Your friend,
Wendell

January 19, 1987

Dear Gary,

I think it would be both surprising and disappointing if we agreed more than we do. If we agreed about everything, what would we have to say to each other? I'm for conversation.

It was good to have your letter and news. I like to think of you and your boys camping on those rivers with the bears, and I hope you'll tell me more about it when we see each other again.

Last summer I saw some grizzlies myself—a momma and two cubs, in Yellowstone. It was hardly a "wilderness experience," since we saw them from the road.

Tanya and I were in England three weeks in November, and we wished for you and spoke of you, remembering our travels with you there. We were a little more leisurely this time. We rented a little car in London and drove SW to Boscastle on the Cornwall coast, looking at the country and the cathedrals, making literary pilgrimages, taking walks, etc. Saw some very nice woodlands this time that would have pleased you, including Gilbert White's "hanger."† We had a very nice visit with John and Truda Lane,† and saw Satish [Kumar] at the Lanes' and at a conference at Dartington, given by Temenos.† [...]

We've been here [at Bucknell University] since Jan. 5. I'm working very hard on a novel.† I *have* to work hard on it because I don't know when I'll ever have this much free time again. Our stay here will be over on March 6. As soon as we get home, Den will be taking off for Kansas, maybe to work in construction with Wes's son, Scott. But who knows. His need now is to be out on his own and see the world a little before he has to settle down. I'm sympathetic with that, and want him to go.

That, of course, both changes the farming situation for me and means that I'll have to stay home more. I'm going to sell the breeding horses and slow down the work schedule some. And staying home more will suit me. I've found all the travel finally to be extremely disorienting—so much so that at times I've had to think hard to remember which season it was.

So I'm not going to go anyplace but to Lexington to teach for a year and a half or so, and then venture out occasionally, but only to save the world, etc., no frivolities.

I'm enthusiastic about going back to farming regular. I have a lot to do and learn before I get too old, and two good colts to break, one this year, one next.

And I remain, dear sir, as ever your loyal friend and admirer.

Wendell

WENDELL BERRY [PORT ROYAL, KY]
TO GARY SNYDER [NEVADA CITY, CA]

September 10, 1987

Dear Gary,

I recently bit into a most profound fortune cookie, and I append the results. I thought you might like to encounter something authentically oriental, for a change.

Confucius say: When person say "love" better make sure word touch wisdom tooth on way out of mouth.

We have been wondering how you and your neighbors are faring in all the fire and smoke. We hope very much that you have not received any damage.

[...] How does one care enough for the natural world to strive to protect it, and yet be reconciled to the damages to it when they occur so as to be undiscouraged and able to go on striving to protect what is left? I know of good instructions about this, coming from several directions, and yet, for me, the difficulty is extreme.

I have begun teaching now, but have not yet settled into it. Since I quit in 1977, I have acquired some more land and other obligations that can't be shirked. It will be a while before I'll know how this new arrangement will work out. Anyhow, I'm glad to be back with my colleagues—some of them—and I'm enjoying my encounters with the students.

We need some more rain here, but otherwise it's a nice time—cooler, the river quiet and clear, the fall jobs getting started.

Our love to Masa, and to you.

Your friend,
Wendell

◇◇◇◇◇

EDITOR'S NOTE: In the margin of this typed letter, Gary Snyder wrote: "This is my Macintosh. It is loyal and obedient most of the time," a comment in regard to Wendell Berry's essay "Why I am Not Going to Buy a Computer" that created a public stir when it was printed in *Harper's* (1987).

GARY SNYDER [NEVADA CITY, CA]
TO WENDELL AND TANYA BERRY [PORT ROYAL, KY]

[March 29, 1988]

Dear Wendell and Tanya,

Springtime warmup weeks—so much bird and animal activity

around the woods right now. Six gray squirrels were running and dashing up in the tall top of a big black oak. Then yesterday I found a young male dead on the ground with a bash on his forehead. Guessed that he had missed a jump, hit a branch right on his head on the way down, and then hit the leafy ground. First time I've ever seen signs that squirrels fall. And the wild turkey flock is making sweeping round-dances in the woods, the toms jumping up and gobbling and fighting at each other. This drouth year has the manzanita in the fullest bloom I've ever seen, over thousands of square miles, and buzzing with bees. But the flowering cherry is ahead by a month and the shortage of rain means we'll skip planting a garden again.

University teaching starts up 1 April and I'm getting my coursework organized. This time the Literature of Wilderness course will directly feed into the book I'm working on, "The Practice of the Wild" and should enable me to finish that project up next winter. I admire how much you can get written Wendell, it seems like a big project for me to write 10 pages of prose. The enclosed piece (a section from the work in progress)† seemed to take all winter. But that's also allowing for the time took out to help Kai recuperate from his car wreck. He got out of pins and braces last week and is pretty much all recovered except for wearing a soft collar to buffer shocks to his neck for another two months. On April 1 he departs for Japan for a one-year scholarship, based at the U. of Ryukyus, which is to say Okinawa. We'll be seeing him off at a potluck in Berkeley, with Jack [Shoemaker] and other friends coming by.

Also I wanted to bring you both up on news in our own family. Brace yourselves for a surprise. But let me say from the front it's good, not bad, and everyone involved is feeling wonderful.

So here's what's happening: Masa and I are realigning our lives, staying close to each other and together on Kitkitdizze land, but about to begin to live with other partners. For over a year now, we have both been seeing other people part of the time, even while living together. There have been no secrets or betrayals from the beginning. This experience together with our new friends has evolved to a clear point of wanting to realign, even while keeping affection, friendship, and our many shared projects. Kai and Gen have known about this almost from the beginning, and are quite supportive.

Nelson Foster, who has been a Zen student of Aitken Roshi's for many years, is Masa's new partner. Nelson lives in Honolulu and has begun to do some Zen teaching work, both here at Ring of Bone and at Koko-an in Hawaii. Nelson and I have been close friends for 10 years, and I welcome his coming to Kitkitdizze, and to Ring of Bone. He will gradually be moving his domicile here over the next half year. My new friend (who was Masa's friend before I got to know her) is Carole Koda. Carole lives in the San Joaquin valley, north of Merced. Carole is full-blood third generation Japanese American. Her grandfather and father founded the rice industry in California, "Cal Rose" and "Kokuho Rose" rice, and Koda farms. Carole and her two daughters, Mika (9) and Kyung-jin (4) will be moving up here over the summer and fall. Carole came to sit at the *zendo* two years ago, and that began our acquaintance. There has been a certain amount of difficulty and pain in these changes, as you can imagine, but for the most part this has been a flowering and discovery of new depths for both Masa and me. We have become deeper and franker with each other as well, and look forward to the richness of this new extended family. Nelson and Masa (it looks to me) share a subtlety of spirit, and a gentleness of style. Carole and I share, among other things, our love of mountains and wilderness, and of poetry.

Our friends are gradually adjusting to this, though it does shake some people. We try to tell them it is not exactly that Masa and I have broken up. It is more interesting and far more intimate than that. A lot of it is new territory, and we are going step by step, finding out what works. The openness, frankness, and continual communication that the four of us manage amongst us in all directions, makes it work. So please don't worry about us, and please welcome Nelson and Carole into our lives.

Knowing your concern for marriage, Wendell, I want to assure you that at least within my own {hunter-and-gatherer/multi-centered universe Buddhist} perspective, we are acting with profound regard for the principle of marriage and its vows and commitments. In full communication and regard for each other, and the young ones.

And Masa's and my works are flourishing. I've been writing poems, she has been doing a lot of dancing, and we both have been well-engaged with our *zendo* projects. It's a good time for us both—

Would have tried to call but leaving for Bay Area and helping Kai out with his last-minute chores is making everything unpredictable so I thought I'd write when I had this moment. Masa sends her love.

29 III 88

Warmly

Gary

PS – Carole Koda is a remarkable woman. More about her later.

WENDELL BERRY [PORT ROYAL, KY]
TO GARY SNYDER [NEVADA CITY, CA]

4/11/88 [April 11, 1988]

Dear Gary,

I'm grateful for your care and kindness in writing to me about your new arrangements. Of course, I will worry about you some, for the same reason that I wish you well: I am your friend. You are as welcome in my life as you ever were, and Carole is as welcome as you are.

Your new essay is good, I think. I have thought often myself of the path and off-the-path, both delightful ideas, and necessary to each other, as you say. When and why does the path become undelightful? Is it a matter of scale? Does that path become undelightful when it has two lanes and a stripe, or before or later? Or is it a matter of speed? For me, actually, it becomes undelightful when it quits being a path and becomes a road. Should a path be wide enough for a team and wagon? I am willing to doubt it. Are you willing for the path to be a path, not a metaphor? I'm inclined to guess that you are.

I've seen squirrels fall out of trees twice. And a friend of mine once saw a squirrel slip on an ice-covered branch and fall and break its neck. This is contrary to my idea of what a squirrel should do, but I haven't thought of any solution.

The last of my lecture trips for a long time is coming up, and soon the semester will be over (on May 4). After that, for two or three weeks at least, I hope to work outdoors every day and think only immediately practical thoughts. I'm tired of mental projects.

Your friend,
Wendell

GARY SNYDER [NEVADA CITY, CA]
TO WENDELL AND TANYA BERRY [PORT ROYAL, KY]

10 V 88 [*May 10, 1988*]

Dear Wendell and Tanya

Thanks for your kind note. I deeply appreciate your spirit of openness and friendship. I'm in touch with Jack [Shoemaker] pretty steadily. Masa and I—I think you realize—are just fine, and will continue to live near each other and work together. [...]
Now I'll stretch your tolerance further w/ this playful poem!

Yours faithfully

Gary

Why I Take Good Care of my Macintosh†

For Wendell

Because it broods under its hood like a
     perched falcon,
Because it jumps like a skittish horse
     and sometimes throws me
Because it is poky when cold
Because plastic is a sad, strong material
     that is charming to rodents
Because it is flighty
Because my mind flies into it through my fingers
Because it leaps forward and backward,
     is an endless sniffer and searcher,
Because its keys click like hail on a rock
& it winks when it goes out,
& puts word-heaps in hoards for me, dozens of pockets of
     gold under boulders in streambeds, identical seedpods
     strong on a vine, or it stores bins of bolts;
And I lose them and find them,
Because whole worlds of writing can be boldly layed out
and then highlighted, & vanish in a flash   at
     "delete"   so it teaches
     of impermanence and pain;
Because my wife likes it,
& because my computer and me are both brief
     in this world, both foolish, and we have earthly fates,
Because I have let it move in with me
     right inside the tent
And it goes with me out every morning
We fill up our baskets,   get back home,
Feel rich,   relax,   I throw it a scrap and it hums.

GS. I. 88

8/24/88 [August 24, 1988]

Dear Gary,

I didn't mean to neglect your letter so long. We have had a pretty busy summer, and I have been saving time by neglecting my friends. Please pardon me.

Thank you for the computer poem. It sounds like a right smart computer. I raise my pencil in a salute to you both.

Our drouth was very bad from March until about the 10th of July. We got rain in the nick of time to save most of the crops and to make some of them exceptional. I have put up plenty of hay and we have the best prospect for fall pasture that we've had in several years.

I built some new fence and made other improvements this summer, and we overhauled our upstairs. We put a big dormer on the back, enlarging the two rooms and adding a bathroom. This was partly to enable us to take care of an aged parent or two, if necessary, but it just greatly increases the pleasantness of the house. One of the rooms will be a sort of library and work room for me—though I will continue to use the old Camp also.[†]

School is starting now. I've come to Lexington today to brace myself for my first classes tomorrow: I have 1 freshman English and 1 composition for teachers.

Except for my father, who is very feeble now, we are all well.

Come to see us when you can and look at our changes.

Your friend,
Wendell

[*September 16, 1988*]†

Camerados—

We went thru the recent forest fire ok but only because the wind blew away. Good luck! Will be doing more brush removal this winter! Now it's cooler and moister.

All's well here,

best,

Gary

1/20/89 [*January 20, 1989*]

Dear Gary,

I'm sorry to have been out of touch for so long.

The usual stuff is going on here, plus some extra. I'm doing more farming than ever, I think. In the fall I taught two composition classes, which involved somewhat too much paper grading. This term, I only have one small class. I've been working hard, preparing to write some lectures and eventually a book about my old compatriot, Harlan Hubbard,† who died last January.

Do you know about Harlan? He and his wife, Anna, lived from 1952 to their deaths in 1986 and 1988 on the Ohio River near here, a mile from any road, supported themselves by their own work, without any modern conveniences or power tools, and yet lived an elegant, abundant life. They were both musicians, Harlan a painter and writer. Their life contradicts just about all the assumptions of modern industrial society. I knew them from 1964, and was friends with them from about 1969. I knew Harlan's three published books,† and had seen some of his painting. But was surprised to find, after I undertook this project, to find that he left, in addition to an unpublished book, perhaps 2500 pages (ts) of a journal, and hundreds of paintings, prints, and drawings. Reading and organizing my notes on all that has been a big job, but I'm about done now. It has been some of the most useful, rich, inspiring reading I have ever done.

We're all fine here, except for my father, who has had a series of strokes, and is seriously disabled now. Our winter, so far, has been unusually warm, like last winter, but wet too, and we see some reason to hope that the drouth may be ended. After mid-July, we got enough rain to make it a pretty good year after all, but from July '87 to July '88 we were severely dry, in spite of a little rain through the winter.

I've been out a while this afternoon, splitting and ricking wood with a few snowflakes flying—wood for next year, mostly locust. Now I have to go out again to milk and finish the feeding.

I hope all is well with you.

Your friend,
Wendell

◇◇◇◇◇

EDITOR'S NOTE: In this letter, Gary Snyder enclosed a draft of the poem "Right in the Trail," with a note that states: "For Wendell and Tanya (who leave no traces)." The poem was later published in *No Nature: New and Selected Poems* (1992).

GARY SNYDER [NEVADA CITY, CA]
TO WENDELL AND TANYA BERRY [PORT ROYAL, KY]

2 III 89 [*March 2, 1989*]

Dear Wendell and Tanya

Coldest of winters—you too—8° here one morn. Snow for 6 weeks. Nanao [Sakaki] wrote and sd Japan was warm all winter! I was feeding the stove and writing away at prose.

We're fine here. The 2 new little girls have rapidly adapted and are at home in the woods.

Now getting ready for spring quarter teaching—more haste—here's a seminar I'm preparing.[†]

When will you come see me again?

fraternally
Gary

WENDELL BERRY [PORT ROYAL, KY]
TO GARY SNYDER [NEVADA CITY, CA]

3/7/89 [March 7, 1989][†]

Dear Gary,

It is kind of you not to withhold good, motherly advice from the bears. Was this bear near your own house there on the ridge? Is that something new? The *only* thing I regret about the poem ["Right in the Trail"] is the word "awesome," which the sports talkers have about used up.

We have coyotes now, did I tell you? They like lamb. We have a dog who will stay with the sheep this time around, which may solve the problem. Let the coyotes eat groundhogs!

I would like to take your course. I like the questions you are asking in it. We'll be out in the Bay Area around April 30. But it'll probably be too short a trip for me to get up to your place. I want to come, though, and will, sooner or later. It would be good to talk with you a while. If you get a chance, come to see us. Bring us news.

Your friend,
Wendell

P.S. We've had a fairly warm winter here too. Now we're lambing and it's cold.

September 6, 1989

Dear Gary,

I just read "The Etiquette of Freedom"[†] for the second time to see if [it] was sure enough as fine as I thought it was the first time. It is. It is a *useful* piece of work. You're a true teacher, because you say things that one *wants* to remember.

Reading, I thought of a few small suggestions to make:

On p. 76, I think your sentence ought to read "Of individuals —following *local* custom, style, and etiquette, ~~of their own~~, without concern . . ."—because I wonder if an individual, as such, can have a custom or an etiquette.

p. 77— "Civilized mythology (medieval Christianity and the Rise of Science)" looks to me like a knot or tangle that requires a lot of picking out. I don't think, for instance, that medieval Christianity was one thing. (The best book I've read on Christianity and nature is Philip Sherrard, *The Eclipse of Man and Nature*, Lindisfarne Press.)

Same page—I don't think [Daniel] Boone was much like Cortés. He was more a creature of this country and he even lived a while as a Shawnee—Blackfish's son—up in Chillicothe. Anyway, your sentence implies that he was in Ky. in old age, but I'm pretty sure he died in Missouri.

p. 113— I wonder if wild nature can accurately be described as a "pathless world."

I don't mean by such quibbles to qualify my high opinion of your essay, which I've copied for my students. I'm especially grateful for your willingness to struggle a while with those daunting terms *nature* and *wild*.

Jack [Shoemaker] told me that you have had pneumonia. I hope you are better and that you are taking proper care of yourself.

We are a good deal occupied these days by various illnesses of our parents.

I have worked all morning in the Camp, and all around it has been mostly quiet. This afternoon I must go help in the tobacco harvest.

Your friend,
Wendell

GARY SNYDER [NEVADA CITY, CA]
TO WENDELL AND TANYA BERRY [PORT ROYAL, KY]

18. IX. 89 [September 18, 1989]

Dear Wendell and Tanya,

Nice to get your letter and Wendell thanks for the suggestions on "Etiquette" and your good words on its behalf. I have incorporated most of your suggestions. Yes, the Sherrard book is really interesting and useful. Well let me bring you up to date—

Carole and I took off for SE Alaska this mid-July and followed John Muir's watery trail[†] around from Frederick Sound over the Sumdum Bay and up the Endicott and Tracy Arms and then to Juneau. This was done in a friend's 65' ketch-rigged old wooden-hulled tug-tender. We left the ship in Juneau and continued on our own over to Gustavus, to pursue Muir into Glacier Bay and right up the ghost of Muir glacier. We rented a sea-kayak and kay-aked six days up the inlet where his glacier was 800' thick when he pulled a sled up it. We were camping in front of the wall of alders on the beaches and tramping through spongy muskeg and eating salmon-berries. Kayaking is a splendid way to drift and float silently through the watery worlds getting to hear the clink and chatter of the little icebergs that broke off the tidewater glaciers, and all the mews and wails and honks of the waterbirds. In fact the birds and their great noise-making was the unexpected bonus of this trip, those waters are so alive.

After I got back I came down with an asthma attack, then bronchitis, and then pneumonia. Dr. says it will be another week before

I'm back into form. So I take naps, don't cut firewood, don't run, and still don't have a whole lot of energy right now.

Kai and Gen are both away at college, Kai's at Berkeley and Gen's at Santa Cruz. Kai is in the Conservation and Natural Resources program at Berkeley, headed by Carolyn Merchant (*The Death of Nature: Women and the Scientific Revolution*)—I used this book in my Davis seminar on "Issues in Nature Literature" this spring, it is a very solid engagement and extension of what Sherrard touches on. He [Kai] is rooming with Lee Swenson whom I think you know, it's great for him. Gen is at Cabrillo Jr. College doing start up studies, and enjoying it so far. He has come a long way, is out of the woods and is a delightful thinker. They were both here all summer doing various work for different households all over the ridge making $7.00 an hour and in constant demand. And mountaineering in their spare time. [...]

We have a surprise early rainstorm, maybe 3 inches already, great for us and a disaster for the valley vineyards.

Hope you both have a good fall,
Gary

WENDELL BERRY [PORT ROYAL, KY]
TO GARY SNYDER [NEVADA CITY, CA]

12/22/89 [December 22, 1989]

Dear Gary,

Carole says you need to see this, my post card of resignation. I'm glad to hear you're coming along ok. But be careful. It is real winter here and has been for a while—the wilderness closing in. We're keeping you in mind.

Wendell

Dear madam or sir:
Your kindest letter

deserves reply,
but I
too often fail
to answer mail.
I do not read
poem or creed
aloud
to any crowd.
I would not stir
for riches, sir
or madam,
if you had'em;
I attest
that it is best
by a sight
that I should write.
Nor do I lecture
or conjecture
about careers
or years
to come.
I am dumb
by predilection
and affection
for the quiet.
I have quit.

—Wendell Berry

◇◇◇◇

EDITOR'S NOTE: Gary Snyder enclosed a note concerning his current work and health condition, along with the following letter to friends dated December 19, 1989.

4 Jan 40090 [January 4, 1990]

Dear Wendell—

Greetings for the New Year. Thanks for your calls and your letter. I'm getting better, but (as part of the process)—for the time feel worse. The nerves and muscles of the side and back are waking up and complaining a lot. Am getting some writing done, anyhow. Looks like the book [*The Practice of the Wild*] will come in on time.

Had a visit from George Sessions and tried to straighten him out, as per your comments on his errors of fact and interpretation. He's in the midst of a very ugly divorce. Am looking forward to seeing you and Tanya again.

Yrz.

Gary

A NOTE TO FRIENDS ON MY CURRENT CONDITION

19. XII. 89

This has been an odd and unexpected fall for me in terms of health. As soon as Carole and I got back from sea-kayaking in SE Alaska (in early August) I came down with what seemed to be asthma. It turned into bronchitis, and then a doctor diagnosed it as pneumonia. After several weeks of medication and rest the pneumonia subsided. An X-ray verified its disappearance, but found an unexpected little spot in one lung. I got a CAT scan for that and sure enough it proved to be a small lesion in the middle lobe on the right side of the sort called a "solitary pulmonary nodule." We consulted with several specialists of various sorts and they all felt that it would be prudent to have it removed and biopsied, since if it did prove to be malignant at this early stage the possibility of total cure would be quite high. I reflected on this for several weeks, and then decided to go ahead and get the surgery. In the meantime I managed to get another chapter of *Practice* done, and in late November I made a trip to the University of Ryukyus in Okinawa to give a paper and a reading and meet with old friends and new scholars. As soon as I got back I went into the Sierra Nevada Memorial Hospital in Grass Valley and had the nodule out. Biopsy showed it to be benign, which is a blessing. Now I am out of the hospital and undergoing the slow and uncomfortable healing that goes with such a drastic incision. It will be three months before I can expect to be strenuously active physically again. As it is, I can type and move the mouse, but believe it or not that is tiring! Still, the slowed-down days have their charm. Much of the time I sit and meditate, incubate, reflect, and mentally explore. To do this in an unstructured way (rather than formal *zazen*) is quite interesting and creative. James Hillman's new book *A Blue Fire*† proved to be exactly the right reading for this time.

There is some finish-up work yet to be done on my prose-work-in progress, *The Practice of the Wild*, and I look forward to re-engaging with that. It must be finished by February. At this point it looks good—

So I clunk around Kitkitdizze. Carole has been a great help and support through this time and so have my stepdaughters Kyung-jin and Mika. Kai and Gen will be up over the solstice holidays and so we will all pump some water and cut some wood ...

Gary

WENDELL BERRY [PORT ROYAL, KY]
TO GARY SNYDER [NEVADA CITY, CA]

January 10, 1990

Dear Gary,

Many thanks for the news. I am sorry for the slowness and

painfulness of your healing, but very glad to know that you are functioning anyhow and getting work done. One thing I haven't yet understood: Was the nodule that was removed the cause of your asthma?

And thanks too for your willingness to talk with George Sessions. I keep finding out from my own persistent combativeness that some conflicts are unnecessary—though I usually find it out too late. Anyhow, there now appear to be a whole slue of kinds of conservationists, and people tend to classify themselves as one kind or another and to treat the preferred kind as exclusive of all the rest. But it seems to me that the classification system begins to break down as soon as you begin to *do* something. For instance, as soon as a deep ecologist takes action to protect wilderness, he or she is practicing what I can only call stewardship: taking care of what you have been given to take care of, or what has been placed within your care. Wilderness is land left alone, but it can't be protected by leaving it alone; to be protected, it has to have human stewards. To me, it appears that this protection has to begin in the human economy, many steps back from that economy's contact with wilderness.

I would like to see a good faith effort among the conservation groups to identify common interests between themselves and the farmers, ranchers, independent loggers, and other small, private land users. I have no doubt that common interests exist, but have been blurred in the rhetoric and the pleasure of combat. It is certain, for one thing, that a "market-oriented economy" is as threatening to small owners and users as it is to wilderness. And it is equally certain that a long-term, decentralized, democratic economy (an ideal "American" enough to be defended in any company) will necessarily be conservative of nature. It is interesting that such a common ground can probably be identified only by a *more* radical understanding of the problem rather than by a compromise of principles or aims.

We had a *very* cold December, and now are having a mild

January. I'm writing and getting out some firewood for next winter.

It was a pleasure to meet Carole on the phone. I look forward to seeing you both in person.

I hope you will be patient with this slow healing.

Our best to you both—to you all.

Your friend,
Wendell

◇◇◇◇◇

EDITOR'S NOTE: The April note mentioned by Wendell Berry is missing.

WENDELL BERRY [PORT ROYAL, KY]
TO GARY SNYDER [NEVADA CITY, CA]

August 12, 1990

Dear Gary,

I intended to answer your April note as soon as I got around to reading the things that accompanied it. I haven't read them yet, except to leaf through and admire the work that Kai put into his "Action Packet."† Before too much longer, I hope, I'll have time to read them. It has been a busy summer. In addition to the usual farming, I have been reading for a new course for the fall semester and writing on a long story. It has got so that I can write only by neglecting the mail and other duties.

But I *did* read your new book of essays [*The Practice of the Wild*] as soon as I could after Dominique sent me the bound proofs. The essays are fine work, as well as useful. They are especially valuable, I think, because of their enthusiasm for the local. The most instructive essay (to me) is "The Place, the Region, and the Commons." The most pleasing are "Ancient Forests of the Far West" and "The Woman who Married a Bear."

173

In addition to their more general values, these essays entertained me a good deal by their difference from mine. Our compositional instincts are somehow radically unlike; you hardly ever make the move that I expect. And so, for me, reading you is full of gratifying surprises—gratifying, because your moves, though not the ones I expect, are always the right moves.

I think your book is indispensable, and I think it will have an effect. If it has an effect, that will be because it leaves no room or excuse to make up for local carelessness by "global concern."

There are only two places in your book at which I disagree.

One is on page 79 [of "Good, Wild, Sacred"] where I think you see agriculture as too exclusive of wildness. Agriculture at its worst is, of course, opposed to wildness—and that, I would argue, is why it is so bad. But at its worst it is neither hospitable to wildness nor in any meaningful sense "cultivated"; it is, at its worst, analogous to industrial mining, which is alien both to wildness and to culture. Gary Nabhan and others have testified to the many necessary connections between wild and cultivated in traditional American Indian agriculture. And a generation ago much hunting and gathering accompanied farming among [...] white (and black) people here —though they lacked, of course, the cultural integrity and sophistication of the Indians.

And on page 41 [of "The Place, the Region, and the Commons"], your definition of "the ideology of monotheism" strikes me as not only far too general and simple, but improbable too. The allegation of uniformity becomes uncomfortable, it seems to me, in the presence of almost any pair of examples you can name: Jesus and Mohammed, Dante and Chaucer, Eliot and David Jones, Billy Graham and E. F. Schumacher, Dorothy Day and Jerry Falwell, Thomas Merton and the Pope. The allegation of "universality" can't even be addressed until you say whether you mean it in the sense of truth or in the sense of force. And does "centralization" apply to theology or to politics? "Centralized" is not an adequate description of, say, a Christian theology that takes God's love to be at once central and surrounding and everywhere between, as Dante's does; or one that takes God to be both transcendent and immanent. Attempts to centralize the politics of Christianity never were very successful. The Protestant rebellion made such attempts unthinkable. Also it is impossible to reconcile the idea of centralization with the anti-state principles of the Anabaptists and other sects, or with the Baptist doctrines of "the priesthood of all believers" and the autonomy of individual congregations. Your definition of the ideology of monotheism seems to me to have been better realized by the empires of polytheistic Rome and atheistic Moscow—or by the present computerized international system—than by any of the "Christian" tyrannies that I know about.

I started this in the woods this morning. Now it is evening, and I'm sitting in the yard with a gin and tonic. A few crickets are singing, and off in the distance I hear a bluejay, some crows, a barred owl, and an automobile. Tanya just came home from a "baby shower." Do you have that kind of weather in the Sierra foothills?

I don't mean to deny that Christian politics or political Christianity has often wished, with varying success, to be uniform, universal, and centralized. It has, and no question about it. But there *is* a question as to whether or not this ambition is a proper one for Christianity which after all, began by opposing God's interests to Caesar's.

The theological parts of your book brought me to a question that I would like to know your answer to: Doesn't polytheism (which you seem to allow) finally imply monotheism? Or, to put it a different way, could a uni-verse (a coherent or integrated nature) have been created by a committee of deities of limited—and therefore contending—powers? I believe that the "Two Cantos of Mutabilitie" of *The Faerie Queene* are connected with this question, which Spenser attempts, with some success, to resolve in the figure of Nature, the "greatest goddesse." These cantos, I think, accomplish both a profound criticism of classical polytheism, and a very significant elaboration of Christian monotheism. I wonder what you think of them—especially the 5th, 6th, 7th, 13th, and 14th stanzas of VII, vii.

I must now hasten to allow the possibility that you haven't time or inclination to be waylaid by such questions from a reader—as I probably wouldn't myself. Anyhow, as you see, your book has waylaid me with some questions, and also much help, encouragement, and pleasure. And so I thank you.

Your friend,
Wendell

WB/tb

WENDELL BERRY [PORT ROYAL, KY]
TO GARY SNYDER AND CAROLE KODA [NEVADA CITY, CA]

5/10/91 [May 10, 1991]

Dear Carole and Gary,

Here beside the Kentucky River, with songs all around us of the sycamore warbler, cardinal, indigo bunting, Baltimore Oriole, wood thrush, robin, and song sparrow, we are thinking of you, dear friends, and wishing you well.

Love,
Wendell

GARY SNYDER [NEVADA CITY, CA]
TO WENDELL AND TANYA BERRY [PORT ROYAL, KY]

10 XI [November 10, 1991]

Dear Wendell and Tanya—

Just back from a visit to Japan—reading poems w/ Nanao, hiking, politicking.

Best wishes to Den for his coming marriage and thank you for *The Discovery of Kentucky*,† a delicious book (w/ *kasuri* design papers ...)

Hope your lives and seasons are going well—here's a summertime report of sorts—†

Warmly

Gary

GARY SNYDER [DAVIS, CA]
TO WENDELL BERRY [PORT ROYAL, KY]

7. V. 93 [May 7, 1993]

Dear Wendell,

I have a moment here at Davis to take breath; have wanted to say hello and thank you for calling (when Carole was recuperating) —I'm sorry I missed you; she appreciated it a lot. And she is pretty much all well now. We are both out in the local forest a lot finishing up our contribution to the forest management plan our whole watershed group† is doing together. As part of our community agreement w/ BLM [Bureau of Land Management].

I'm teaching another 5 weeks and then a year's sabbatical—I hope you and Tanya and Mary and Den and their families are all doing fine—

best to you—

Gary

WENDELL BERRY [PORT ROYAL, KY]
TO GARY SNYDER [NEVADA CITY, CA]

July 11, 1993

Dear Gary,

It was good to have your letter. I hope all's well with you and Carole and the children.

Here we go on with the same efforts as before. So far, the year has been a good one. We have the best lamb crop ever, a good garden, lots of pasture, etc. My mind wanders back and forth between fields and woods, farming and forestry. Sometimes I think I'm learning a little, gaining a little ground. We're involved in a couple of local economic and community projects that may finally come to some sort of realization. They go slowly, but I think that's the way I'd rather they would go.

I wish we could get together sometime for some talk and an exchange of local news. On next May 24 I'm supposed to give a speech to the Peninsula Open Space Trust. Will you be in the Bay Area around that time, or at home? That's a bad time of year for me to be long away from home, but I'd like to extend the trip a day or two to come up to Kitkitdizze again if possible—and if I can forestall other people's ideas about what I ought to do.

Den and his wife, Billie Carol, had a little girl, Emily Rose, on May 2. So we have four granddaughters now.

Your friend,
Wendell

GARY SNYDER [NEVADA CITY, CA]
TO WENDELL BERRY [PORT ROYAL, KY]

7. VIII. 93 [*August 7, 1993*]

Dear Wendell

Good to hear from you. I hope the Kentucky River didn't come right up to your front doorstep!

After kicking endless tangles of life's red tape out of the way over the last year I'm finally into the real work of organizing and writing the final stages of a 38-year-long poetry project[†] and I'm as happy as a pig in shit. It is downright *relaxing* to be doing the work you want to do, no matter how hard you might work at it. It looks great. (Although Richard Nelson wd. never venture to say such a thing, he refuses to say one word about a MS he's working on, until it's totally done.)

I've stayed away from some gatherings and conferences etc. that were really tempting to keep on track. Including the megatechnology gathering in San Francisco† which I gather you went to. I was taking care of other visitors to the Davis program that weekend.

Wendell, as far as I can tell now I'll be here May 24 and thereabouts and Carole and I would love to see you. Put it down and so will we. And congratulations to Den the father!

Carole is in Guatemala with her older daughter Mika studying Spanish for 3 weeks, and I live in blessed obscurity for the time— I think the neighbors think I'm also gone. Say hello to Tanya and see you down the trail—

best—

Gary

WENDELL BERRY [PORT ROYAL, KY]
TO GARY SNYDER [NEVADA CITY, CA]

September 22, 1993

Dear Gary,

Thanks for your letter. We're still planning to be in the Bay Area on and around May 24th. We'll hope to come up for at least a little while. I'd like to see and hear what is going on with you and your place.

I met George Sessions last May in San Francisco [at the megatechnology and development conference] and like him very much.

Fall is with us here, the garden about finished and the fall chores under way. I'm teaching this semester, to the improvement of what I am not sure. We hope all is well with you and Carole.

Your friend,

Wendell

WB/tb

31. I. 94 [*January 31, 1994*]

Dear Wendell,

I'm wondering how you and Tanya did through the cold snap. I was talking with Jack Shoemaker earlier this morning, I'm dictating this to my little black box while driving home from Berkeley, and he said that you had several days of isolation and silence which doesn't sound like too bad a thing. I was in Indianapolis this week doing a residency for the Indiana Humanities Council, and of course the weather is warmer and wet now, but I heard good stories of the cold spell.

We are looking forward to your and Tanya's visit in May. Apparently your dates are not yet sure so I should tell you that I have one date, May 24th, when I am to be in San Francisco participating in a benefit program regarding old growth forest in the Sierra Nevada. There is also a possibility that I might go to Yellowstone to speak to the annual gathering of the Greater Yellowstone Ecosystem Alliance. They themselves have not yet decided if they can bring me, or what the dates are. I have been invited three years running in the past, and so we are trying to work it out so that I might actually go this time. Assuming that we'll find some dates that are agreeable to us, I want to assure you that the little guest room will be there for you and Tanya, and we want to put you up and keep you as long as you can stay, talk about art and nature and all that, and share some stories from recent years. I will be back from four or five weeks in Africa in the first part of May, and so will probably be somewhat addled myself. [...]

If Steve [Sanfield] arranges for you to do a reading at North Columbia that's great, we'll be there (along with lots of other people). Clear day today, heading east on I-80, grass greening out and clear enough to see the snowy high Sierra all the way across the valley. But—threat of drought again. Let me know your plans for May when they get clear.

Yrz.

Gary

2/17/94 [*February 17, 1994*]

Dear Gary,

I've tried to call you up several times and no luck, so I thought I'd better write to say that I've agreed with Steve [Sanfield] to read on the ridge† on the night of May 27. [...]

Would it suit if Tanya and I stay with Steve on the night of the 27th and then come over and spend the night of the 28th in your guest room? I do long to sit down with you and Carole for some quiet and leisurely talk—yes, of art and nature and all that.

Our winter has been in several ways difficult, but now we're looking forward to the lambs, who will begin to arrive in a couple of weeks.

Wendell

20. II. 94 [*February 20, 1994*]

Dear Wendell,

I just had a charming chat with a young man named Todd at the Orion Society offices in New York. He had called to invite me to attend the ceremonies in your honor/John Hay award in April. I had to tell him that—as pleased as I am to be invited—I expect to be in Africa. I guess I told you that, with Kai and Gen, taking advantage of Kai's year-long experience there. So congratulations to you on that, and I still expect to see you and Tanya here in May.

And good to talk on the phone—

Yrz.

Gary

◇◇◇◇◇

EDITOR'S NOTE: This letter was written after Wendell and Tanya Berry visited Kitkitdizze in May 1994. During their trip, they camped with Gary Snyder and Carole Koda in the Black Rock Desert of Nevada.

WENDELL BERRY [PORT ROYAL, KY]
TO GARY SNYDER [NEVADA CITY, CA]

5/31/94 [May 31, 1994]

Dear Carole and Gary,

I'm really sorry we can't sit out in that desert and talk and eat and laugh and walk around from now on.

Carole, Tanya and I both were solidly pleased to have your good company for a while and to get to know you a little.

Gary, our talk heartened me. We obviously can't, mustn't, be optimistic. But how good to think, beyond the thought of victory, of making some happy, useful sense with companions!

Both of you, come to see us when you can.

And *many* thanks.

Your friend,

Wendell

P.S. As it happened, I had without knowing it an account of Drum's purchase[†] in my briefcase. I read it flying home. It is *very* important. [...]

9. VI. 94 [June 9, 1994]

Dear Wendell and Tanya—

Brief though it was—we enjoyed our trip [to the Black Rock Desert] with you enormously. After such a long spell of not seeing each other, we just picked right up!

KJ[†] loved getting the poem from you, but was a bit baffled. I'm enclosing a poem of hers—from last year—(if it's a poem.) And my 1988 record of Dooby Av.[†]

Soon again!

Gary

[PS] Carole says hello and she'll write.

6/28/94 [June 28, 1994]

Dear Gary,

KJ's poem tikkled me.[†] And it was good to revisit Doobie Lane in your piece.

I've just learned about the Menominee in Wisconsin,[†] who have been logging and living from the same 220,000 acres of woods for 140 years and have as much timber standing as when they began. I hope to fly up there soon to see for myself.

Yes! May it not be so long to next time.

Wendell

◇◇◇◇◇

EDITOR'S NOTE: The following letter concerns Gary Snyder and Carole Koda's idea for the publication of *Three on Community:*

Gary Snyder, Wendell Berry, and Carole Koda, a chapbook published by Limberlost Press (Boise, Idaho) in 1996. The book contains the following essays: Gary Snyder's "Crossing Into the Watershed," Wendell Berry's "Conserving Communities," and Carole Koda's "Dancing in the Borderland: Finding our Common Ground in North America."

GARY SNYDER [NEVADA CITY, CA]
TO WENDELL BERRY [PORT ROYAL, KY]

22. VII. 94 [*July 22, 1994*]

Dear Wendell,

Carole and I have just finished reading your essay "Conserving Communities."† In a way I wish I had been able to read it before you visited, because it would have been enjoyable to talk about those ideas further. But they will be around a long time, suffice it to say I think you are on a marvelously strong track there.

I appreciate your small but potent point, that the community can and must include non-human members. (The problem I have always had with "biocentric deep ecology" rhetoric is its ungroundedness. As soon as it gets down to cases, it has to be a community exercise.)

So: when and where will this be published, so that I can point people toward it? If there were going to be an anthology of some sort, I would love to see your paper "Conserving Communities" next to my little essay "Coming Into the Watershed"† to hammer the points home. I trust you have seen the latter. Once again, thank you for pointing the way to the very core of things.

Hi to Tanya.

best—

Gary

[PS] You and I are both quoted in the *Wall Street Journal* recently—I heard—not unfavorably but as "neo-luddites."

13 XII 94 [*December 13, 1994*]

Dear Wendell,

I couldn't wait until the *Audubon*† came out for you to see this —it's what I sent them—a really useful exercise for me in recalling what I thought/think I'm doing.

Still burrowed into *Mts. & Rivers* now—

Solstice and Christmas greeting to you and Tanya,

Gary

12/16/94 [*December 16, 1994*]

Dear Gary,

I think your piece on Kitkitdizze is first rate and very welcome. Thanks for sending it.

The neighbor who was going to pick my corn didn't get around to it before the ground got too muddy for a tractor. So I'm shucking the two acres by hand. Good work, though hard on the hands, and I wish I'd done it earlier.

It's raining today.

Happy Solstice, Xmas, and New Year to you dear people!

Wendell

18. II. 95 [*February 18, 1995*]

Dear Wendell,

Just had a call from Tom Lyon† responding to my letter, that he would be quite willing and happy to do the little foreword for our 3 essay chapbook. Rick Ardinger[†] is also quite pleased and getting ready to go ahead with it. You should send your essay to Tom —address [enclosed] if you don't have it. [...] Best to you—

Gary

[PS] Wendell—let me know your views on format, binding, etc. I had a title idea: *Place, Community, and Race* and am still working at it.

GARY SNYDER [NEVADA CITY, CA]
TO WENDELL BERRY [PORT ROYAL, KY]

I. III. 95 [March 1, 1995]

Dear Wendell

I get a sense (here) that [Rick] Ardinger is appreciating our collection.[†] I've about finished "Mts and Rivers" too—

Am seeing if a good title comes along.

Yrz.

G.

GARY SNYDER [NEVADA CITY, CA]
TO WENDELL BERRY [PORT ROYAL, KY]

13 III 95 [March 13, 1995]

Dear Wendell—

Here's a copy of Tom Lyon's foreword.[†] If it suits you—(Carole and I very much like it)—we'll pass it on to Limberlost, and the booklet will be launched. I include here also a copy of Rick's recent letter to me (if I didn't send it to you already—my memory fools me sometimes)—which is very appreciative.

More rains here: we're fine, but the valleys are floating—

best,

Gary

◇◇◇◇◇

EDITOR'S NOTE: Robert Hass, U.S. Poet Laureate 1995–1997, invited Wendell Berry and Gary Snyder to participate in an event titled "Watershed: Writers, Nature, and Community" (1996), cosponsored by the Library of Congress and The Orion Society in Washington, D.C. The event also included Pattiann Rogers, Scott Russell Sanders, Linda Hogan, Richard Nelson, Barry Lopez, Terry Tempest Williams, William Kittredge, Gary Paul Nabhan, Annick Smith, Rick Bass, James Galvin, Joy Harjo, Peter Matthiessen, Lucille Clifton, Cornelius Eady, and Rachel Bagby.

GARY SNYDER [NEVADA CITY, CA]
TO WENDELL BERRY [PORT ROYAL, KY]

12. IV. 95 [*April 12, 1995*]

Dear Wendell—

I forwarded your "yes" to Bob Hass. He takes up that job in October. He has your address— [...]

best,
Gary

WENDELL BERRY [PORT ROYAL, KY]
TO GARY SNYDER [NEVADA CITY, CA]

4/24/96 [*April 24, 1996*]

Dear Gary,

Here are some xerox copies of logging documents that have been useful to me and may be to you. Also a copy of the *Draft Horse Journal* with my piece on Charlie Fisher[†] and another article on horse logging.

It was good to see you in Washington—though how one gets there from here I don't know. And we were happy to see Gen if only for a moment. Tell Carole she must come to see us and bring you.

187

Your friend,
Wendell

5/4/96 [*May 4, 1996*]

Dear Gary,

This is by my friend, Gary Anderson.† I believe his numbers are sound. I hope all's well with you. Here the spring has been wet, cold, and late. We haven't yet planted a seed in the garden or worked a foot of the ground.

Your friend,
Wendell

6/23/95 [*June 23, 1995*]

Dear Gary,

I wrote it down that possibly I'll go to Washington DC in April to Bob Hass's meeting. I assume I'll hear from him when he has dates, etc.

"Finding the Space in the Heart" is just a splendid poem. And I am glad to be taken so happily back to that playa.†

Wendell

[*May 7, 1996*]

Dear Wendell and Tanya—

Great to see you both! Wendell thanks for the logging and draft horse stuff—

Wes J. coming to Davis this week—

Yrz—

Gary

WENDELL BERRY [PORT ROYAL, KY]
TO GARY SNYDER [NEVADA CITY, CA]

Port Royal, Ky. 40058
June 2, 1996

Dear Gary,

I think this book was among the ones you passed on to me in Washington. Probably you don't know who Neil is, and I'm a fool for not selling this autographed copy—but here it is, in case I'm wrong.

Douglas Haynes[†] was here today. I walked him through the woods and through the mud. He's a good young man, I think, and I believe you'll find him worthwhile.

We're rotting and drowning here, but otherwise fine. I hope you all are even better than we are.

Wendell

P.S.— Saw Drum Hadley at the Land Inst. last weekend. Am very happy to report that there has been no noticeable improvement.

GARY SNYDER [NEVADA CITY, CA]
TO WENDELL AND TANYA BERRY [PORT ROYAL, KY]

11. XI. 96 [November 11, 1996]

Dear Wendell and Tanya,

Jack [Shoemaker] told me that you and Tanya had been out on Chincoteague,[†] and that you-all had had a good visit. I was out there once some years ago, when giving a talk at Salisbury College, and spent a day walking up the long beach. It's very lovely, and quite different from the feel of walking the Pacific coast, though I couldn't explain how.

Marion Gilliam[†] called and said they were going to give me the John Hay award this year. I said okay, realizing it is perhaps a somewhat complicated exercise but deciding to do it anyway. I'll call in a few days[†] to ask you your advice, what goes on, how to best suggest its set-up.

We have a sprig of yew needles on the Buddha-altar. In the little vase. Carole picked them up in a walk down along a creek—they are only found here at creekside—to help her appreciate them, and aid her reflection on the work of her cure. One of the main chemicals they're giving her in her monthly therapy at the hospital is derived from the yew tree, it's a recent discovery, called Taxol in the trade. We've been reflecting on the interconnected accidents of the universe, or purposes as it may be, that put a chemical in a tree that's best known as a bow-wood that specifically targets cancer cells of certain types. This may be her best hope for really cleaning this stuff up.

She's doing strong and well, a clear focus on her life, and a lot of grace. But it is uncomfortable and unpleasant a good part of the time.

Thanks for your words and insights on *Mountains and Rivers*—I know how strange and even weird it may seem to many people, and how remote or obscure some of the connections might be. I'm sure that's no problem for you, but still it's out on some edge. And, I think you're right, a lot of folks aren't going to see many of the connections: I just hope they can see enough, that they can stay with it, along the way. I've loved the sense of almost musical composition, completion that it has given me to finish it. And now, so many things neglected for the last five years around the place—people don't believe me when I say (when asked what I'm going to do next) I'm going to clean up the place! But that's exactly what I mean.

Warm greetings to you and Tanya, I'll be on the phone soon. And, for whatever it's worth, here's my own account of travels in India†— back in the early 60s—maybe help prepare you a little for that trip.

Yours, and hello to Tanya—

Gary

WENDELL BERRY [PORT ROYAL, KY]
TO GARY SNYDER [NEVADA CITY, CA]

12/14/96 [December 14, 1996]

Dear Gary,

It turns out I'm not going to India in January, after all. But I *have* read your book on your Indian travels, and I thank you for sending it. It is a good book and I learned a lot from it.

To settle my thoughts about *Mts. and Rivers* I wrote a little essay† that I think will be published eventually in *Sewanee Review*. It is very positive about the book, but of course I don't know whether or not you will think I like it in the right way. I sent Jack [Shoemaker] a copy.

The John Hay award is good news. When I got it, I tried to turn it to practical account by getting a lot of people together at Shakertown (Pleasant Hill) to talk about community economies. One never knows if what might help does help, but at least it was pleasant enough (as honors go) and did no lasting damage. John Hay's book on terns, *The Bird of Light*,† is a good one, by the way, if you haven't read it. It stays in your mind.

We hope things are going all right with Carole. The biggest yew tree I ever saw was in Gilbert White's churchyard in Selborne. They planted yews in the churchyards so they could have bow-wood without poisoning the livestock. I guess that was necessary in the days of the commons. Probably you know all that. But here's something you don't know yet. The mayor of Elizabethtown, Ky., told me that she received a phone call from an irate person out in the country who wanted to know, "What're you going to do about them Texas Jews?" It took her a while to figure out that the caller meant "Taxus Yews," the trimmings of which the city had evidently dumped where cattle could get at them.

Anyhow, more power to Taxol, to Carole, to churchyard yews, and to Texas Jews.

Things are going ahead here at an unsurprising rate, and our complaints are more or less normal.

Your friend,
Wendell

GARY SNYDER [NEVADA CITY, CA]
TO WENDELL BERRY [PORT ROYAL, KY]

17. XII. 96 [December 17, 1996]

Dear Wendell,

After a couple of weeks of heavy rain in California we have one of those totally clear days where the wind has blown away what might be left of smog and cloud and you can see every detail of the distant foothills. We've been crossing paths, or collaboratively, at long-distance lately—I'm thinking of our two responses to W. T. Anderson's article† in *Mother Jones*, I must say he got more attention from us both than he probably deserves. Still, things like that shouldn't go unanswered. As Jack S. [Shoemaker] says, his article starts out fairly reasonably, nothing to make an argument over and becomes unaccountably mean-spirited. And Jack told me that you said that they cut a good part of your response as well. Looks like the Right and the Left is willing to gang up on nature, each from their own particular sort of ignorance. Anyhow: best Solstice season wishes to you and Tanya, to Mary, and Den and their families. And to all the horses, cows, sheep, and barn cats out there. And the suckers in the Kentucky River. We're unaccountably cheerful here, in that Carole—for all the discomfort of it—is weathering the chemotherapy with considerable grace, hasn't lost her hair, and has a wonderful sense of her own life.

And I can't tell you how much I appreciate your delicate, sensitive, and to the point—your interim comments on *Mountains and Rivers*—Jack gave me a copy of it in Santa Rosa, also where he introduced me, and it is so gratifying that you have got the sense of it so much as I myself felt it to be. Remarkably confirming.

I'm still about to call you and talk about the John Hayes Fellowship [*sic*: John Hay Award] and get your advice how to best manage those guys. I need to make some decisions with them fairly soon... What between doing some book-traveling, finishing teaching, and helping Carole I haven't had much time to think about it. Also, it makes me unaccountably happy that I got you and Tanya out to the Black Rock Desert.

Yours,
Gary

WENDELL BERRY [PORT ROYAL, KY]
TO GARY SNYDER [NEVADA CITY, CA]

1/22/97 [*January 22, 1997*]

Dear Gary,

I've had to write the Orion Society that I can't come out to help honor you [for the John Hay Award] on April 25-27. At best, that would be a troublesome time for me to get away, but I also have a speech to make on the night of the 25th. Of course I honor you anyhow and wherever, but I'm truly sorry to have to be absent from Practicing the Wild.

One way or another, I hope we'll be together again pretty soon.

My mother died on Jan. 3 after a short time in the hospital. She was ill and old and good, and I can wish for nothing different, but

I do feel the change. Aside from that, and except for expectable ailments among the grandchildren, we are all right.

I hope Carole's treatment and Carole herself are coming along ok.

Your friend,
Wendell

GARY SNYDER [NEVADA CITY, CA]
TO WENDELL AND TANYA BERRY [PORT ROYAL, KY]

14. IV. 97 [April 14, 1997]

Dear Wendell and Tanya,

I've been thinking to write you for quite some time. I tried to call several times during the high water some weeks back, and always got a busy line—figured you must have something pretty serious going on and so left you alone. Jack [Shoemaker] told me that the water came up to the barn but I guess no big damages. And the stairs up to your writing cabin.

Carole's doing pretty well, back to her full weight and basic health, and all we have to do now is wait and see if there are any recurrences. There's a good chance not.

I'm just on my way back from visiting Freeport, Illinois, where I gave a talk at Highland College, and a lecture that is endowed by Dr. Earl Boyer—a very much alive and kicking octogenarian retired veterinarian. Doc Boyer likes to come to the lectures that he himself has endowed, and I had dinner with him and many a good talk. He's an amiably passionate and somewhat eccentric guy who hates global corporations, and the effect of capitalism on the environment. So the theme this year, to which I was required to hew, was capitalism, ethics, and the environment. When I had realized I had been given a license to take off and beat up on capitalism all I wanted to, I did—with some restraint—and tried to make some positive comments as well—but it was kind of fun. And read some poems. And dedicated one poem to Allen Ginsberg's memory,† and talked a little bit about Allen.

The other person I met there was Dan Smith† and his wife Cheryl; and his brother Tim. You apparently know Dan's work. They have 300 some acres that they took over from their father, and are milking 120 cows. Dan is about 40—a wonderful guy, genuine poetic talent, tremendously hard worker, who is very excited about his life and work. He's doing rotation grazing with his cows, has them turned out in the open most of the time, after having tried industrial dairy shut-down and liquid manure slurry tanks for awhile. He's got a lot of money invested in equipment that just sits there now. And he's very happy about having a lower vet bill, lower electric bill, and healthier cows. I guarantee you would like him, if you ever get a chance to meet him. His wife, Cheryl—like any good farmer's wife these days—teaches kindergarten, and is a lady of beauty, discipline, straight posture and bright eyes. They hosted a potluck for me, the good Doctor Boyer, and a bunch of faculty from the community college. It does warm one's heart to see such cultural and agricultural energy brought together.

And I was reminded that for a period of time, partly under the influence of your example and writings, I wrestled with thoughts about the American agricultural economy and community, but pulled away from it a little as I, of necessity, got drawn into West Coast forestry and public land issues. I was really moved by Dan Smith's pride in the health of his cows, as part of the "backwards step" he took toward grazing in the pasture. Trying to keep farming going in America is such a poignant effort. Well, you know all about that.

I hope Den and Mary are well. I'm looking forward to not doing much intellectual work this summer at all, quick trip to Japan to give a poetry reading, and the rest of the time engaged with remodeling and building around the place—add on another 600 square foot semi-detached building, put in an inside toilet! I had thought I could get to the 21st century still with an outhouse—but it's not to be. New space—a decent guest bedroom—bigger living room with a bigger table—you'll have to come party with us.

Yr old friend—
Gary

WENDELL BERRY [PORT ROYAL, KY]
TO GARY SNYDER [NEVADA CITY, CA]

4/23/97 [*April 23, 1997*]

Dear Gary and Carole,

We were happy to have your news, and especially to know that Carole is doing all right. We would love to see you both. It would be fine to go for a walk here together—or anywhere else.

I know that Allen Ginsberg's death is a sorrow to you, Gary, and I am sorry. Jack told me some of the details over the phone. It is good that he was able to get away without interference from reporters and the like.

I'm glad you enjoyed your visit to Freeport, Ill. The rural Midwest is having a time of it. Maury Telleen says, "It looks like we've fought a war here, and lost." Contract farming and the industrialization of livestock production are advancing very fast. But this other thing is happening too—what you saw at Dan and Cheryl Smith's.

These days, in all my public involvements, I'm mainly following my belief that if we could develop truly local and native economies in the countryside—agrarian and sylvan economies—we would almost naturally solve a lot of our problems. That certainly is only a belief—I can't prove it. But I *don't* believe in the other, the global, economy.

We had water in four buildings, including my Camp house, where I write. There was no severe damage, but a lot of upheaval and mess. Some fences were damaged. My steps here at the Camp floated away; I'm getting in, for the time being, by gangplank. Some people lost cattle. In the Licking R. valley, some people were drowned. We got off light, and are grateful.

A flood, of course, is exciting too, even when it is messing up your place and your routine. It is a major wilderness event come smack into the middle of everybody's homelife. And you have to take it as a comment: "Well, well," it says, "I didn't know *you* were here. When did you put up these fences? Did you think I'd need *steps* to get into your house?"

I hosed out the Camp and went back to work before the floor was dry. I'm writing a pretty big novel—the autobiography of Jayber Crow,† the Pt. Wm. [Port William] barber—and am about half finished, I hope.

We and our descendants are doing ok and staying busy. I hope all's well with the two of you and your young ones.

Your friend,
Wendell

P.S. Come to see us if you can. Maybe there's a chance we'll get out there in the fall.

GARY SNYDER [NEVADA CITY, CA]
TO WENDELL AND TANYA BERRY [PORT ROYAL, KY]

15. XII. 97 [December 15, 1997]

Dear Wendell and Tanya,

I realize that Jack [Shoemaker] has probably been keeping you up on our situation to some degree, but here's a further update:

As many of you know Carole had pretty drastic surgery last summer trying to eliminate a rare cancer cell in her abdomen called pseudomyxsoma. She was recuperating all fall, but couldn't gain any weight. That was because she had to live with an ileostomy

—that's a hole in your side that drains the small intestine. The body has a hard time taking up nutrition in those circumstances—

December 11 she went back to the Washington Hospital Center (DC) for another surgery to check for recurrence and reconnect her GI tract back to normal. She'll be there until early January it seems, because they are going to give her abdominal chemotherapy washes. And it takes quite a while to restart the large intestine. Her sister Mary Anne, daughter Mika, and I will all be there at various points. It will be early January when she comes home, most likely.

And little bit of news from Gary. I was diagnosed with moderately advanced prostate cancer back in April, and have been doing several kinds of treatment since. I'll be done with treatment for a while after March, and then just watch and see how it goes. The Docs say with luck I should be fine for some years. I didn't start telling friends til recently because I wanted to wait until Carole was through the worst of her own situation, can't have too many soap operas going. I was having a little prostate trouble last winter, which had me go in for a physical, and that's when I decided to get a PSA test. Good thing. And be sure to take your Saw Palmetto caps, laddies! (No kidding.)

And through all this summer I managed to keep on track with a 600 s.f. addition to the Kitkitdizze house, on the west, and some basic re-working of the old house, enlarging the main room. Indoor toilet and taking out the fire pit. We slept on the deck of the barn and cooked outdoors most of the summer, and now we're in our very new-feeling place, though Carole's away for Solstice. . . and a very convivial and cheery Solstice season to you all. Gary

15. XII. 97

We have had, in many ways, a rich time together this summer and fall in spite of—or because of—these challenges to our health and life. Last summer we also did some very beautiful and convenient and totally compatible work on the house including a 600 sq. ft.

addition. We all wish a great solstice season and light and rebirth to you-all, and especially love to you and Tanya,

Gary

◇◇◇◇◇

EDITOR'S NOTE: There is a letter missing from Wendell Berry dated December 22, 1997.

WENDELL BERRY [PORT ROYAL, KY]
TO GARY SNYDER [NEVADA CITY, CA]

Port Royal, Ky. 40058
3/31/98 [March 31, 1998]

Dear Carole and Gary,

I thought I would send along the enclosed [*Sewanee Review*], which may not be the most popular magazine in N. California. I'm glad to have my piece on *Mts. and Rivers* published at last. [...]

We hear from you all by way of Jack [Shoemaker] and Jane [Vandenburgh], and have you often in our thoughts.

After a warm winter, we're having maybe too early a spring. The redbuds are blooming, also the cherries, pear trees, etc. The pastures are green. We have 54 lambs.

Our love to you both.
Wendell

◇◇◇◇◇

EDITOR'S NOTE: While reading the issue of the *Sewanee Review* containing Wendell Berry's "Some Interim Thoughts on Gary Snyder's *Mountains and Rivers Without End*," Gary Snyder came across a piece by R. S. Gwynn titled "Ballade of the Yale Younger Poets of Yesteryear." The poem repeatedly asks "And where is Lindley Williams Hubbell?" By way of response, Snyder attached a copy of a letter written to George Core, editor of the *Sewanee Review,* explaining to Core and the journal's readers that Hubbell was a poet and translator who received a Yale Younger Poets award in 1927. In 1953, he moved to Kyoto, Japan. He became a Japanese citizen and acquired his Japanese name—Shūseki Hayash—in 1960. He taught Shakespeare and English literature at Doshisha University from 1953 to 1970. Snyder met Hubbell in 1956, while studying Zen Buddhism in Kyoto, Japan.

GARY SNYDER [NEVADA CITY, CA]
TO WENDELL BERRY [PORT ROYAL, KY]

3. V. 98 [*May 3, 1998*]

Dear Wendell—

Thank you for sending the winter *Sewanee Review*—with your strange and wonderful review. I liked it so much.

And, as per enclosed, a poem on p. 177 that I ran across took me into some unexpected territory of our own. Carole is slowly improving—yet—and seems to be fine for now. Warm greetings to you and Tanya,

Gary

WENDELL BERRY [PORT ROYAL, KY]
TO GARY SNYDER [NEVADA CITY, CA]

5/8/98 [*May 8, 1998*]

Dear Gary,

I know from talking to Jack [Shoemaker] yesterday that you are now in Washington, but I'll go ahead and write you while your letter to me is fresh.

I'm glad you got the *Sewanee Review*, and am delighted with your letter in reply to R. S. Gwynn, which is just and proper. George Core surely ought to publish it.

Here, we have been wet for 3 weeks or more, which has made gardening difficult but given a great abundance of grass. The grazers are happy.

We had our 3rd annual forestry field day[†] on the 5th and maybe 125 people turned up. Our people need to see good forestry as a necessary part of good farming, and maybe they're beginning to. And the work on local food economy is going ahead.

I've just been reading about you in Peter Coyote's book.[†] It's a valuable book, I think, but troubling—a tribe without elders.

We're glad to hear that Carole is improving, however slowly. We send her our love, tell her.

Your friend,
Wendell

GARY SNYDER [NEVADA CITY, CA]
TO WENDELL BERRY [PORT ROYAL, KY]

25. V. 98 [May 25, 1998]

Dear Wendell,

Thanks for your quick note back about the letter I wrote re: Lindley Hubbell. Here's a xerox of the letter Core responded with. I don't think, from the sound of it, he's going to print it—that's a pity.

And when I sent that to you I had fully intended to add in a letter of appreciation for the *Sewanee Review* piece by you. It got sealed and mailed somehow before I put it all together properly. Your way of talking about *Mountains and Rivers* has such probity, and deep honesty, and an accuracy that reflects the weirdness of the project and the way I am in fact curious about it and unsure of it myself. The whole poem is an exercise in intuition, faith, and trust—in a way. So you caught all that and reflected it in a correspondingly low-key tone. I really enjoy the way this worked out.

Carole is a bit down, feeling she hasn't made much progress in the last two months. She has I think, but it is certainly subtle and we have to constantly remind ourselves that the doctor warned her it might take a full year. So she stays close to her bedroom, goes out and works a bit in the garden or the rest of the house when she's feeling well, but needs rest and can eat just the proper food only, much of the time. We had assumed that she'd be much better by now, so that I had committed myself to a few trips in northern California way last winter, and I regret it now, because it's a strain on both of us when I'm away.

On the inner side of things, the time this has given us together and the honest depth of feeling all this provokes, is really a gift.

I hope that all is well with you and Tanya, the rest of your family. I was in Washington, D.C., early in the month, I worry a dab about Jack [Shoemaker . . .]. But maybe it'll be alright—

Your friend,
Gary

GARY SNYDER [NEVADA CITY, CA]
TO WENDELL BERRY [PORT ROYAL, KY]

20 August [August 20, 1998]

Dear Wendell and Tanya,

I've wanted to send you the Black Rock Press book[†] for a long time. The *Kyoto Journal* "Inaka" (="rural"—"country") issue is more recent. It has some selections from Carole's family history.[†] We just delivered our youngest, Robin, to a very nice boarding high school in the Sanpete Valley of Utah—"Wasatch Academy"—Carole went too. Love and Excellent wishes to you—

Gary

Port Royal, Ky. 40058
August 24, 1998

Dear Carole and Gary,

I have the thought of the two of you pretty often in my mind, like an unanswered letter, so here is a bit of an answer, incomplete as it must necessarily be.

This afternoon on my river-porch I have read the selections from Carole's family history in *Kyoto Journal* with admiration for that gathering and for those people and what they did—and also with sorrow for our government's (still ongoing) inability to recognize a settled community.

And I've read Gary's poems so beautifully made into *Finding the Space* by Black Rock Press. Such a book has an important influence on reading, giving grace. And the poems, this time, seemed just reassuringly good. They keep admitting one deeper in.

Thank you for those gifts.

And also, again, for taking Tanya and me to the Black Rock lake bottom. It was, besides generous, very canny and clever of you to take a sappy fellow like me to a place perfectly sapless.

This year, Mary started a farmers' market on the courthouse lawn at New Castle. It has been successful. Mary and her family have made pretty significant money there. So have others. But *also* everybody likes it. The people who come to buy linger and talk. And so forth. This encourages me. Maybe there is some kind of law in it. If you get the economy right, you don't have to plan the gathering and the talk.

It is a hot, dry afternoon here on the river, but breezy.

Our love to you people. I wish we could see you.

Wendell

◇◇◇◇◇

EDITOR'S NOTE: From January to November of 1999, Wendell Berry and Gary Snyder were involved in a conversation about logging on public lands with Bill Devall. Devall sent both writers a proposal titled "A Campaign to End Commercial Logging on Public Lands" and asked for their feedback in order to create a more comprehensive set of arguments, ideally drawing from the work of social scientists and philosophers in the deep ecology movement. Although Berry was appreciative of Devall's commitment to public forests, his letter—dated January 23, 1999—was critical of the extreme stance of the document and its overall lack of attention to the sustainable use of woodlands. Berry sent Snyder a copy of his letter to Devall, along with copies of three additional statements showing where he has stood as a conservationist, particularly in regard to woodland restoration. During the same time period, Devall sent several questions to Snyder, the responses to which—dated May 16, 1999 —indicate that Snyder did not view the extreme nature of Devall's plan to be feasible. Snyder pointed out, for example, that there were numerous issues of social and economic particularity that were not addressed in the zero cut plan.

WENDELL BERRY [PORT ROYAL, KY]
TO GARY SNYDER [NEVADA CITY, CA]

5/19/99 [May 19, 1999]

Dear Gary,

Here are three statements that show about where I have stuck as a conservationist. If these cause you to think anything I should know, please tell me.

We're all right here. Our love to you both.

Wendell

◇◇◇◇◇

EDITOR'S NOTE: In response, Snyder sent Berry a copy of his reply to Bill Devall on June 16, 1999.

WENDELL BERRY [PORT ROYAL, KY]
TO GARY SNYDER [NEVADA CITY, CA]

June 24, 1999

Dear Gary,

Thanks for sending me your reply to Bill Devall. It is a good reply. The problem with "zero cut" is that it is too simple. *Somebody* is going to have to think of good ways of using forests. Agreeing on the details is not so important right now as facing the problem. What I am most eager for is to see the good examples studied both ecologically and economically by conservationists, forest ecologists, and woods workers.

You asked me to report on my visit to the Democratic Policy committee.[†] I can't of course report *results*, but I can say that the seven of us who testified were attentively and even understandingly heard by several senators. I believe that maybe there is a little better chance now that the issues of agriculture will be discussed publicly in something like their real gravity. This is, as you know, not a time for optimism.

I'm home now with no trips scheduled until the latter end of September so I'm looking forward to getting some work done here without too much haste. We hope all is well with you and Carole and we send our love to you both.

Your friend,
Wendell

P.S. I'm holding November 3rd and November 10th, 2000, for a reading out there. Right?

WB/tb

5. VII. 99 [*July 5, 1999*]

Dear Wendell,

I had a nice note from Jim Dodge[†] about his basic enjoyment of
the "Fire and Grit" event,[†] and from the sound of it all went well.
I hope it was okay for you, too. I'm personally glad I stayed home,
I've done heroic work cleaning out excess books and papers from
my old barn here, and am feeling exceeding virtuous. And thanks
for the quick comment on the Democratic Party policy committee.

You are on for November 10th, a Friday, the year 2000. Is that
okay? The plan would be a Friday evening event, at the [North
Columbia Schoolhouse] Cultural Center, maybe with a conversation on stage at the second half—maybe with me if that interests
you. Or someone else. And a Saturday morning seminar, invited
people, followed by a lunch. You and Tanya would stay here at Kitkitdizze as our guests, it is a much more comfortable house now.
Indoor plumbing, other amenities. And I would hope you could
stay for another night if possible—Saturday—so we could go for a
Saturday afternoon walk, and have a more relaxed time for dinner.
[...] Steve and Sarah [Sanfield] could join us if you'd like. That's the
outline of it—let me know.

We had a hit of high 90s weather here, but it's gone back down
to the 70s and 80s—though very clear—which is absolutely delicious. For some reason, the foothill's cherry trees fruited remarkably well this June and our trees put out so much that even the birds
couldn't get them all and so we got a lot for ourselves. Everyone is
reporting this. Apparently raccoons will climb high up into trees
because we have been finding raccoon droppings full of cherry pits
as well. I'm studying pond biology quite a bit right now, my 25-year-
old pond which started out as bare clay bottom is now full of various water weeds, not to mention all sorts of bugs; the viviparous

mosquito-fish which I planted myself, and a population of bullfrogs which seems to have driven away all other frogs. I got a special kind of rake with ropes on it and cutters on the teeth—three feet wide—that with two people you can supposedly cut and pull lots of pond weeds out of your pond. Having my sturdy younger daughter home gives me a partner at this.

And, continuing to clean up notes and scribbles, hoping to see if there are any good poems or essays that have already been launched and forgotten, rather than grazing new stuff off the top. A good summer to you and Tanya—

Gary

WENDELL BERRY [PORT ROYAL, KY]
TO GARY SNYDER [NEVADA CITY, CA]

7/10/99 [July 10, 1999]

Dear Gary,

November 10, 2000, is fine. And, as you know, I am always glad to converse with you. And anything that will suit you and Carole will suit Tanya and me.

A rainy morning here. Fledgling Carolina wrens raised under the porch roof here at the Camp left the nest this morning—an anxious time for the parents.

Love to you both.

Wendell

◇◇◇◇◇

EDITOR'S NOTE: Gary Snyder's letter was written after meeting with Wendell Berry at the Lensic Performing Arts Center in Santa Fe, New Mexico. The Lannan Foundation hosted a reading and conversation with the two writers that was moderated by Jack Shoemaker.

16 XI 99 [November 16, 1999]

Dear Wendell and Tanya

Back to some dark rains—catching a cold—and full of great thoughts about our time together.

Thanks for the forestry letter to Chris.† Here's a quick set of responses I wrote back to Bill Devall, of Arcata. Pretty much on the same track as you. Carole and I wish you a good warm thanksgiving.

Gary

Port Royal, Ky. 40058
Thanksgiving morning [November 25, 1999]

Dear Gary,

I'm very glad to see your letter to Bill Devall. Maybe it's not "realistic" to propose an economy that is compatible with the survival of *all* worthy things—but I think that is the economy I am going to work for.

Would you mind if I show your pages to Bill D. to the Heartwood people here?

Except for the preparatory moments at the theater—when our "conversation" seemed the most unknown thing in all the future—I loved all that crossing of paths in Santa Fe.

Since then I've been hopping about like a pea on a hot griddle—obligations everywhere. Now, maybe, it's easing up somewhat.

Our love to you both.

Wendell

6. XII. 99 [December 6, 1999]

Dear Wendell—

Please, feel free to xerox, show that letter I wrote to Bill Devall, to anyone who you think might benefit from it. I hope I might be allowed to do the same with yours? Solstice season rapidly rushing up on us—a very fine Christmas to you and Tanya, Mary and her family, Den and his family—

Your friend,
Gary

12/10/99 [December 10, 1999]

Dear Gary,

I think you can properly show my letter [to Bill Devall] to anybody you'd like to see it—but it might seem a discourtesy to let it get published. And I'm glad to be able to make the same use of your letter to Bill Devall.

I've had the flu and for a while was properly humbled, but am getting better.

And yes! To all of you dear people we wish a most happy Christmas.

Your friend,
Wendell

17. XII. 99 [December 17, 1999]

Dear Wendell,

Reflecting back on our brief talk about Dan Daggett, and the dilemma of family ranching, and then catching up on my reading I came across this piece by Larry McMurtry.† It's a very sober and balanced perspective, I think—throws more light on the question —ironically, his father the rancher's big fear was that "the farmers are coming!" The solstice season draws nigh and we have a bit of snow on the ground now. Since August there has been a full grown tom wild turkey around the area with one leg that dangles uselessly. I hadn't thought he'd last long, but I see him still every few days hopping a step at a time and somehow surviving. I guess he can fly, but with only one leg he can't scratch! When I see the other turkeys scratching I pity the poor guy. Our very best to you and Tanya—

Gary

Port Royal, Ky. 40058
12/23/99 [December 23, 1999]

Dear Gary,

Thank you. I read that piece by Larry McMurtry. What he seems not to understand is that histories like his father's, and the studies and statistics that Larry refers to, are not peculiar to W. Texas. They are common throughout the rural economy of the U.S., and increasingly so over the last 50 or 60 years. Overgrazing, everywhere, is the result of overproduction, which is the result of low prices, which are the result of overproduction. The same for overplowing. And this process is necessary to the excessive profits of the agribusiness corporations, who of course encourage the process. As soon as I can get it copied, I'll send you a speech by Eddie Albert,[†] which gives some pertinent history.

I like your essay, "Grace," which I've re-read 3 times since I got your *Reader*.[†] Apparently, none of the great traditional religions (as I gather from Coomaraswamy,[†] who seems to have known them all) will countenance "trade-offs." They all hold in one way or another that everything good must be saved. This is, as you say, tough. And it is exactly the difficulty that needs to be faced by the conservationists. To suppose that wilderness and wildness can be saved by plundering the land-using economies is only to repeat the old mistake of the industrial capitalists.

Well, it is cold here now. I got laid low by the flu for two weeks but am better now, and everybody else is healthy. I hauled in the last load of sawed wood yesterday, and lit fires in the stoves at the house for the first time.

May you and Carole be warm.

Your friend,
Wendell

P.S.—The Amish have defied the statistics and the studies (so far) by maintaining their subsistence economies and the practices of neighborhood.

◇◇◇◇◇

EDITOR'S NOTE: In the following letters, Gary Snyder and Wendell Berry start to make plans for a visit from Berry that would involve a reading at North Columbia Schoolhouse Cultural Center in November 2000.

17. IV. 00 [*April 17, 2000*]

Wendell—

Just a quick note, I know you've been in touch with John McLeod[†] about your fall schedule. Jack Hicks[†] wants to know if you would like to come to UC Davis after the ridge. That could be the Monday, Tuesday, or Wednesday if you like, following on your time here—he says any of those—and they will pay you real money to do that, plus set up to sign books. Do you want to think about this? Nice apple blossom cool rain here right now with wild turkeys gobbling out under the oak trees—

Yours ever,
Gary

Port Royal, Ky. 40058
4/21/00 [*April 21, 2000*]

Dear Gary,

I wish I could go to Davis and do something for Jack Hicks, but the schedule won't allow it. We'll have to fly to Seattle on Sun., Nov. 12. Tell Jack I'm sorry.

I understand that I'm to do something for you on Nov. 10 and Nov. 11.[†] We'll have a chance to walk around and look at the woods, I hope. I guess we'll rent a car at S.F. and leave it on Sun. at Sacramento.

It makes me happy to think of being up there with you and Carole again.

Your friend,
Wendell

7. IX. 00 [September 7, 2000]

Dear Wendell,

I hope you and Tanya are well. I am finishing up a lot of little details before leaving for Korea and Japan, some talks to give and readings, and a lot of old friends to touch base with. I'll be gone from the 22nd of September till the 20th of October, and it occurred to me it wouldn't hurt if we got some things in place earlier rather than later—for your visit out our way in November. So please have John McLeod (or do it yourself if that's better) send a basic publicity bundle to Michael Garitty [...] the director of the North Columbia Cultural Center, where our event will take place, so that he can be blocking out press release and poster information. (And I'll be sending a copy of this letter to John McLeod too.)

I guess John is the one to make sure that there will be books for sale at the event, do you have any sense of what you'd like to have there beyond *Jayber Crow* and *Life is a Miracle*? The Cultural Center hall will hold 200 people, maybe a little more—and we don't necessarily expect to fill it, being way out where we are. Our publicity is good though, and we'll have an enthusiastic and attentive audience for sure. We'll estimate potential book sales on that basis—

Carole and I just returned from a relaxing five day trip to the Bay Area looking at the Chinese archeology show at the Asian Art Museum, the Thiebaud retrospective, and the many new exhibits in the S.F. Museum of Modern Art. We haven't done a trip like this in quite a few years, it's very civilized! We'll talk to you on the phone before I leave, Wendell—

Best,
Gary

18. IX. 00 [September 18, 2000]

Hi Wendell,

How do you like this: a grey squirrel which has now for ten days been regularly climbing up into our apple trees, first the Gravenstein, then the Jonathan, now the Pippin and severing apples so that they fall on the ground and then immediately a four-point buck comes along and eats some of the apples. And the rest of the time he lounges in the shade of the trees. What a deal!

I'm writing to add to my previous note, in regard to Steve Sanfield, I had a nice chat with Steve a few weeks back and explained to him that you wouldn't have much time here, and said that we would host a dinner for you and Tanya to which I would invite him and Sarah, and he need not worry about making some social efforts on his own. He seemed quite content with that.

Changing; most everybody I know has decided that since Bush is going to take California anyway, we're all going to vote for Ralph Nader and make our anti-globalization point. Gone from the 23rd Sept. to 20 October, be in touch when I get back.

Gary

[PS] Wendell, wrote this before talking on the phone to you ...

18. IX [September 18, 2000]

Dear Wendell,

Nice to talk yesterday. Here's a map to my place—hope it's legible—(comprehensible)—call if there's any trouble.

And am sending you this odd little piece[†] on immigration I wrote a bit back—cool equinox, good Halloween.

See you November,

Gary   Carole's best too …

WENDELL BERRY [PORT ROYAL, KY]
TO GARY SNYDER [NEVADA CITY, CA]

Port Royal 40058
9/22/00 [September 22, 2000]

Dear Gary,

We got the stuff. Thanks.

Your piece on "Migration/Immigration" is useful. It gets at least beyond the current political "debate" between sentimentality and greed.

Mexicans are everywhere here now, doing all the work that we are too good to do for ourselves. I think it is the same sorry old mistake again, but this time with another subservient race, and not just "the south" but the whole U.S.

I love your story of the squirrel and the deer. Long live interracial cooperation!

Our love to you people.

Wendell

◇◇◇◇◇

EDITOR'S NOTE: Wendell Berry's letter was written shortly after his visit to Kitkitdizze and reading at the North Columbia Schoolhouse Cultural Center.

WENDELL BERRY [PORT ROYAL, KY]
TO GARY SNYDER [NEVADA CITY, CA]

11/20/00 [November 20, 2000]

Dear Gary and Carole,

It was almost entirely good to be up there with you two and your neighbors—my one regret being that Tanya missed it.[†]

I guess I must have been somewhat distracted by Tanya's absence, for I left some gifts that your friends gave me—in, as I remember, a big paper sack. It pains me to think I could be so careless. If you can use the things, please accept them as a gift from me.

Gary, I think you'd have liked the Grassbank Conference in Santa Fe. The Quivira Coalition† and some ranchers appear to be doing good work. Our friend Drum Hadley was there and in good form.

Love,
Wendell

GARY SNYDER [NEVADA CITY, CA]
TO WENDELL AND TANYA BERRY [PORT ROYAL, KY]

27. XI. 00 [*November 27, 2000*]

Dear Wendell,

You and Tanya are back home by now—and gone through the ceremonies of Thanksgiving—hope all went well. Kai was ten days in Siberia attending and teaching at a GIS conference in Khabarovsk, he says a totally European style city only ten miles from the Chinese border. His wife came down from Corvallis with the little girl, and we had a family Thanksgiving in our house for the first time since Carole and I married. In the past Carole and I always went to one of her family/relative's homes. It was exhausting, but great fun.

Thank you for coming to North Columbia and Kitkitdizze, I have never seen our local folks so thoroughly engaged before, during, and after a visit like they were this time. Here is a clipping† on the North Columbia Schoolhouse for its 125th birthday—will give you a sense of where it is you were. I hope we are able to visit again before too long—

Your friend,
Gary

4. I. 02 [*January 4, 2002*]

Dear Wendell and Tanya,

Into the new year now—our warmish days right now with lots of rain, overflowing ponds and scrappy wild turkeys under the oaks. Happy new year to you both; it's been awhile since we were in touch. Wendell, I got *Sonata at Payne Hollow*† and was really intrigued by it. Have followed Harlan Hubbard's life and works a bit from afar, thanks to you and Gray Zeitz.† This little (beautifully produced) piece is on the order of a Noh drama—precisely, with the travelers entering a known landscape, and then encountering the spirits of that place. But you know all of this—and so, I'm one of the few (not so few maybe) who see that, and applaud it. Thank you for doing this, and sending it to us!

I'll share thoughts with you later, when the spirit moves me, on our life in North America/the globe/since last fall and on. I've been thinking and working on that quite a bit—and on the side, helping to organize a conference on Sierra Nevada forestry. Carole is doing about the same, keeping up her spirits, not always comfortable. She sends her love to you guys and all of us here on the Ridge appreciate that there are a few other comrades here and there in the wider world that share in the vision of what we're stumbling along trying to do.

Yours in the world,
Gary

Port Royal, Ky. 40058
1/29/02 [January 29, 2002]

Dear Gary,

I'm really pleased to have your response to my little play, and am especially glad you saw the Noh influence. Of course I know I can't write an actual Noh play, but that little volume of the Pound-Fenollosa translations[†] has shimmered on my mind for years.

We're staying plenty busy here, but all our bunch are coming along ok. I'm writing speeches at present, and seem always to be involved in something public to do with agriculture or conservation. I'm helping to put together a "forest field day" in this area that will have more to do with forest ecology and intelligent logging than our previous ones.

Here is a copy of a letter I just wrote to *The Hudson Review*. Do you know Michael Lind? I think his "comment" is shockingly bad.[†]

Our love to Carole and you.

Wendell

P.S.—Gary, have you ever been to Okinawa. From time to time the history of Pt. Wm. [Port William] and other concerns start me reading again about W.W. II. I just read George Feifer's heart-breaking account of the battle, and then Yanagi's account[†] of the intact island culture before the war. What that war did and what it showed us about us humans is a perpetual horror and amazement to me.

Nathan Coulter fought on Okinawa. That's what started me reading about it. But the fact of the battle certainly dwarfs anything anybody might know or say about it.

Also: I'm coming to S.F. Feb. 22–24, leaving the 25th, to talk to the Sierra Club Board about agriculture, but avoiding any speaking or reading otherwise. If you're going to be down to the Bay at that time and we could possibly eat a meal together, please let me know.

◇◇◇◇◇

EDITOR'S NOTE: Gary Snyder's sister, Anthea Corinne Snyder Lowry, was killed in an auto accident south of Petaluma, California, in 2002. In "For Anthea Corinne Snyder Lowry," a poem from *Danger on Peaks* (2004), Snyder memorialized his sister in the following way:

> She was on the Marin County Grand Jury, heading to a meeting, south of Petaluma on the 101. The pickup ahead of her lost a grass-mower off the back. She pulled onto the shoulder, and walked right out into the lane to take it off. That had always been her way. Struck by a speedy car, an instant death.

> White egrets standing there
>   always standing there
>   there at the crossing

> on the Petaluma River

GARY SNYDER [NEVADA CITY, CA]
TO WENDELL BERRY [PORT ROYAL, KY]

[March 20, 2002]

Dear Wendell

Quick question—did I ever send you a copy of my (late) sister's book on the chicken farms of Petaluma?† If not—I must!

Yrz. ever Gary

219

4/8/02 [April 8, 2002]

Dear Gary,

I didn't know about Thea's death until I got your card and then talked with Jack [Shoemaker] today and found out what had happened. Though I only met her briefly a time or two, she is vivid in my memory. Besides horrified and saddened, I'm very moved to think that in her last moments in this world she was helping somebody in trouble. I'd be *glad* to have a copy of her book on the chicken farms of Petaluma.

Your friend,
Wendell

GARY SNYDER [NEVADA CITY, CA]
TO WENDELL BERRY [PORT ROYAL, KY]

26 II '03 [February 26, 2003][†]

Dear Wendell and Tanya—

Brush-piles smouldering—noise of logging at a neighbors—everybody talking about these times. Your "Citizens' Response"[†] gave Carole and me heart—it is perfect. I hope it goes out further—but —our people are largely sort of hypnotized at the moment. But for those who are speaking/acting/up—lots of them here in our county —some bussed to the San Francisco marches.[†]

Be well, persevere —
love from Gary and Carole

4/6/03 [April 6, 2003]

Dear Gary,

Your poem, "For Philip Whalen" is very moving to me, for the stated reasons, also because I know it takes fifty-some years to write such a poem. Thanks.

We have green grass, some new leaves, three rows in the garden, 35 lambs, and some love left over to send west to Carole and to you.

Wendell

◇◇◇◇◇

EDITOR'S NOTE: It is unclear when the following letter from Gary Snyder was sent. Snyder wrote a note with it that reads: "Yikes! Found this unsent still in a corner of the outgoing mailbag. Sorry! G."

GARY SNYDER [NEVADA, CA]
TO WENDELL BERRY [PORT ROYAL, KY]

7. VII. '03 [July 7, 2003]

Dear Wendell and Tanya

The Gift of Gravity; too—Thank you for that. "The Cold Pane" a long-time favorite/many others familiar; but a fine mix here.†

And you, both bearing your witness to our world condition, as subsistence—as moral practice, as a steady strength. I love our long-distance friendship—

Carole's and my love, Gary

◇◇◇◇◇

EDITOR'S NOTE: Wendell Berry was scheduled to participate in a panel discussion titled "Fast Food World: Perils and Promises of the Global Food Chain" at the University of California, Berkeley (2003). The Slow Food panel included five speakers: Michael Pollan, Eric Schlosser, Carlo Petrini, Wendell Berry, and Vandana Shiva.

WENDELL BERRY [PORT ROYAL, KY]
TO GARY SNYDER [NEVADA CITY, CA]

Port Royal
10/21/03 [*October 21, 2003*]

Dear Gary,

Tanya and I will be coming out to Berkeley, probably on Nov. 22, to take part in a Slow Food panel on campus on the 24th and talk with Michael Pollan's students on the 25th, returning home on the 26th. We tried out the thought of a short visit with you and Carole, but we can't be out there long enough to make it work. We're sorry for that of course. Is there any chance that either or both of you will be coming down to the Bay at that time? When I told Michael we were thinking of visiting you, he said to invite you to attend the Slow Food event and have dinner with us afterward at Chez Panisse.

Whether we see you and Carole or not, we wish we could see you, and we are often thinking and speaking of you. Our love to you both.

Wendell

GARY SNYDER [NEVADA CITY, CA]
TO WENDELL BERRY [PORT ROYAL, KY]

31 X [*October 31, 2003*]

Dear Wendell—

Got your message—we're on the Mendocino Coast in fact, catching up on reading and writing. Nov. 23 through Thanksgiving Kai and his family will be with us, down from Oregon—so we won't be able to go to Berkeley. Alas! Thanks for letting me know.

Yrz

Gary

6. VIII. 04 [August 6, 2004]

Dear Wendell,

I hope you are all recovered now. I know it was some weeks ago, I had been in touch with Jack Shoemaker. I recently received—as a forward on email, your great piece† offering some advice to the Kerry campaign and reminding everyone again of the basic and true meanings of American democracy.

It says something about our times that we have to remind people of it. And of course Carole and I still have, have it pinned up, your statement ["A Citizen's Response ..."] that was in *The New York Times* with its properly 18th century design. Would that people would listen, and would that they would remember.

Carole's about the same, lately knitting little sweaters for recently born babies—usually children of the children our children grew up with; and making a few baby quilts as well. And now she and I are busy training our new poodle pup, an apricot female ten weeks old, using a very gentle and animal-psyche friendly system. In a month we'll be going to Italy for three weeks. I've had some contacts there—especially bioregionalists—who have been inviting me for many years. Carole really has long wanted to travel there and she's going to risk it no matter what. We'll be pretty well taken care of as we move about from Rome to Pitigliano (where a book festival will be held)—to Gubbio for a bioregional conference held on a farm—to Firenze, Siena, and then up to the Austrian border to see the museum of the Ice Man. And then back to the Po Valley where my friend [Giuseppe] Moretti† has a 15 acre farm and spend a bit of time with him.

Any shred of advice you might give us about Italy we'd much appreciate. A nice translation of *Turtle Island* recently came out *L'isole Tartaruga*. Can you think of any people you know there who would appreciate getting a copy that I wouldn't know or think of? I do not know too many people to be suggesting this book to. Lawrence Ferlinghetti, who has gotten his childhood Italian up to pretty good speed again, says he liked it.

Warm greetings to Tanya, we are much looking forward to your visit to the West Coast in February.

Your friend,
Gary

◇◇◇◇

EDITOR'S NOTE: In 1961–62, Wendell Berry and his family lived in Florence, Italy, and in southern France while on a Guggenheim Fellowship. In a previous letter, Berry had enclosed a speech titled "Tuscany," which was delivered at Pisa in 2003 and then published in *Citizenship Papers* (2003).

WENDELL BERRY [PORT ROYAL, KY]
TO GARY SNYDER [NEVADA CITY, CA]

August 17, 2004

Dear Gary,

It makes me happy to think of you and Carole in Italy. We have just one real and dear friend there: Giannozzo Pucci. [...] Giannozzo and his wife, Maria Novella, and their children live on a farm outside of Fiesole above Florence. He has been a Green member of the Florence city council, knows English, [...] has read widely and thought deeply and carefully, and is a generous, gentle, very sweet and likeable man. I'd bet he knows about you. I'm sending along a couple of his writings† that will give you some sense of him. He'd welcome a copy of *L'isole Tartaruga*. I'll be more than glad to write to him for you. But maybe I should know when you'll be in Florence before I do that?

I have a great liking also for Carlo Petrini, founder of Slow Food, but I don't know him as well. Alice Waters would be the one to put you in touch with him. Carlo has no English, but people around him do. He is at Bra.

It's good to think of Carole knitting those sweaters, and of the two of you training the poodle pup.

Here we're keeping busy at the usual stuff, in some astonishingly cool weather for August. I've been writing a few poems, but mostly speeches (which is to say essays), and I'm getting tired of speeches.

And so, yes, it's consoling to look forward to being with you and Carole again in February, and while we wait we'll look forward also to *Danger on Peaks*.

Our love to you both,
Wendell

GARY SNYDER [NEVADA CITY, CA]
TO WENDELL BERRY [PORT ROYAL, KY]

15. X. 04 [*October 15, 2004*]

Dear Wendell,

A brief report back to you from our tour through Italy, Carole and I landing in Rome and there for four days in an elegant borrowed apartment right downtown near the Piazza Navona, then to Pitigliano in Tuscany for a reading and some discussion, then to meetings at a farm in Umbria south of Gubbio. And then Carole took the train to Milan and flew back home—not wanting to try her luck much farther—and I went on for a book signing and a few days in Firenze. There, of all things, at the Edison Bookstore when

I was doing a reading and signing from *Tartaruga*, I was greeted by G. Pucci and his wife; and Teddy Goldsmith. They were planning the launch of the first issue of *The Ecologist* Italian version the very next day (but I couldn't go). Mr. and Mrs. Pucci were charming, as was Goldsmith. And I remembered you had mentioned his name. He in turn said to me, "Wendell and Tanya stayed at our place when they were first in Italy, and just last year too"—

So I must thank you again for sending that information, your essay ["Tuscany"], in advance. After Firenze I went with my friend Giuseppe Moretti in his little car up to his farm just south of the Po River and not far from Mantova. He was born there, and his family have been farmers in that region forever. He is now an ardent bioregionalist and alternative agriculture—alternative everything —thinker. Giuseppe and I drove up to Bozano, well into the south Tyrol/upper Adige River country, to spend a day with the museum where the "Man in the Ice" is kept and displayed.† I had really wanted to see this and to study it. We took a return route that went through and over the Dolomites through a number of German-speaking alpine farm and ski areas, and swung back to Mantova and his farm. It was altogether wonderful, I met great people and learned many little lessons. Flew back from Milan, and have been scrambling around catching up and trying to be ready for the coming winter ever since.

So thanks again, I'm assuming Jack [Shoemaker] has sent you a copy of my new book [*Danger on Peaks*] but if not I surely will. Hello from Carole and me to you and Tanya—see you in February—

Hi to Tanya—
may you all be well!
Gary

◇◇◇◇◇

EDITOR'S NOTE: On November 24, 2004, Wendell Berry sent Gary Snyder a letter complimenting him on the publication of *Danger on Peaks*. That note is missing.

GARY SNYDER [NEVADA CITY, CA]
TO WENDELL AND TANYA BERRY [PORT ROYAL, KY]

17 Jan 05 [*January 17, 2005*]†

Dear Wendell—

I'm looking at your note of November 24 (—ha, I'm catching up!) Good words for *Danger . . . grazie*. Carole's doctor visit in November was reassuring—and though she's no better, she's handling her daily difficulties with skill. And, see you soon!

Very best to Tanya and you,

Gary

GARY SNYDER [NEVADA CITY, CA]
TO WENDELL AND TANYA BERRY [PORT ROYAL, KY]

1. IV. 05 [*April 1, 2005*]

Dear Wendell and Tanya

Here's my letter to Daniel Kemmis,† finally, which I held off sending till I had read yours. And I didn't get to reading yours until recently, as I was finishing up my paper for the Koreans.† I do think the letter to Daniel K.† is extremely important for all of us, and I hope it will be published and made available. My Occidental hat is off to you, and my Oriental side is making a deep *namaste* bow to you. You are an invaluable spokesperson for the sanity and virtue that was once strongly in our culture. Also thank you for your further comments on *Danger on Peaks*, you have seen deeply into what I hoped it would be.

Carole has recently shifted over to direct tube feeding into a vein near her heart instead of solid food; her digestive system is not able to handle much of solids any more. It all happens during the night, and in the daytime she is mobile. We're hoping this gives her more energy and much less discomfort. The newer system has a little day-pack and an electric DC/AC pump that will put food in your body anywhere you go. The old one hung from a pole.

So, with more energy and mobility, she decided she wanted to make a push and go look at the wildflowers blooming in Death Valley. We drove down, got a room at the ranch at Furnace Creek, and were sauntering (and crawling) in the splendid wildflower fields on the bajadas, flowers that are the result of bigger than usual winter rains. Lots of cars from L.A. were in the valley enjoying the fields of Desert Sunflower too. We managed to identity another dozen species in addition to the dominant desert gold. What a strange and lovely space. It is very clear and clean but VERY salty. Drove back north on the wide fast and open desert mountain highway 95. Carole managed the whole trip with no significant trouble.

April 1. Foolish greetings ...
Gary

WENDELL BERRY [PORT ROYAL, KY]
TO GARY SNYDER [NEVADA CITY, CA]

Port Royal, Ky.
4/14/05 [April 14, 2005]

Dear Gary,

Thank you for your letter. I said to Tanya, "Gary's letter is really moving to me." And she agreed that there are not many people whose approval matters much to me any more.

And I like your letter to Daniel [Kemmis], which I think will require him to think harder than my letter did.

I know we've got to be practical and try to outvote these capitalist totalitarians, but I hate to see the Democrats try to do it by becoming more like their opponents: "Oh, yes, I too wish to shoot a lot of people."

We love your report on your and Carole's trip to Death Valley in bloom. As it happened, my friend Bob Weeden, a biologist who has worked much in Alaska, made the same pilgrimage with his wife, evidently at the same time. "From 3500 ft. down to below sea level there were square miles of flowers. Tall yellow ones, big enough to stop speeding tourists, tiny blue or white or pink or yellow belly flowers to bring you to your knees." And he quoted a poem, I suppose his own:

> I like things that are little and brown,
> Beetles and sparrows and mice.
> For to see them well you must kneel down,
> And a humbling science is nice.

Here we are mostly all right, I alone being a little out of kilter with "prostate trouble," minor but distracting.

We have small leaves, green grass, new lambs. And lots of wild woods flowers, like the desert ones making the most of a "window of opportunity," here the brief time between too much cold and too much shade.

Our love to Carole and to you.
Wendell

August 11, 2005

Dear Gary and Carole,

I look upon your birthday card as a birthday *gift*. Thank you. Yes: 71. Three score and ten, and any more after that is "for good measure." Here is a recent poem[†] also for good measure.

Every day we think of the two of you.

Yours faithfully,
Wendell

VII

I know I am getting old and I say so,
but I don't think of myself as an old man.
I think of myself as a young man
with unforeseen debilities. Time is neither
young nor old, but simply new, always
counting, the only apocalypse. And the clouds
—no mere measure or geometry, no cubism,
can account for clouds or, satisfactorily, for bodies.
There is no science for this, or art either.
Even the old body is new—who has known it
before?—and no sooner new than gone, to be
replaced by a body yet older and again new.
The clouds are rarely absent from our sky
over this humid valley, and there is a sycamore
that I watch as, growing on the river bank,
it forecloses the horizon, like the years
of an old man. And you, who are as old
almost as I am, I love as I loved you
young, except that, old, I am astonished
at such a possibility, and am duly grateful.

12/12/05 [December 12, 2005]

Dear Gary,

I'm much indebted to you for the copy of Drum's book,† which I've only just now got around to. It is vivid poetry, and entirely unlike anybody else's. But to me it seems original in the right way, for I imagine it as entirely like the landscape and the life it comes from. I'm reading it eagerly, with pleasure, and of course remembering the time you and Drum came here [in 1983], and Drum's "rehearsal" in the dining room of the Springs Motel in Lexington, and his reading at the university that so pleased and delighted everybody. So my pleasure now and my gratitude are complex, like the growth in an old fencerow.

As soon as I finish the book I'll write to Drum, c/o his publisher.

Through the fall I worked my way through a bit of teaching, a big bunch, variously collected, of public obligations. Now my life is becoming private again and I'm settling down at home and writing more prose, for a change, that is not a speech. I'll continue to have some public obligations that I can't get out of, but mostly local, and I hope more widely spaced. To all invitations to travel I'm now rendering the beautiful monosyllable "No."

We have some snow on the ground here, and seem to be starting a colder winter than we've had lately.

I'm continuing, in Kentucky, to bang myself like a drumstick on the need to develop local food and forest economies. The need is great and could easily become desperate, but the making of such economies will be a long, hard job. It's impossible not to be reminded often of the craziness of such an endeavor, but I'm by no means working alone, and there is some evidence of progress.

We hear from you and Carole pretty often via Jack [Shoemaker], and we have you often in our thoughts. And now as we're coming to the time of longer light, we send our greetings and love to you both.

Wendell

P.S. I forgot to say above that your foreword to Drum's book is admirable, just right.

GARY SNYDER [NEVADA CITY, CA]
TO WENDELL AND TANYA BERRY [PORT ROYAL, KY]

15. XII. '05 [December 15, 2005]

Dear Wendell and Tanya—

Well, warm greetings across this broad land—for the Solstice—for Christmas, and for life going on. *Blessed Are the Peacemakers.*[†] Steve and Sara [Sanfield] described a lovely afternoon with you recently —we crossed path at our Ridge redneck bar and restaurant. Carole sends her love—; hanging in. I much appreciate your poem on being young and old. Great good wishes dear friends—

Gary

WENDELL BERRY [PORT ROYAL, KY]
TO GARY SNYDER [NEVADA CITY, CA]

Port Royal, Ky. 40058
9/14/06 [September 14, 2006]

Dear Gary,

Kitkitdizze is one of the places where my mind has gone to the ground, and I felt deeply and familiarly happy to be there again. I liked our mind-leveling conversation on Sunday morning, brief as it was. My awareness of Carole's absence[†] made her in a way present to me, and I was thankful for that. And so, once again, I am much indebted to you. When you get a chance come to see us.

Your friend,
Wendell

15. IX .06 [September 15, 2006]

Dear Wendell,

Such a pleasure to have you here! I really appreciate the effort you made to stay a day longer and visit Steve [Sanfield] and me (also I am grateful that you gave me the push to go over and see Steve myself, it actually felt very good).

The broadside poem[†] you gave me—calligraphed by Christine C.—marks a great step forward in Occidental culture. One of the few poems I've ever seen—that is almost a prayer—reaching for a way to speak to the point that Rasmussen's Eskimo informant was making when he said "All our food is souls."[†] Explaining why Eskimos had to be very careful. And it's just a good poem, anyhow. I like the word "shooter."

Somehow I never got to asking you about how Tanya was, what she was up to, please accept my regrets for that—and let her know I hope she's doing well and wish her well. It was nice to hear about Mary and Den, each in their way, I will see what I can do about getting more information for you about Bob Erickson's furniture work, and anything else along those lines you'd like me to keep an eye out for. On your several visits to San Juan Ridge did we ever manage to get you over to see Lennie Brackett's[†] traditional and rather elegant Japanese house? That, and also the State Park hydraulic mining village North Bloomfield with all of its gear would be worth another trip here for you. I think.

Okay: cooler weather has come, and I'm still catching up on mail.

Best to you—
Gary

September 29, 2006

Dear Gary:

I'm much taken with your remarks about my hog killing poem. I take it more seriously now than I did when I wrote it, and I think it probably *is* a prayer. And though none of us here could have put it as elegantly and as truly as the Eskimo you quote—"all our food is souls"—we felt something of the same anxiety, and that is what the poem comes from. It was written in the time when four or five households of us were getting together every fall to kill maybe fourteen hogs. I think that every experienced person among us would be anxious that the deaths should not be painful, and that meant, among other things, that they should never have to be shot twice. Our way of putting it was that they should not be made to squeal. The one who did the shooting was my old neighbor Marvin Ford, known as "Mob." Mob bore a lot of responsibility, and he felt it. The hogs to be killed would be penned in the barn lot. Mob would pick one, and walk slowly around as the hog moved, waiting for the moment when the hog would lift its head and look straight at him. Then he shot. Never a squeal. The hog would be dead by the time it hit the ground. So I think my poem has a cultural source.

Tanya is fine, and was much interested to hear my report of our trip to your place. She and I first visited you there sometime in the late 70s, nearly thirty years ago!

No, you never did take us to see either the Brackett house or the mining village. So that's something to look forward to next time.

Your friend,
Wendell

dpc†

[PS]

Gary, I got your packet of things to read,† and I'll read them soon. For now, we're leaving tomorrow morning to go to Chicago, Kansas (Wes's)†, Montana, Wyoming. Home the 18th.

WENDELL BERRY [PORT ROYAL, KY]
TO GARY SNYDER [NEVADA CITY, CA]

10/24/06 [October 24, 2006]

Dear Gary,

Without venturing a guess as to your wish for the enclosed documents, I am simply fulfilling my commission. I do not know Becky.†

It has been winterish here, though today, with the sun out, it was possible to sweat at work if you kept your jacket on.

Your friend,
Wendell

WENDELL BERRY [PORT ROYAL, KY]
TO GARY SNYDER [NEVADA CITY, CA]

November 5, '06 [November 5, 2006]

Dear Gary,

Thanks for the essay by C. A. Bowers. I don't much care for the word "environment," since I have a significant portion of mine inside my skin. But if "Environmental Conservatives" can put me into the same company as you, Wes [Jackson], and Vandana Shiva,† the name is secondary and I am grateful. It's a useful essay, I think.

I recently re-read *Paradise Lost*, VII because of something I was writing, but with your reference to Rasmussen's Eskimo friend ("all our food is souls") very much at the front of my mind. And so

I found that in his account of the creation Milton used the word "soul," each time quoting Genesis 2:7, at least 3 times, once of Adam, and twice of not-human creatures. See VII: 388, 392, 528.

It has been raining here this fall like a California winter.

Your friend,
Wendell

WENDELL BERRY [PORT ROYAL, KY]
TO GARY SNYDER [NEVADA CITY, CA]

Port Royal (Lanes Landing)
December 7, '06 [December 7, 2006]

Dear Gary,

Thank you for the article by Tu Weiming and the booklet by Giuseppe Moretti, both of which have been a help to me.

I've also read with great interest your albatross essay (I've mislaid the magazine and don't have the exact title) in Satish's *Resurgence.*[†] I read that, it happened, just as I was re-reading and re-re-reading "The Rime of the Ancient Mariner" ("I shot the albatross.").[†]

"The Rime" astonished me this time by its excellence, which I underestimated before. It is pertinent to your essay, and I recommend it.

Also, apropos of your essay, I enclose a copy of a lecture by S. H. Nasr,[†] an eminent scholar of Islam. I don't know if my underlinings will be in your way or not, but notice at least the marked passages in the middles of pp. 13 and 19.

This is a bitter cold windy day here. I've been writing another damned speech the last two weeks, and am thoroughly weary of it. It's a pleasure to call back those vivid hours with you and your neighbors.

Your friend,
Wendell

11/23/07 [*November 23, 2007*]

Dear Gary,

It was good to hear your voice during the Counterpoint conference call, and I've been meaning to write to you ever since.

When *Back on the Fire* came, I began by dabbling around in it, being busy and as usual misled by various distractions, but then I settled down and read it from cover to cover, as I was supposed to. It is a good, I meant to say excellent, useful, entirely readable collection. I'm grateful for the humor in it—your reply to the homosexuals,† I'm sure, will be ever fresh and perfect in my mind—and I'm particularly grateful for your continuing attention to land use and the economy.

I'm presently reading a book that Wes Jackson swears by—Stan Rowe's *Home Place*;† do you know it?—and now I'm ready to swear by it too. It doesn't entirely escape, as maybe it couldn't, the ugly, academic vocabulary of the various "centrisms," and on some issues inevitably there is more to be said, as (I think) on abortion, but it is the best, clearest defense imaginable of what he calls the Ecosphere.

I hope you're doing all right. We're all right here.

Your friend,
Wendell

16. XII. 07 [*December 16, 2007*]

Dear Wendell and Tanya,

Very nice to get your note, and yes—that was an okay conversation we all had—all around—in conference with Jack [Shoemaker] and Charlie [Winton], but I must say I don't have much access to finding new investors[†] for them living back here where I do and not knowing many actively middle-class people in the urban world. In fact, I just had an email yesterday from Jack Shoemaker elaborating on the need to get some more money together and wondering what I could do. Frankly I don't even know (it's my own fault, I haven't really asked) what becomes of the small amount of money I invest myself—if there is some formula for dividends if the company ever makes any money. I should find out if I'm going to recommend this thing to others.

A mini-example, I guess, of the world at large. My dental hygienist, a right-winger, was shocked when I told her the other day that capitalism works just fine with totalitarianism as well, or better, than with democracy. Thinking of both China and Nazi Germany. Apparently, that had never occurred to her, but I'll give her credit, she agreed that might be true.

We've had a pretty dry fall, though not a drought, maybe 12 inches of rain so far. There's plenty of time over the winter to make up the annual average. I've missed my timing again though and didn't catch the right dry window to burn a couple of major brush piles right on the edge of the new storm coming in. Now those big brush piles are so soaked that they'll be hard to start unless we get a mid-winter dry spell (which has been known to happen). The trouble is, as the fire guys and the agencies have all found out, the workable window for prescribed burning on wild lands is generally too small to be able to count on it annually and get significant acreage low-burned in order to reduce large-fire hazard. It looks like the answer is either mechanical mastication, which is very expensive, or just rolling with the blow when the big fires hit. In fact the counties and the insurance companies could tackle that if they wanted to— especially with southern California—by having gnarlier restrictions on new home development in high fire chaparral habitat. 60,000 new homes are scheduled to be built over this coming summer in basically the same kind of southern California brush lands that burned 2,000 houses just last month.

I didn't mean to get into a West Coast rant—what I'm really enjoying is working on an essay on walking to go into Tom Killion's new book of prints of Mt. Tamalpais. Do you have a copy of that Killion book I did with him called "High Sierra"?[†]

Well, Christmas and Solstice greetings to you and Tanya, your children and grandchildren, and all of your clan for this year. I hope things are going tolerably well and continue so. I'm doing fine with my dog in the back and heated corner of my little house, and actually beginning to catch up on some work.

Yours,   convivial nights—

Gary   short days—

midwinter cheer

WENDELL BERRY [PORT ROYAL, KY]
TO GARY SNYDER [NEVADA CITY, CA]

1/5/07 [*sic: January 5, 2008*]

Dear Gary,

You certainly are right about capitalism and totalitarianism. And no doubt the brush lands and landslides of California are better habitats for Buddhists than for capitalists. And I can think of a lot of places where I would rather live with Buddhists than with capitalists. If you know any Buddhist-capitalists, don't tell me.

We're being slowly rained on here today and it's fairly warm. The ground is thawing and will be muddy soon, which will make me wish for freezing weather.

The news says deep snow in the Sierras, and we hope you and your neighbors are doing all right.

I'm enclosing a piece on forestry I wrote for two Ky. papers.[†] The Pioneer Forest is the best documented sustainable forestry project I know about. There's more to be said about it. I'm going to see if *Orion* could use an expanded version.

Bald eagles are appearing, these days, beyond my Camp house

windows, and black bears are said to have arrived upriver in the east end of our county.

Your friend,
Wendell

19 VI 08 [June 19, 2008]

Dear Wendell

A woman Dana Goodyear† may call you. She's writing for the *New Yorker.* I hope this isn't too much of a bother. Best wishes to you, Tanya, and all—

Gary

◇◇◇◇

EDITOR'S NOTE: Gary Snyder mentions a letter from Wendell Berry dated May of 2007. This letter does not exist. Snyder was referring to Berry's letter from January 5, 2008 (misdated by Berry as 1/5/07). Snyder misread the date as May 1, 2007.

15. II. 08 Parinirvana Day† [February 15, 2008]

Dear Wendell,

I'm going to use this letter just to respond to one thing: the note you sent me in May of last year, 07, and the essay on the pioneer forest. The one in Salem, Missouri.

Truth is I finally got to reading it, which is a sign that I am getting more on balance in the current world. It is very interesting, and I appreciate what you said in your letter—the best documented such sustainable forest project in your part of the world. Also, it's very different from West Coast pine and Doug fir zone forestry which is so much more industrial. However, with the growing number of small and medium sized private forest and land owners—many of whom originally thought to just "preserve" their forest land but who are now pushed to wonder again what might be done with it to just reduce the hazard of wild fire, this is interesting. And coming to be relevant.

So one question is would you permit it to be republished in the Yuba Watershed Institute newsletter, *Tree Rings*. That's not much of a venue, it only has a circulation of a couple of hundred, but it goes out to people in the industry and in public lands management as well as concerned citizens. We've held two large gatherings here on the question of sustainable forestry—sponsored by the Tahoe National Forest Supervisor Steve Eubanks—and though a lot of it was in the service of Forest Service rhetoric, a number of good ideas came through. I know that Steve, now that he is retired from being the supervisor and from the Forest Service, will appreciate your essay enormously. I'm assuming it will come out in a forthcoming book as well. (Or maybe it already has!)

Cold spell letting up now, the snow is melting and patchy, I don't need the 4X to get out any more, and I'm forging ahead on my work with the Mt. Tamalpais book. Best wishes to you and Tanya and all—

Gary

WENDELL BERRY [PORT ROYAL, KY]
TO GARY SNYDER [NEVADA CITY, CA]

2/20/08 [*February 20, 2008*]

Dear Gary,

Of course you can print my little Pioneer Forest article in *Tree*

Rings. It'll be an honor, and I'll have my typist friend email it to you so it won't have to be retyped. Would you say "By permission of the author"? Maybe better to just let it go.

I want eventually to enlarge that piece, maybe for *Orion*. That might give me a chance to talk about good forestry practice by knowledge, familiarity, with the forest rather than by application of rules.

Cold, windy, and gray here on the river this afternoon. We've had a good deal of freezing weather, with a lot of rainy spells in between, almost no snow. It's about lambing time.

Thank you for the account of Parinirvana Day.

Your friend,
Wendell

July 19, 09 [July 19, 2009]

Dear Gary,

Your letter and the book on Tamalpais [*Tamalpais Walking: Poetry, History, and Prints*] are very dear to us, and we thank you. The book is beautiful. Tanya loves it and has kept it at hand ever since it came. That mountain presided over her childhood and she has many familiar memories of it. I have a good many memories of it too, but for me it keeps the charm of strangeness that it had for me when I first went there in 1958, when I was 24. For me, this is the familiar place, and I sink deeper into it as I grow older. When we came back here to live in 1965, I was warned that I was wasting my time and throwing away better opportunities, because I "already knew this place." In fact, I had only begun to know it. And the wonderful thing is that, after being here for another 45 years, I still have only begun to know it.

Anyhow, when Tanya relinquishes that book, if she hasn't worn it out, I'll keep it by me for a while. And as you suggest, I hope we'll walk again on that dear old mountain when we re-visit California. We will be coming out again probably in the last of Oct., and staying until the 5th or 6th of Nov. If you're down at the Bay at that time, maybe you will walk with us.

I was planning to spend most of this Sunday in the woods. But we're expecting a high today of 75°, and it's simply too chilly this morning to be comfortable sitting outdoors. So I'm spending the day reading and answering the mail in my old Camp house by the river, which is a good place to be any day.

Climate change is beyond my competence. I have to trust other people on that. I do know competently that oddities of weather have become more frequent. But I keep thinking that the most serious issue is economic. If the climate were permanently stable and we had an unlimited quantity of non-polluting fuel, our "way of life" would still be wrecking the world. As it is, this part of the world is being worse wrecked by mining coal than by burning coal.

This year we've had, for the first time in several years, a well-watered growing season. And so our garden, pastures, and woodlands are abounding.

Your comment on the present "drought" in California reminds me that it was a very dry time out there when Tanya and I made our first visit to your place.† It must have been in the late 70s. 1977? On that trip I asked Tanya's uncle, a geologist and a good outdoorsman, how seriously dry he thought it was. He said with a fine defiance, "It's not too dry for the native plants, and that's all that matters to me." So by his standard, you're exactly right.

We'll be happy if we see you out there this fall. And remember that if you come this way, we'll be glad as always to see you here.

Yes indeed, yours faithfully,
Wendell

15 VIII '09 [August 15, 2009]

Dear Wendell—

Well thanks for your letter. Of course I'm really glad that Tanya found the *Tamalpais* book ok! It has done very well in the Bay Area —talk about niche markets!

I'm doing a fundraiser at a private home in Mill Valley on Sept. 26—for Heyday Press—with Tom K. and another at the O'Hanlon Center (where Tanya once lived) on Nov. 12, Thursday. Tom Killion with—

Big interests want to resurrect the possibility of a "peripheral canal" and also reduce protection for the endangered Delta Smelt— and other life forms—"Drouth" language is good politics right now in California. (I'm all for a new Calif. constitutional conference)

Ok—back from a family trip w/ Kai and grandkids to Vancouver BC— "urban adventuring"

best always
Gary

8/23/09 [August 23, 2009]

Dear Gary,

It's Sunday morning, unusually cool for August, and I'm in the woods for the day with some things to read, my lunch in a paper sack, a canteen of water, etc., all in my old pack basket. The year is turning toward fall now, and white snakeroot and the goldenrods are starting to bloom. We've had lots of rain and everything is very green, but there's much wreckage in the woods, big broken-off limbs and fallen trees from the hurricane that came last fall and an ice storm in the winter.

I don't think our trips to the Bay area are going to coincide the least bit, and I'm sorry for that. We'll have been there and gone when you're there on Nov. 12. It's a loss to us not to be able to visit the mountain and the O'Hanlon's place with you.

Ann and Richard O'Hanlon, as poor young artists, bought that place cheap before the Golden Gate Bridge was built. And you're right, it was a place very important to Tanya in the California years of her growing up. And then she and Mary and I lived there at low rent in a tiny house, almost a playhouse, during my years of Stanford, 1958–1960. And so it became an important place also to me. I did my writing in a little studio just up the hill from the big studio that is now a gallery, and where I guess they'll have your reading or speaking. When we were there last, the little studio was still standing. I heated it in the winter with Presto Logs (as I think they were called—cylinders of pressed saw dust) sliced up with a hatchet.

It is interesting that normal rainfall is producing "drouth language" in the politics of California. In Kentucky the "normal" catastrophe of coal has produced a political language of "clean coal." And so forth. We are getting a bad case of fantasy politics. I wonder how close to ungovernable this nation is.

Well, anyhow, it *is* a fine day in the woods.

Your friend,
Wendell

GARY SNYDER [NEVADA CITY, CA]
TO WENDELL BERRY [PORT ROYAL, KY]

30. VIII. 12 [*August 30, 2012*]

Dear Wendell,

I hope you and Tanya are doing well—and all the family and the stock as well. Jack [Shoemaker] gave me your handsome new collected poems, what a good book and how well brought together. And congratulations for that excellent essay, paper, on Thomas

Jefferson [the Jefferson Lecture]† which I read shortly after you gave it I guess, Jack sent it to me as a pdf. It's been a dab hotter here this summer than usual, and I guess it must have been pretty extreme at your place; but what occupies my consciousness more of the time is being prepared for wildfire. Though: this isn't that different from every other summer. However, with all the other fires that have been going around the state and the West, there's a good chance that if we had one near our part of the woods the fire crews and equipment might be elsewhere, so for that reason I put in and am keeping up an 8-hydrant 5,000 gallon water tank—4,000 feet of buried 3" line—dedicated firefighting system on our 100 acres here. The challenge is, getting out and practicing now.

Also Jack [Shoemaker] and Charlie [Winton] told me that our meeting was scheduled for the end of October and you would be out in the Bay Area right about that time. I had not let Jack know of the changes in my plans that came about so that I would not be here; it's not his fault that he scheduled it. Anyway, I'll be up in Oregon finishing up at Oregon State University and then finally spending a few days with my son and grandchildren, first chance in a year.

Kai I am very pleased to say has taken up snow peak mountaineering, took some lessons in it with the Mazamas, and now has climbed four or five of the major West Coast peaks. It's an excellent way to really see the landscape out here and it makes you feel (I will testify at any rate) really good.

I'm beset, as I'm sure you are, by numerous requests, but I try to hold the line so that I can finish up a couple more writing projects before I get too close to (as Gore Vidal put it) the exit. Sorry I'll miss you in Northern California this time, I hope you and Tanya get a chance maybe to get up for a moment on the top of Tamalpais and look over the whole Bay . . .

Yours,

Gary

And greetings to Tanya

◇◇◇◇◇

EDITOR'S NOTE: Wendell Berry sent Gary Snyder a copy of the summer 2013 issue of *Farming* magazine. Berry is photographed on the cover of that issue with a horse and a mule.

GARY SNYDER [NEVADA CITY, CA]
TO WENDELL BERRY [PORT ROYAL, KY]

[*July 13, 2013*]

Wendell—thanks! for the magazine.

But why is it horses have small ears and big feet & mules have big ears & small feet—?

Gary

WENDELL BERRY [PORT ROYAL, KY]
TO GARY SNYDER [NEVADA CITY, CA]

7/16/13 [*July 16, 2013*]

Dear Gary,

A horse is the child of a male and female horse, as you'd expect. A mule is the child of a female horse and a male ("jack") ass. The mule gets his (or her) bigger ears and smaller feet from the jack. The mule's ears are always conspicuously bigger than those of his (or her) mother. The foot difference is not so conspicuous when the mule comes from a smaller-footed mare or one of saddle or racing breeds.

A friend of mine gave me a bird house to put near the small porch in the woods where I'm sitting. The bird house has been taken over by flying squirrels. Sometimes one of the squirrels comes to the opening and regards me, and I regard him or her back. I am unsure how either of us is affected by this.

Wendell

p. vii   "Dear Gary": from letter dated January 19, 1987.

p. vii   "Dear Wendell": from letter dated August 28, 1985.

p. ix   "binocular vision": from letter dated March 11, 1983. In an interview published in *Conversations with Wendell Berry* (2007), Berry also makes the following statement: "Gary Snyder and I agree on a lot of things, but his point of view is different from mine and it has been immensely useful to me. Some differences make for binocular vision."

p. ix   "impulse to speak": from letter dated July 22, 1980.

p. x   "draws on": Gary Snyder, *The Real Work: Interview & Talks, 1964–1979*. Wm. Scott McLean, ed. (New York: New Directions, 1980), p. 124.

p. xii   "a book by a young writer": Jack Shoemaker, "A Long Shelf," in *Wendell Berry: Life and Work*, Jason Peters, ed. (Lexington, KY: Univ. Press of Kentucky, 2007), p. 316.

p. xii   "an impulse of reverence": Wendell Berry, *A Continuous Harmony* (New York: Harcourt Brace Jovanovich, 1972), p. 35.

p. xii   "reading for pleasure": from letter dated July 24, 1973. Jack Shoemaker had sent Berry some pamphlets of Snyder's *Six Sections from Mountains and Rivers Without End* (Berkeley, CA: Four Seasons Foundation, 1970).

p. xii   "to help with work": from letter dated November 1, 1973.

p. xiii   "moving event": Wendell Berry and Gary Snyder, "Poetry Reading at the San Francisco Museum of Modern Art, March 3, 1977," Audio Recording (San Francisco, CA: The Poetry Center at San Francisco State University, 1977).

p. xiii   "I have been keeping": from letter dated April 9, 1974.

p. xiv   "The day that Gary": Wendell Berry and Gary Snyder, "Poetry Reading at the San Francisco Museum of Modern Art, March 3, 1977."

p. xvi   "delighted": from letter dated February 17, 1975.

p. xvi   "music": from letter dated July 25, 1976.

p. xvi   "Well, last spring": Wendell Berry and Gary Snyder, "Poetry Reading at the San Francisco Museum of Modern Art, March 3, 1977."

p. xviii   "native to this place": In reference to Wes Jackson, *Becoming Native to This Place* (Lexington, KY: Univ. Press of Kentucky, 1994), an expanded version of the University of Kentucky Blazer Lecture he delivered in 1991. The book was reprinted by Counterpoint Press in 1996.

p. xx   "We are going to visit": from letter dated December 23, 1976.

p. xx   "*distant* neighbors": from letter dated March 20, 1977.

p. xx   Wendell Berry, "Life on (and off) Schedule," *Organic Gardening and Farming* (August 1977), pp. 44–51.

p. xxii   "spiritual survival": Gary Snyder, "The Etiquette of Freedom," in *The Practice of the Wild* (San Francisco, CA: North Point Press, 1990), p. 21.

p. 3   July 7, 1973: Snyder's note was sent on a poetry postcard of "Clear Cut" (Detroit, MI: The Alternative Press, n.d.), a poem later published in *Turtle Island* (1974).

p. 3   *Continuous Harmony*: Wendell Berry, *A Continuous Harmony* (1972).

p. 3   *Ghost Dance*: Weston La Barre, *Ghost Dance: Origins of Religion* (New York: Doubleday & Co., 1970).

p. 4   Jack Shoemaker: a mutual friend of Wendell Berry and Gary Snyder, and long-standing publisher of their work through Sand Dollar Books, North Point Press, Pantheon, Shoemaker and Hoard, and Counterpoint Press. For more on this relationship see Jack Shoemaker, "A Long Shelf," in *Wendell Berry: Life and Work*, Jason Peters, ed. (Lexington, KY: Univ. Press of Kentucky, 2007), and interviews with Shoemaker in *The Etiquette of Freedom: Gary Snyder, Jim Harrison, and* The Practice of the Wild (Berkeley, CA: Counterpoint Press, 2010).

p. 4   40 acre farm: Berry discussed the purchase of this additional acreage in his Elliston Lectures at the University of Cincinnati, given while he was the poet-in-residence in 1974.

p. 5 December 6, 1973: Snyder's note was sent on a Smithsonian Institution postcard of a Chinese painting by Chao Yung titled *Horse and Groom* (AD 1347).

p. 5 Tanya Berry: Wendell Berry's wife.

p. 5 Stewart Brand: editor of *The Whole Earth Catalog* and founder of *CoEvolution Quarterly*; also a Lindisfarne Fellow.

p. 5 Lawrence Ferlinghetti: poet, publisher, and cofounder of City Lights Books.

p. 5 Michael McClure: poet and playwright of the Beat Generation.

p. 6 *Spring and Asura*: Kenji Miyazawa was a Japanese modernist poet and author of *Spring and Asura* (1922), which Snyder translated in *The Back Country* (1968).

p. 6 Den Berry: Wendell and Tanya Berry's son.

p. 6 "To Gary Snyder": published in *Apple* 9 (1974) and *To What Listens* (1975). Berry gave a copy of *To What Listens* to Snyder with the inscription "To Gary / with greetings / from across the way. Wendell." A slightly different version of this poem was later published in *A Part* (1980).

p. 6 "Poem for Den": this poem was not published.

p. 6 One of my neighbors: in reference to Owen Flood. Berry dedicated *Farming: A Handbook* (1970) to Owen and Loyce Flood, and wrote about the Floods in "Does Community Have a Value?" in *Home Economics* (1987). He also dedicated *Three Memorial Poems* (1977) to Owen Flood, who passed away in March of 1974.

p. 7 "Its hardship": This quote is the concluding line of section two of Berry's poem *Work Song* titled "A Vision." The poem was later published in *Clearing* (1977).

p. 8 February 17, 1975: Berry's note was sent on a poetry postcard of "Falling Asleep" (Austin, TX: Cold Mountain Press, 1974), a poem later published in *A Part* (1980).

p. 8   agriculture book: Wendell Berry, *The Unsettling of America* (1977).

p. 8   Bob G.: Bob Greensfelder, a classmate of Snyder's from Reed College who lives at San Juan Ridge.

p. 9   Masa: Masa Uehara Snyder, Snyder's wife.

p. 9   *People's Land*: Peter Barnes, *The People's Land: A Reader on Land Reform in the United States* (Emmaus, PA: Rodale Press, 1975).

p. 9   *Old Jack*: Wendell Berry, *The Memory of Old Jack* (1974).

p. 10   on my book: Gary Snyder, *The Old Ways: Six Essays* (1977).

p. 10   agriculture book: Wendell Berry, *The Unsettling of America* (1977).

p. 10   Steve: Steve Sanfield, a poet and storyteller from San Juan Ridge.

p. 11   Gen: Gen Snyder, Gary and Masa's son.

p. 11   Kai: Kai Snyder, Gary and Masa's son.

p. 12   *Kuksu: Journal of Backcountry Writing,* a literary magazine founded and edited by San Juan Ridge poet Dale Pendell.

p. 12   Fred Martin: was managing editor at New Directions.

p. 12   Gaia biosphere: In the early 1970s, Lindisfarne Fellow James Lovelock and Sidney Epton were among those who formulated the Gaia Hypothesis, which proposed the earth to be a self-regulating community of living organisms. This theory was linked to Lovelock's earlier work from the 1960s that investigated whether or not Mars was once a life-supporting planet.

p. 13   poem from you: Gary Snyder, "Berry Territory," first published in *New Directions Anthology* 35 (1977). The poem appeared in a somewhat different form in *Axe Handles* (1983).

p. 13   farming book: Wendell Berry, *The Unsettling of America* (1977).

p. 13   Jon Beckmann: was publisher of Sierra Club Books from 1973 to 1994.

p. 13   Sim Van der Ryn: a researcher and builder in sustainable architecture and bioregional design. He is a Lindisfarne Fellow and founder of the Farallones Institute, a center that designed and managed the Integral Urban House, a 1970s self-reliant urban homestead in Berkeley, California.

p. 14   Bob Callahan: was publisher of Turtle Island Books.

p. 14   friendliness between us: Berry published letters in *CoEvolution Quarterly* (Summer 1976) expressing his disapproval of the journal promoting the feasibility of inhabiting space colonies. Stewart Brand printed his ambivalent response to the letters.

p. 14   University: Berry was in the English Department at the University of Kentucky 1964–1977 and 1987–1993.

p. 15   Odum's: Howard T. Odum, *Environment, Power, and Society* (New York: Wiley, 1971).

p. 15   *Energy* book: *Energy and Power: A Scientific American Book* (New York: Freeman, W. H. & Co., 1971).

p. 15   Brown's: Jerry Brown, Governor of California, 1975–1983.

p. 15   read poesy *together*: Snyder and Berry would read poetry together for the first time on March 3, 1977, at the San Francisco Museum of Modern Art.

p. 16   For W.B.'s *Unsettling of America*: An abbreviated version of this statement later appeared on the book jacket of *The Unsettling of America* (1977).

p. 19   40077: In the 1970s, while Snyder was working on *Turtle Island,* he began using a self-created dating system that he called Homo Sapiens Dating, or Upper Paleolithic Dating. It is based on the principle that since different calendars (Chinese, Jewish, India, Meso-America) date in accord with their own mythologies, it might also serve contemporary, postmodern human beings to consider a calendar based on when the first aesthetic or spiritual seeming objects begin to show up in the archaeological record. Such are the southwestern European and North African cave wall paintings, and various objects that represent fish, or animals, or birds. Based on what was known forty years ago, Snyder selected the number 40,000 to mark the start of the twentieth century. Later cave paintings have since been discovered with animal art that is dated even earlier. For that and other reasons, Snyder has stopped using the dating system.

p. 19   might freeze across: January 1977 was the coldest month in the

Ohio Valley's history. Long stretches of the Ohio and Kentucky rivers froze across.

p. 19   California Arts Council: Snyder was appointed to the Board of the California Arts Council by Governor Jerry Brown and served from 1974 to 1979.

p. 19   agricultural disaster: At the bottom of this letter, Snyder has drawn an indigenous pictograph of "rain clouds."

p. 19   Ramanujan's translations: A.K. Ramanujan was an Indian poet, translator, and scholar. He was the editor and translator of several books, including *The Interior Landscape: Love Poems from a Classical Tamil Anthology* (1967).

p. 20   George Hart's study: George Hart, *The Poems of Ancient Tamil: Their Milieu and Their Sanskrit Counterparts* (Berkeley, CA: Univ. of California Press, 1975).

p. 20   draft of an article: Wendell Berry, "Life on (and off) Schedule," *Organic Gardening and Farming* (August 1977).

p. 21   Jerry Goldstein: was editor of *Organic Gardening and Farming* at Rodale Press.

p. 23   your interview: in reference to Snyder's interview with Peter Barry Chowka in the *East West Journal* (Summer 1977), reprinted in *The Real Work: Interviews & Talks, 1964–1979*, Scott McLean, ed. (1980). In this interview Snyder also spoke of the importance of Wendell Berry and his work.

p. 24   an essay disapproving: Wendell Berry, "The Specialization of Poetry," in *The Hudson Review* 28 (Spring 1975); later published in *Standing by Words* (1983).

p. 25   Grand Coulee: In the 1930s, Snyder's father was a labor organizer for workers at Grand Coulee Dam, at the time the largest multiuse dam project in the world.

p. 25   Jarold Ramsey: the compiler and editor of *Coyote Was Going There: Indian Literature of the Oregon Country* (Seattle, WA: Univ. of Washington Press, 1977).

p. 25   William Stafford: was Oregon Poet Laureate from 1975 to 1990.

p. 25 Warm Springs Indian Reservation: At Reed College, Snyder and Dell Hymes did fieldwork with anthropology professors David and Katherine French at Warm Springs Indian Reservation. After graduating from Reed, Snyder worked on the reservation (1951, 1954) as a timber scaler and choker setter, which shaped his book *Myths & Texts* (1960).

p. 25 book on Asia and nature: In 1970, Snyder began an environmental history book for the John Muir Institute that was later titled *The Great Clod* project. Although the book was not completed, sections of it were published in *CoEvolution Quarterly* (Fall 1978) and *The Gary Snyder Reader* (1999).

p. 27 egb: Eva Grace Brumett, a neighbor who typed Snyder's dictated letters and worked as his assistant for several years.

p. 27 Enclosure: Gary Snyder, "True Night," in *Axe Handles* (1983).

p. 28 *Ishi*: Theodora Kroeber, *Ishi in Two Worlds: A Biography of the Last Wild Indian in North America* (1961).

p. 28 Lao Tzu: a Chinese philosopher and teacher of Taoism; also spelled as Lao-tsu throughout the letters.

p. 28 Maury Telleen: was an agrarian, editor, and founder of *The Draft Horse Journal*. Berry dedicated *The Unsettling of America* to Telleen and wrote about him in "Going Back—or Ahead—to Horses" (1980) in *The Gift of Good Land* (1981). When Telleen passed away in 2011, Berry wrote a memorial that was published in *The Draft Horse Journal* and later in *It All Turns on Affection* (2012).

p. 28 Rodale Press: Berry was contributing editor at Rodale Press from 1977 to 1979, publisher of *Organic Gardening and Farming* and *New Farm*.

p. 28 Stephen Brush: an anthropologist, then at the College of William and Mary.

p. 29 some haikus: Steve Sanfield sent a group of poems titled "Drought" (1976).

p. 29 Larry Korn: a student of Masanobu Fukuoka, who helped edit the English-language version of *The One-Straw Revolution: An Introduction to Natural Farming* (Emmaus, PA: Rodale Press, 1978).

p. 29   Banyan Ashram: Gary Snyder, "Suwa-No-Se Island and the Banyan Ashram," in *Earth House Hold* (1969).

p. 30   Leroy Quintana: author of *Hijo del pueblo: New Mexico poems* (1976).

p. 30   benefit reading: "Words for Whales: A Greenpeace Benefit," March 23, 1978; an audio recording of the event is archived at the University of California, Davis.

p. 30   brand new play: Michael McClure's *Minnie Mouse and the Tap-Dancing Buddha* was being performed at the Magic Theatre in San Francisco.

p. 30   Maidu: indigenous tribes and bands of the central Sierra Nevada.

p. 31   *satori*: the attainment of comprehension and enlightenment for Zen Buddhists.

p. 31   I send a poem: Wendell Berry, "The River Bridged and Forgot," later published in *The Wheel* (1982).

p. 32   I enclose a translation: Wendell Berry, "Ronsard's Lament for the Cutting of the Forest of Gastine," a partial translation of Ronsard's *Elegy XXIV*, later published in *A Part* (1980).

p. 32   nature of evil: Snyder wrote about the question of evil in "Buddhism and the Coming Revolution" in *Earth House Hold* (1969).

p. 33   editorial meeting: This issue of the *Journal for the Protection of All Beings*, guest edited by Snyder, Meltzer, Ferlinghetti, and McClure, was copublished with *CoEvolution Quarterly* (Fall 1978).

p. 33   for plants and trees: William LaFleur, "Sattva: Enlightenment for Plants and Trees in Buddhism."

p. 33   Asia book workings: Gary Snyder, "'Wild' in China."

p. 33   poem by Peter Blue Cloud: "Rattle."

p. 33   bird watching journals: Peter Warshall, "Puffins and Peregrines: Excerpts from my Farallones Journal."

p. 34   poem appear both places: The poem was published in *The Hudson Review* (Spring 1979).

p. 34   Peru trip: Wendell Berry, "An Agricultural Journey in Peru" (1979), in *The Gift of Good Land* (1981).

p. 36 Leander Poisson: Leander Poisson and Gretchen Vogel Poisson later published *Solar Gardening: Growing Vegetables Year-Round the American Intensive Way* (White River Junction, VT: Chelsea Green Publishing, 1994).

p. 37 New Alchemy: The New Alchemy Institute was a twelve-acre research farm founded by John and Nancy Jack Todd and William McLarney. It was established in 1969 to investigate organic agriculture, aquaculture, and shelter design. John and Nancy Jack Todd are also Lindisfarne Fellows and authors of *Eco-Cities to Living Machines: Principles of Ecological Design* (Berkeley, CA: North Atlantic Books, 1994).

p. 38 Robert Aitken: was a Zen teacher and social activist who co-founded the Honolulu Diamond Sangha (1959) with his wife Anne Hopkins Aitken. Aitken also taught *sesshins* at the San Juan Ridge community and the Ring of Bone Zendo at Kitkitdizze.

p. 38 *koans*: Buddhist training stories, phrases, or riddles that invite meditation and clarity.

p. 39 Hokkaido: The northernmost and second largest island of Japan.

p. 39 going together to Alaska: Gary and Masa Snyder were scheduled to teach, read poetry, and perform dance in Ketchikan, Sitka, and Juneau with the Southeast Alaska Conservation Council.

p. 40 a teacher: Harold Cassidy was a retired professor of chemistry at Yale University, living in Madison, Indiana. He was a leader in a local fight against the building of the now-abandoned Marble Hill Nuclear Power Plant at Marble Hill, Indiana. In June of 1979, Berry was among eighty-nine protesters arrested at the nuclear plant for crossing a property fence in an act of civil disobedience.

p. 40 Southern Baptist Theological Seminary: in reference to "The Gift of Good Land," a speech sponsored by the Clarence Jordan Institute for Ethical Concerns at Southern Baptist Theological Seminary (1979).

p. 41 *The Arrogance of Humanism*: David Ehrenfeld, *The Arrogance of Humanism* (New York: Oxford Univ. Press, 1978).

p. 41 Gary Nabhan: This trip to Arizona with agricultural ecologist and Lindisfarne Fellow Gary Nabhan was later discussed in Berry's

"Three Ways of Farming in the Southwest" (1979) in *The Gift of Good Land* (1981). Berry offered a further discussion of Nabhan's work on agriculture in Arizona and New Mexico in "Getting Along with Nature" (1982) in *Home Economics* (1987).

p. 42   Gregory Bateson: was an anthropologist, social scientist, and Lindisfarne Fellow, whose books *Steps to an Ecology of Mind* (1972) and *Mind and Nature* (1979) intersected across many fields. Bateson died in 1980 at the Lindisfarne Guest House at Green Gulch Farm, part of the San Francisco Zen Center.

p. 42   a copy of a paper: Gary Snyder, "Poetry, Community, and Climax," in *The Real Work: Interviews & Talks, 1964–1979* (1980).

p. 43   a little book: Peter Blue Cloud, *Back Then Tomorrow*, preface by Gary Snyder (Brunswick, ME: Blackberry Press, 1978).

p. 43   recently published B.A. thesis: Gary Snyder, *He Who Hunted Birds in His Father's Village: The Dimensions of a Haida Myth* (1979).

p. 44   University of Hawaii: Gary and Masa Snyder were visiting artists with the InterArts Hawaii program. They participated in a symposium titled "Poetry and Dance of Life and Place." While there, Snyder read poetry with W. S. Merwin at the Mid-Pacific Institute in Honolulu.

p. 44   electric fence: Berry also wrote an article about fences for *Organic Gardening and Farming*, titled "A Short Tour around the Subject of Fences" (May 1978).

p. 44   new poems: in reference to Berry's Sabbath poems, an ongoing practice started in 1979. Sabbath poems from 1979 to 1997 are in *A Timbered Choir* (1998), 1998–2004 in *Given* (2006), and 2005–2008 in *Leavings* (2010). The poems are now collected in *This Day: Collected and New Sabbath Poems* (2013).

p. 45   The pages in the Fall '78: Gary Snyder, "'Wild' in China," reprinted in *The Gary Snyder Reader* (1999).

p. 46   Michael Harner: Michael Harner and Alfred Meyer, *Cannibal* (New York: Morrow, 1979).

p. 46   Fukuoka's work: Masanobu Fukuoka, *The One-Straw Revolution:*

An Introduction to Natural Farming, Larry Korn, ed., preface by Wendell Berry (Emmaus, PA: Rodale Press, 1978).

p. 49   the enclosed essay: Wendell Berry, "The Gift of Good Land," in *Sierra Club Bulletin* (1979), later published in *The Gift of Good Land* (1981).

p. 49   Larry Stains: a journalist and editor of *New Shelter* from 1978 to 1982.

p. 49   an agronomist and a botanist: Timothy Taylor, an agronomist at the University of Kentucky; Bill Martin, a botanist at Eastern Kentucky University. Observations from this trip were later developed in Berry's essay "The Native Grasses and What They Mean" (1979) in *The Gift of Good Land* (1981).

p. 50   Judy Hurley: was an activist and teacher in Santa Cruz. Snyder met her while studying Zen Buddhism in Kyoto, Japan.

p. 50   article for *Shelter*: This article was not written.

p. 50   Chuang-tzu: a Chinese philosopher of the fourth century BCE.

p. 51   M.C. Bateson: Mary Catherine Bateson, an anthropologist and Lindisfarne Fellow.

p. 51   *sangha*: community activities, assembly, or gathering.

p. 51   *Mountains and Rivers Sutra*: Dōgen Kigen was a thirteenth-century Buddhist teacher and founder of the Sōtō school of Zen in Japan, whose work became important to Snyder's *Mountains and Rivers Without End* (1996). Snyder also wrote about Dōgen's *Mountains and Rivers Sutra* in "Blue Mountains Constantly Walking" in *The Practice of the Wild* (1990).

p. 51   the enclosed: Berry enclosed a typescript of the Sabbath poems of 1979.

p. 52   my brother: John M. Berry, Jr., lawyer and farmer, was involved in the Kentucky State Senate from 1974 to 1982.

p. 52   Green Gulch: Green Gulch Farm, part of the San Francisco Zen Center (1972) and home to the Lindisfarne Guest House.

p. 52   the sake of a novel: Wendell Berry, *Remembering* (1988).

p. 53 any place else: Berry later addressed these issues in "The Loss of the University" (1984) in *Home Economics* (1987)

p. 54 *Heraclitean Fire*: Erwin Chargaff, *Heraclitean Fire: Sketches from a Life Before Nature* (Concord, MA: Paul & Co. Pub. Consortium, 1978).

p. 56 Thomas Merton: was a Trappist monk of the Abbey of Gethsemani in Kentucky. He was a poet, essayist, and student of comparative religion interested in establishing a dialogue between Christianity and Zen Buddhism. After moving to Lanes Landing in 1965, Wendell and Tanya Berry met Merton though a mutual friendship with photographer Ralph Eugene Meatyard.

p. 56 "prayer has been valid": from T.S. Eliot, "Little Gidding," in *Four Quartets* (1945).

p. 59 "meat" for our use: in reference to Genesis 9:2–3.

p. 59 Meister Eckhart: a thirteenth-century Dominican mystic. Twentieth-century Zen Buddhists such as D. T. Suzuki have noted similarities between Eckhart's teachings and Buddhism.

p. 60 Catholic Workers: The Catholic Worker movement was founded in 1933 by Dorothy Day and Peter Maurin.

p. 60 Trappist Monks: a cloistered and contemplative order of Cistercian monastics.

p. 60 the little piece I have enclosed: Snyder enclosed a homily written by Fr. Willigis Jäger, OSB, titled "This is my Body." The talk was delivered in 1979 at the So. Leyte *sesshin* led by Yamada Roshi. In a marginalia note, Snyder described Jäger as "a Christian-Zen priest."

p. 60 Turtle Island: An indigenous name for North America; see the "Introductory Note" to Snyder's *Turtle Island* (1974).

p. 61 my new book: Gary Snyder, *The Real Work: Interviews & Talks, 1964–1979* (1980).

p. 63 [all?]: This bracketed word does not note an editorial question of legibility. It is in Berry's letter and questions Snyder's rendering of Genesis 9:2–3.

p. 64 "atoned": The question of "atonement" or being "at-one-ment" with the maker was also taken up in Berry's "A Secular Pilgrimage" and "Discipline and Hope" in *A Continuous Harmony* (1972).

p. 65   "dissociation of sensibility": from T.S. Eliot's essay "The Metaphysical Poets" (1921).

p. 68   David Padwa: founder of Agrigenetics Corporation (est. 1975).

p. 69   Teilhard evolutionists: Pierre Teilhard de Chardin was a French philosopher, paleontologist, and Jesuit priest who proposed that the universe was evolving toward a maximum level of consciousness and technological complexity. His theories on original sin and evolution were condemned by the Magisterium of the Catholic Church.

p. 74   last essay I did: Gary Snyder, "Poetry, Community, and Climax" in *The Real Work: Interviews & Talks, 1964–1979* (1980).

p. 75   "secret history of the Mongols": Jack Shoemaker published *The Secret History of the Mongols*, a translation done by Paul Kahn, based on a translation by Francis Cleaves (North Point Press, 1984). Snyder and Shoemaker had typescripts of the text in 1979–1980, while preparing to edit and revise it for publication.

p. 76   Genesis 9:10

p. 77   Bill Devall: was a sociologist and environmental philosopher, as well as a central participant in the Deep Ecology movement.

p. 78   George Sessions: an environmental philosopher at Sierra College.

p. 81   essay on the atom bomb: Teilhard de Chardin, "Some Reflections on the Spiritual Repercussions of the Atom Bomb," in *The Future of Man* (New York: Harper & Row, 1964).

p. 81   R. Buckminster Fuller: was an architect, Unitarian minister, systems theorist, and futurist, well known for popularizing the geodesic dome and shelter.

p. 81   C. S. Lewis's trilogy: *Out of the Silent Planet* (1938), *Perelandra* (1943), and *That Hideous Strength* (1945).

p. 81   Edward Abbey: a novelist, essayist, and controversial environmental activist. Berry wrote an essay titled "A Few Words in Favor of Edward Abbey" (1985) that is published in *What Are People For?* (1990).

p. 82   The stanzas from Dunbar: In addition to a revised manuscript of the Sabbath poems (c. 1979–1980), Berry enclosed "From Dunbar," a poem that was not later published.

p. 83   Wes Jackson: an agronomist and geneticist who cofounded The Land Institute (est. 1976) with his first wife, Dana Jackson. Wes and Dana Jackson are also Lindisfarne Fellows. Berry dedicated *Home Economics* (1987) to Wes Jackson.

p. 83   an article about them: Wendell Berry, "New Roots for Agricultural Research" (1981), in *The Gift of Good Land* (1981).

p. 84   *Time* article: Melvin Maddock, "In Tennessee: The Last Garden," *Time* (December 1980).

p. 84   a little permission here: Snyder requested permission to use the passage "My feet are cold . . . so are mine" from Berry's *Sayings and Doings* (1975). Snyder quoted this passage in "The Old Masters and the Old Women: Foreword to Sōiku Shigematsu's *A Zen Forest,*" later reprinted in *A Place in Space: Ethics, Aesthetics, and Watersheds* (1995).

p. 84   George Gaylord Simpson and P. B. Medawar: Their reviews of *The Phenomenon of Man* are reprinted in *Darwin*, Philip Appleman, ed. (New York: W. W. Norton & Co., 1979).

p. 87   Means: In addition to P. B. Medawar's review of *The Phenomenon of Man,* Snyder sent an article by Russell Means, a prominent Oglala Sioux activist and founder of the American Indian Movement (AIM). Based on the conversation between Berry and Snyder, the article under discussion was likely "For America to Live, Europe Must Die," a speech that Means delivered in 1980 at the Black Hills International Survival Gathering in the Black Hills of South Dakota.

p. 88   some of my old work: Berry was revisiting two of his early novels, *Nathan Coulter* (1960) and *A Place on Earth* (1967), to be published as revised editions with North Point Press.

p. 88   Leonard Peltier: a Native American activist and member of the American Indian Movement (AIM). In 1977, Peltier was controversially convicted and sentenced to two consecutive life terms for the shooting of two FBI agents during a conflict on the Pine Ridge Indian Reservation in 1975.

p. 90 Bill Thompson: The correspondence between William Irwin Thompson and Berry concerned arguments about the role and place of technology in Christian eschatology. There was also a discussion of Berry's essay "Standing by Words," the opening lecture given at the Lindisfarne Fellows Conference in 1978. The lecture was then published by Lindisfarne Press (1980) and printed in *The Hudson Review* (Winter 1980–81).

p. 90 June 9, 1981: Snyder's note was sent on a postcard from the Okinawa Prefectural Museum.

p. 91 *Small Farm* [*sic: New Farm*]: Snyder was referring to the *New Farm*, published by Rodale Press, where Berry was formerly a contributing editor.

p. 94 busy with a long essay: "Poetry and Place" (1982), published in *Standing by Words* (1983).

p. 95 Lindisfarne in Colorado: The Lindisfarne Association had moved to Crestone, Colorado. Their 1982 annual meeting, which Berry and Snyder attended, was titled "The Land: Its Ecological Development and Its Economic Understanding."

p. 95 *Zendo* building project: Ring of Bone Zendo, named after a line in Lew Welch's poem "I Saw Myself." Welch disappeared from Kitkitdizze during a period of severe depression in 1971. Snyder's poems "For/From Lew" and "For Lew Welch in a Snowfall" speak of Welch's absence and ongoing presence at Kitkitdizze.

p. 96 Kathleen Raine: a British poet, literary critic, Lindisfarne Fellow, founder and editor of *Temenos*, and founding member of the Temenos Academy. In 2003, Raine passed away and Berry dedicated *This Day: Collected and New Sabbath Poems* (2013) in her memory. Berry also wrote an essay in appreciation of Raine titled "Against the Nihil of the Age" (2001) later published in *Imagination in Place* (2011).

p. 97 "Energy flowing ...": from R. Buckminster Fuller, *Synergetics 2: Explorations in the Geometry of Thinking* (New York: Macmillan, 1979).

p. 98   "People, Land, and Community": published in *The Schumacher Lectures*, Volume II, Satish Kumar, ed. (London: Blond and Briggs, 1984); a later version of the essay was published in *Standing by Words* (1983).

p. 99   "Onearth" invitation: In 1982, the Findhorn Foundation purchased Findhorn Bay Caravan Park in Moray, Scotland. That same year, the foundation organized the "Onearth Planetary Village Gathering," which Berry and Snyder spoke at.

p. 99   Mr. Young: Dudley Young, a literary critic at University of Essex. Young sent Berry an article titled "Life with Lord Lowell at Essex University," *PN Review* 28 (1982).

p. 99   Michael Hamburger: a poet, translator, and literary critic.

p. 100   R. Doudna: Roger Doudna, a representative of the Findhorn Foundation and Soil Association. The Soil Association in Edinburgh is the Scottish office of the United Kingdom's largest organization for the promotion of healthy, sustainable food, organic farming, and land use.

p. 101   My paper's finished: Gary Snyder, "Wild, Sacred, Good Land," in *The Schumacher Lectures*, Volume II, Satish Kumar, ed. (1984); a later version of the essay was published as "Good, Wild, Sacred" in *The Practice of the Wild* (1990).

p. 101   the ballad: Snyder enclosed a ballad from a British reader who attended the Schumacher Lectures titled "Upon Hearing Wendell Berry and Gary Snyder Speak at the Schumacher Lectures in Bristol."

p. 101   Jerry Martien: a bioregional writer and activist from the North Coast of California. He is the author of *Pieces in Place* (1999), foreword by Gary Snyder, and *Shell Game: A True Account of Beads and Money in North America* (1996).

p. 105   a stranger's letter: Berry enclosed a thoughtful letter written in regard to *The Unsettling of America* (1977) and *The Gift of Good Land* (1981).

p. 105   British agricultural travels: Wendell Berry, "Irish Journal" (1982), published in *Home Economics* (1987).

p. 105 the ideogram: Masa Uehara Snyder designed the ideogram for *Standing by Words* (1983).

p. 108 Drummond Hadley: a poet and rancher from a southwestern ranch bordering Arizona, New Mexico, and Mexico.

p. 110 inclusion in the book: *Meeting the Expectations of the Land: Essays in Sustainable Agriculture and Stewardship*, Wes Jackson, Wendell Berry, and Bruce Colman, eds. (San Francisco: North Point Press, 1984).

p. 111 Gene Logsdon: writer on agriculture, columnist, novelist, and farmer from Upper Sandusky, Ohio. Berry dedicated *The Gift of Good Land* (1981) to Logsdon.

p. 113 David Orr: a Taoist poet, creek-walker, ideal reader, and inspiring friend. Orr was born in Kentucky in 1942, taught for a number of years at the University of Louisville, spent more than a decade as an inventor and information technology expert, and died in California in 1989.

p. 113 Tom and Ginny Marsh: Wendell Berry wrote an article about Tom and Ginny Marsh titled "An Excellent Homestead" (1979), later published in *The Gift of Good Land* (1981). Tom was a potter from Borden, Indiana, who taught in the Fine Arts department at the University of Louisville. Ginny is a practicing ceramicist who worked and taught collaboratively with her husband until his death in 1991.

p. 114 *Nō* plays: an elevated form of Japanese musical drama that has been performed since the fourteenth century. The plays are an expression of shamanistic performance that invoke the spirit realms. Snyder attended several *Nō* performances while living in Kyoto, Japan, during the 1950s and 1960s. The style of the plays shaped *Mountains and Rivers Without End* (1996).

p. 114 Hawaii bird stamp: This comment concerns the end of Snyder's previous letter about listening to Hawaiian birdsong in Honolulu. The stamp was of a Hawaiian goose and hibiscus.

p. 115 David Jones: David Jones, *The Sleeping Lord and Other Fragments* (London: Faber and Faber, 1974).

p. 116 Wes's book: Wes Jackson, *New Roots for Agriculture* (San Francisco, CA: Friends of the Earth, 1980).

p. 116   *Stone Age Economics*: Marshall Sahlins, *Stone Age Economics* (New York: Water de Gruyter, 1972).

p. 119   *The Tree of Life*: H.J. Massingham, *The Tree of Life* (London: Chapman and Hall, 1943).

p. 119   "The Old Faith": in Frank O'Connor, *More Stories by Frank O'Connor* (New York: Knopf, 1954).

p. 121   I want you to see this: Wendell Berry, "Two Economies" (1983), later published in *Home Economics* (1987).

p. 124   Morris Graves retrospective: Morris Graves, a painter from the Pacific Northwest and founder of the Northwest School style of painting, noted for its regionalism and mysticism. The mentioned retrospective was "Morris Graves: Vision of the Inner Eye" (1983–1984), organized by the Phillips Collection, Washington, D.C.

p. 124   *The Great Transformation*: Karl Polanyi, *The Great Transformation: The Political and Economic Origins of Our Time* (1944).

p. 125   I'm enclosing here a xerox: Luke Breit, "Sharon Dubiago: Psyche Rides the West Coast," *Poet News* (January 1984). The enclosed article spoke of a reading with Sharon Dubiago and Wendell Berry at University of Wisconsin. Snyder marked a place in the article where Dubiago states that when she meets Berry for a debate she "is going to talk about 'Feminism and Ecology,' which I don't know a fucking thing about." The article went on to claim that Snyder declined to participate in a debate with Dubiago, after an invitation allegedly came following an article that Dubiago published about the lack of women poets represented from the San Juan Ridge area titled "Where is the Female on the Bearshit Trail?"

p. 125   Alaska Humanities Forum: Snyder was working as a consultant with Gary Holthaus, Executive Director of the Alaska Humanities Forum. Snyder gave readings in southeastern Alaska and visited numerous villages along the Kobuk River in northwest Alaska.

p. 127   ten years ago: Snyder had attended a previous Wilderness Institute conference titled "The Right to Remain Wild" (1975). His talk "Clouds and Rocks" was published in *Right to Remain Wild, a*

Public Choice: Proceedings of a Conference, November 17–19, 1975 (Missoula, MT: Univ. of Montana Press, 1975).

p. 133 Subsistence equals Sacrament: Snyder wrote about eating as sacrament in "Grace," an essay published in *CoEvolution Quarterly* (Fall 1984), and later included in *The Practice of the Wild* (1990).

p. 134 What kind of economy would cherish trees?: This question gets developed in "Conserving Forest Communities," delivered at the Kentucky Forest Summit (1994) and published in *Another Turn of the Crank* (1995).

p. 135 Your new poem: in reference to Snyder's previously enclosed poem, "Night Song of the Los Angeles Basin," later published in *Mountains and Rivers Without End* (1996).

p. 136 Richard Brothers: an advocate of bioregionalism and sustainable forestry from southern Oregon. Brothers had published an article in *In Context* titled "Respectful Forestry: Forestry Ecosystems Could Serve Us Generously if We Would Work with Them" (Winter 1984).

p. 137 *Driftwood Valley*: Theodora C. Stanwell-Fletcher, *Driftwood Valley* (1946). Berry wrote an introduction for this book in 1989, when it was published as part of the Penguin Nature Classics series, edited by Edward Hoagland. The book was later reprinted by Oregon State Univ. Press in 1999.

p. 138 indeed go to Alaska: Berry was considering working with Snyder for the Alaska Humanities Forum.

p. 138 And here's the essay: "Preserving Wildness," published by the Wyoming Outdoor Council (1986), and later in *Home Economics* (1987).

p. 138 the two fat papers: Richard Sylvan, "A Critique of Deep Ecology," *Discussion Papers in Environmental Philosophy* no. 14 (Department of Philosophy, Research School of the Social Sciences, Australian National Univ.: Canberra, 1985); Warwick Fox, *Approaching Deep Ecology: A Response to Richard Sylvan's Critique of Deep Ecology* (Hobart: Centre for Environmental Studies, Univ. of Tasmania, 1986).

p. 139   Arne Næss: Norwegian philosopher and key thinker in the Deep Ecology movement.

p. 139   Roderick Nash: author of *Wilderness and the American Mind* (New Haven, CT: Yale Univ. Press, 1967) and *The Rights of Nature: A History of Environmental Ethics* (Madison, WI: Univ. of Wisconsin Press, 1989).

p. 140   Richard Nelson: a cultural anthropologist whose work focuses on indigenous cultures of Alaska; *Make Prayers to the Raven: A Koyukon View of the Northern Forest* (Chicago, IL: Univ. of Chicago Press, 1983).

p. 140   David Brower: was founder of the Sierra Club Foundation and the John Muir Institute for Environmental Studies.

p. 141   *Nature and Madness*: Paul Shepard, *Nature and Madness* (San Francisco, CA: Sierra Club Books, 1982).

p. 142   Ursus Arctos: scientific name for the brown bear.

p. 143   Edgar Anderson: an American botanist. His books *Introgressive Hybridization* (1949) and *Plants, Man, and Life* (1952) were early contributions to botanical genetics.

p. 143   *Deep Ecology*: Bill Devall and George Sessions, eds., *Deep Ecology: Living as if Nature Mattered* (Layton, UT: Gibbs Smith, 1985).

p. 144   how you live, how you work: Issues pertaining to conservation, environmentalism, agrarianism, and work are addressed in several of Berry's later essays, including "Conservation is Good Work" (1992) in *Sex, Economy, Freedom, and Community* (1993), as well as "In Distrust of Movements" (1998) and "The Whole Horse"(1996) in *Citizenship Papers* (2003).

p. 148   "the human form divine": William Blake, a line from "The Divine Image" in *Songs of Innocence* (1789).

p. 148   sexual discipline: These issues are later developed in Berry's "Sex, Economy, Freedom, and Community" (1992) and "The Conservation of Nature and the Preservation of Humanity" (1995).

p. 148   Laurens van der Post's account: Laurens van der Post, *The Lost World of the Kalahari* (New York: Harcourt Brace Jovanovich, 1977).

p. 152 leave for Pennsylvania: Berry was writer-in-residence at Bucknell University in early 1987.

p. 152 wild and cultured: Gary Snyder, *The Practice of the Wild* (1990).

p. 154 Gilbert White's "hanger": Gilbert White was an eighteenth century naturalist and author of *Natural History and Antiquities of Selborne* (1789); the "hanger" is a wood on the side of a steep hill.

p. 154 John and Truda Lane: The Lanes hosted Wendell and Tanya Berry during their stay in Devon. John was an artist and writer, former art editor for *Resurgence*, and a trustee at Dartington Hall, which, in 1990, became home to Schumacher College, an international center for ecological studies. Truda Lane is an artist whose work is published in *Life Lines: Selected Drawings of Truda Lane* (Resurgence Books, 2010).

p. 154 Temenos: *Temenos* journal was established by Kathleen Raine, Keith Critchlow, Brian Keeble, and Philip Sherrard in 1980. The Temenos Academy, of which Berry is a fellow, was founded in 1990.

p. 155 working very hard on a novel: Wendell Berry, *Remembering* (1988).

p. 157 The enclosed piece: Gary Snyder, "On the Path, Off the Trail," in *The Practice of the Wild* (1990).

p. 161 *Why I Take Good Care*: This poem was published in *Turn-Around Times* (March 1988) and reprinted ten years later in *IT Times* (January 1998), both student technology magazines at University of California, Davis. In these two publications, the poem was not dedicated to Wendell Berry.

p. 162 the old Camp: a small cabin near Lanes Landing on the Kentucky River. In 1963, after the Camp was flooded several times and fell into neglect, Berry reconstructed the cabin, moving it to higher ground. He tells the story of the Camp in the title essay of *The Long-Legged House* (1969), and continues to use it as a place for writing.

p. 163 September 16, 1988: Snyder's note was sent on a poetry postcard of "Pollen" (Gary Snyder V 87), printed by "the unspeakable vision of the individual" (California, PA: 1988).

p. 163   Harlan Hubbard: Wendell Berry, *Harlan Hubbard: Life and Work* (1990). This material was also delivered through the Blazer Lectures at the University of Kentucky in 1989.

p. 163   three published books: At the time, Harlan Hubbard's published books included: *Shantyboat* (New York: Dodd, Mead, 1953), *Payne Hollow: Life on the Fringe of Society* (New York: Crowell, 1974), and *Harlan Hubbard Journals, 1929-1944*, Vincent Kohler and David F. Ward, eds. (Lexington, KY: Univ. Press of Kentucky, 1987). Additional publications now include: *Shantyboat Journal* (1994) and *Payne Hollow* (1996), both edited by Don Wallis and published by the Univ. Press of Kentucky, as well as Harlan Hubbard's *Shantyboat on the Bayous* (Lexington, KY: Univ. Press of Kentucky, 1990).

p. 165   a seminar I'm preparing: Snyder enclosed a description for "A Seminar on 'Issues and Problems in Nature Literature.'"

p. 165   March 7, 1989: Berry enclosed the poem "Sabbaths III (Santa Clara Valley)," published in *Sabbaths 1987–90* (Ipswich, UK: Golgonooza Press, 1992) and in *This Day: Collected and New Sabbath Poems* (2013).

p. 166   "The Etiquette of Freedom": Gary Snyder, "The Etiquette of Freedom," in *The Practice of the Wild* (1990).

p. 167   John Muir's watery trail: John Muir's journeys through Alaska (1879-1880, and 1890) are mapped and recorded in John Muir, *Travels in Alaska* (New York: Houghton Mifflin Co., 1915).

p. 171   *A Blue Fire*: James Hillman, *A Blue Fire: Selected Writings of James Hillman*, Thomas Moore, ed. (New York: HarperCollins, 1989).

p. 173   "Action Packet": Kai Snyder and Mary Cadenasso, *Action Packet: A Directory for Environmental Action* (Berkeley, CA: Conservation and Resource Studies Dept., UC Berkeley, 1990).

p. 177   report of sorts: Snyder enclosed a copy of notes concerning travels made during the summer of 1991. These include descriptions of a trip that Snyder and Carole Koda made to Haines, Alaska, and a three-day sea kayak trip made with Richard Nelson of Sitka, Alaska. The second half of the notes is a series of reflections about a mountain-climbing trip in the High Sierra that Snyder made with Carole and Kai.

p. 177   *The Discovery of Kentucky*: Wendell Berry, *The Discovery of Kentucky* (1991).

p. 177   watershed group: The Yuba Watershed Institute (est. 1990) is a cooperative management agreement with the U.S. Bureau of Land Management and the Timber Farmers Guild of North America for the joint management of forestland on ten parcels in Nevada County, California.

p. 178   38-year-long poetry project: Gary Snyder, *Mountains and Rivers Without End* (1996).

p. 179   gathering in San Francisco: Berry was one of forty-six participants engaged in a San Francisco conference called "Megatechnology and Development" (1993). Conference proceedings, including a second meeting in Devon, England, were edited by Stephanie Mills as *Turning Away from Technology: A New Vision for the 21st Century* (San Francisco, CA: Sierra Club Books, 1997).

p. 181   read on the ridge: Berry enclosed an invitation from Steve Sanfield, asking him to read at North Columbia Schoolhouse Cultural Center on May 27.

p. 182   Drum's purchase: In 1993, Drum Hadley began a conversation with the Nature Conservancy to manage Gray Ranch, a 502-square mile ranch in southwestern New Mexico that is home to diverse grasslands, as well as unique woodland and riparian communities. In subsequent months, Hadley became a founding director of the Animas Foundation, a private land management organization that purchased the ranch from the Nature Conservancy.

p. 183   KJ: Kyung-jin (Carole Koda's daughter). Snyder enclosed a poem by her called "Praise Poetry" (January 1993).

p. 183   record of Doobie Av.: DeWayne Williams and Gary Snyder, *Dooby Lane: A Testament Inscribed in Stone Tablets by DeWayne Williams* (Reno, NV: Black Rock Press, 1996).

p. 183   KJ's poem tikkled me: Part of KJ's poem was about tickling, repeatedly spelled as "tikkled."

p. 183   Menominee in Wisconsin: Berry developed this research in

"Conserving Forest Communities" (1994) in *Another Turn of the Crank* (1995).

p. 184   "Conserving Communities": Wendell Berry, "Conserving Forest Communities," later published in *Another Turn of the Crank* (1995).

p. 184   "Coming Into the Watershed": Gary Snyder, "Coming Into the Watershed," also published in *A Place in Space: Ethics, Aesthetics, and Watersheds* (1996).

p. 185   *Audubon*: Gary Snyder, "Kitkitdizze: A Node in the Net," later published in *A Place in Space: Ethics, Aesthetics, and Watersheds* (1996). The enclosed copy has a note reading "version of 4. XII. 94 replaces earlier," followed by "This copy for Wendell—Gary XII. 94."

p. 185   Tom Lyon: professor of English at Utah State University from 1964-1997, and editor of *Western American Literature*.

p. 186   Rick Ardinger: coeditor at Limberlost Press.

p. 186   appreciating our collection: Snyder enclosed an enthusiastic letter from Rick Ardinger, who described the collaborative project as an important bioregional primer.

p. 186   Tom Lyon's foreword: Snyder enclosed a copy of Tom Lyon's foreword for *Three on Community*, as well as a letter from Lyon.

p. 187   Charlie Fisher: Wendell Berry, "Trees for My Son and Grandson to Harvest," later published as "Charlie Fisher" in *The Way of Ignorance* (2005).

p. 188   Gary Anderson: of Hardin County, Kentucky, owns and operates a small-scale, sustainable logging operation with draft horses. Gary Anderson, Troy Firth, Wendell Berry, and Jason Rutledge spoke on a panel together about the advantages of low-impact horse logging through the Healing Harvest Forest Foundation in Copper Hill, Virginia.

p. 188   "Finding the Space in the Heart": Gary Snyder, "Finding the Space in the Heart," in *Mountains and Rivers Without End* (1996). The poem traverses ridges, canyon edges, and the "playa" of "the long gone Lake Lahontan," a massive lake of the Pleistocene period that once covered much of northwestern Nevada, including the Black Rock Desert, where Wendell and Tanya had camped with Gary and Carole in 1994.

p. 189 Douglas Haynes: a poet and essayist from Wisconsin.

p. 189 Chincoteague: Chincoteague Island, Virginia.

p. 190 Marion Gilliam: founder of *Orion* and The Orion Society.

p. 190 I'll call in a few days: Wendell Berry received the John Hay Award in 1994.

p. 191 account of travels in India: Gary Snyder, *Passage through India* (1983).

p. 191 I wrote a little essay: Wendell Berry, "Some Interim Thoughts on Gary Snyder's *Mountains and Rivers Without End*," published in the *Sewanee Review* (Winter 1988) and later in *Imagination in Place* (2010).

p. 191 *The Bird of Light*: John Hay, *The Bird of Light* (New York: W. W. Norton & Co., 1991).

p. 192 W. T. Anderson's article: Walter Truett Anderson, "There's No Going Back to Nature," *Mother Jones* 21.5 (September–October 1996). Snyder and Berry wrote responses to Anderson's article that were published together in the subsequent issue of *Mother Jones* 21.6 (November–December 1996).

p. 195 Allen Ginsberg's memory: Ginsberg had passed away a few days earlier, on April 5, 1997.

p. 195 Dan Smith: a dairy farmer and poet. His book of poems, *Home Land*, was published in *Human Landscapes: Three Books of Poems* (Huron, OH: Bottom Dog Press, 1997).

p. 197 autobiography of Jayber Crow: Wendell Berry, *Jayber Crow* (2000).

p. 201 forestry field day: Berry organized several local forestry events sponsored by the United Citizens Bank and Brown-Forman.

p. 201 Peter Coyote's book: Peter Coyote, *Sleeping Where I Fall* (Washington, D.C.: Counterpoint, 1998).

p. 202 Black Rock Press book: Gary Snyder, *Finding the Space* (Reno, NV: Black Rock Press, 1996).

p. 202 Carole's family history: Carole Koda, "Homegrown," *Kyoto Journal* 37 (1998), an article of selections from Koda's book *Homegrown: Thirteen Brothers and Sisters, a Century in America* (1996). Snyder's foreword to Koda's book, titled "Grown in America," was published in *Back on the Fire* (2007).

p. 205 Democratic Policy committee: On June 23, 1999, Berry spoke at a meeting of U.S. Senators of the Democratic Party titled "Agriculture Issues and American Farmers." The intent was to hear testimony from farmers and rural business leaders about the agriculture crisis that was ruining small farms.

p. 206 Jim Dodge: novelist, poet, and professor at Humboldt State University who has also written essays on bioregional thought and practice.

p. 206 "Fire and Grit": an Orion Society conference held at the U.S. Fish and Wildlife Service National Conservation Training Center in Shepherdstown, West Virginia.

p. 208 Chris: in regard to a letter sent to Chris Schimmoeller, director of Kentucky Heartwood from 1992 to 2002. Heartwood, founded in 1991, is a regional network of community organizations located throughout the Midwest and eastern United States. They are committed to community activism and woodland preservation. The enclosed letter concerned Berry's unwillingness to support the proposal of a "zero cut" wilderness forestry policy in Kentucky.

p. 210 Dan Daggett: author and conservationist whose book *Beyond the Rangeland Conflict: Toward a West That Works* (Reno, NV: Univ. of Nevada Press, 1998) profiled ten rancher-conservationist partnerships that demonstrate ways local communities are working to restore sustainable land use.

p. <?> this piece by Larry McMurtry: Larry McMurtry, "Death of the Cowboy," *New York Review of Books* 46.17 (November 4, 1999).

p. 211 Eddie Albert: an actor and activist. He delivered a speech titled

"Civilization Rests on Topsoil," later published in *The Mother Earth News* (May–June 1980).

p. 211 "Grace": Gary Snyder, "Grace," in *The Gary Snyder Reader* (1999).

p. 211 Coomaraswamy: Ananda Coomaraswamy, an English and Ceylonese philosopher and metaphysician, as well as a curator of fine art and a prolific scholar on traditional arts, cultures, and religions.

p. 212 John McLeod: was publicity director at Counterpoint Press.

p. 212 Jack Hicks: professor of English at UC Davis and former director of the Nature and Culture program.

p. 212 Nov. 10 and Nov. 11: in reference to the reading and conversation with Snyder that Berry would give at North Columbia Schoolhouse Cultural Center.

p. 214 odd little piece: Gary Snyder, "Migration/Immigration: Wandering South and North, Erasing Borders, Coming to Live on Turtle Island," *Wild Duck Review* (Winter 1998), later published in *Back on the Fire* (2007).

p. 215 Tanya missed it: Tanya Berry was sick and had to stay in a motel in Nevada City, while Wendell stayed with Carole and Gary at Kitkitdizze.

p. 216 Quivira Coalition: in reference to the Quivira Coalition conference "Grassbanks and the West: Challenges and Opportunities," Santa Fe, New Mexico (November 2000). The coalition, founded in 1997, is an organization committed to collaboratively restoring ecological, social, and economic health on western lands.

p. 216 Here is a clipping: Carol Feineman, "Pupils Return to Historic North Columbia Schoolhouse," *The Union* (November 20, 2000).

p. 217 *Sonata at Payne Hollow*: Wendell Berry, *Sonata at Payne Hollow* (Monterey, KY: Larkspur Press, 2001); illustrations for this book were made from woodcuts by Harlan Hubbard.

p. 217 Gray Zeitz: printer and designer of handmade books and broadsides at Larkspur Press.

p. 218 Pound-Fenollosa translations: *Certain Noble Plays of Japan: From the Manuscripts of Ernest Fenollosa*, chosen and finished by Ezra Pound, with an introduction by William Butler Yeats (1916), reprinted by New Directions (1959).

p. 218 "comment": Michael Lind, "Comment: Our Country and Our Culture," *The Hudson Review* (Winter 2002). Berry's response to Lind's essay was later published in *The Hudson Review* 55.1 (Spring 2002), followed by a reply from Michael Lind.

p. 218 heart-breaking account: George Feifer, *The Battle of Okinawa: The Blood and the Bomb* (1992), and Yanagi Sōetsu, *The Unknown Craftsman: A Japanese Insight into Beauty* (1989). Berry consulted these books when writing *Hannah Coulter* (2004).

p. 219 book on the chicken farms: Thea S. Lowry, *Empty Shells: The Story of Petaluma, America's Chicken City* (Novato, CA: Manifold Press, 2000).

p. 220 February 26, 2003: Snyder enclosed the poem "For Philip Zenshin Whalen," later published in *Danger on Peaks* (2004). Whalen passed away in 2002.

p. 220 "Citizens' Response": Wendell Berry, "A Citizen's Response to the National Security Strategy of the United States," a full-page advertisement placed by *Orion* in *The New York Times* (February 9, 2003); later published in *Citizenship Papers* (2003).

p. 220 San Francisco marches: In January 2003, an estimated 150,000 to 200,000 people had marched through San Francisco in protest against the Iraq War.

p. 221 *The Gift of Gravity*: Wendell Berry, *The Gift of Gravity* (Old Deerfield, MA: Deerfield Press, 1979).

p. 223 your great piece: Wendell Berry, "Some Notes for the Kerry Campaign, If Wanted," *Orion* (2004); later published in *The Way of Ignorance* (2006).

p. 223 Giuseppe Moretti: a key figure in the Italian bioregional movement. He had arranged for the translation of Snyder's poetry and articles into Italian.

p. 224 a couple of his writings: Berry enclosed a piece by Giannozzo Pucci titled "The Dream of Florence."

p. 226   "Man in the Ice": Ötzi, the "Man in the Ice," is a well-preserved natural mummy of a man who was discovered by hikers in the Ötztal Alps of Austria and Italy in 1991.

p. 227   January 17, 2005: Snyder's note was sent on a card of Tom Killion's woodcut print, *Piute Canyon and Mt. Humphreys, John Muir Wilderness* (1993), distributed by Seabright Press.

p. 227   Daniel Kemmis: Berry and Snyder both responded to letters from Kemmis, author of *This Sovereign Land: A New Vision for Governing the West* (2001), a former mayor of Missoula, Montana, and a former Minority Leader and Speaker of the Montana House of Representatives. At the time, Kemmis was considering declaring Democratic Party candidacy for the U.S. Senate election in 2006.

p. 227   my paper for the Koreans: in reference to "Writers and the War Against Nature," a paper Snyder gave at a conference titled "Writers Making Peace" in Seoul, Korea (2005).

p. 227   letter to Daniel K.: Berry's letter to Daniel Kemmis was published in *The Way of Ignorance* (2005), along with Kemmis's response.

p. 230   Here is a recent poem: Wendell Berry, "VII" (Sabbaths 2005), from *Leavings* (2010) and in *This Day: Collected and New Sabbath Poems* (2013).

p. 231   Drum's book: Drum Hadley, *Voice of the Borderlands*, foreword by Gary Snyder (Tucson, AZ: Rio Nuevo, 2007).

p. 232   *Blessed Are the Peacemakers*: in reference to Wendell Berry, *Blessed Are the Peacemakers* (2005).

p. 232   Carole's absence: In June of 2006, Carole Koda passed away at Kitkitdizze.

p. 233   The broadside poem: Wendell Berry, "For the Hog Killing," in *A Part* (1980) and *New Collected Poems* (2012).

p. 233   "All our food is souls": This passage was quoted by Snyder in "Grace," as published in *CoEvolution Quarterly* (Fall 1984).

p. 233   Lennie Brackett's: a designer and builder of Japanese houses in Nevada City.

p. 234   dpc: David Charlton was handling some typing for Berry from dictation and handwritten drafts, as was his wife, Tanya Charlton.

p. 235   packet of things to read: In a previous letter, Snyder had enclosed several documents, including an article by C. A. Bowers, "Some Thoughts on the Misuse of Our Political Language," *Educational Studies* 40.2 (October 2006); an article by Tu Weiming, professor of Chinese history, philosophy, and New Confucianism, who had written about Wendell Berry; and a booklet by Giuseppe Moretti, a key figure in the Italian bioregional movement.

p. 235   Wes's: The Land Institute; Salina, Kansas.

p. 235   Becky: A reader sent Berry a note about Christ Church Cathedral in Nashville and wanted Berry to tell Snyder about a Blessing of the Animals service. Berry also forwarded a homily sent by the reader titled "Are There Animals in Heaven?" In the margin of the document, Snyder wrote the following comment: "Next: To hope for the non-human world to bless us."

p. 235   Vandana Shiva: an environmental and economic activist based in Delhi, India.

p. 236   albatross essay: Gary Snyder, "Writers and the War Against Nature," *Resurgence* 239 (November–December 2006), later published in *Back on the Fire* (2007).

p. 236   "I shot the albatross.": from Samuel Taylor Coleridge, "The Rime of the Ancient Mariner" (1798).

p. 236   lecture by S. H. Nasr: Seyyed Hossein Nasr, "The Spiritual and Religious Dimensions of the Environmental Crisis" (London: Temenos Academy, 1999).

p. 237   reply to the homosexuals: Gary Snyder, "Fires, Floods, and Following the Dao," in *Back on the Fire* (2007).

p. 237   *Home Place*: Stan Rowe, *Home Place: Essays on Ecology* (1990), revised edition with foreword by Wes Jackson (Edmonton, AB: NeWest Press, 2002).

p. 238   finding new investors: In 2007, Counterpoint Press was reestablished from Washington, D.C., to Berkeley, California, through the merging of three independent presses: Counterpoint, Shoemaker & Hoard, and Soft Skull Press.

p. 239   Tom Killion's new book: The two books mentioned are Gary Snyder and Tom Killion, *Tamalpais Walking: Poetry, History, and Prints* (Berkeley, CA: Heyday Books, 2009), and Gary Snyder and Tom Killion, *The High Sierra of California: Poems and Journals* (Berkeley, CA: Heyday Books, 2005).

p. 239   a piece on forestry: Wendell Berry, "Better Ways to Manage, Study Robinson Forest," *Lexington Herald-Leader* (December 28, 2007), and "Sustainable Forestry: Lessons for Kentucky," *Louisville Courier-Journal* (December 29, 2007).

p. 240   Dana Goodyear: a journalist who wrote an article on Gary Snyder and Kitkitdizze titled "Zen Master: Gary Snyder and the Art of Life" for the *New Yorker* (October 20, 2008).

p. 240   Parinirvana Day: Snyder enclosed an essay titled "Parinirvana, 'Going on in to Nirvana' or possibly, 'Death Beyond Death' Day," which provides the cultural significance of this traditional Buddhist day.

p. 243   visit to your place: Berry wrote about this drought in "Life on (and off) Schedule," an essay about his first visit to Kitkitdizze in 1977.

p. 246   Jefferson Lecture: Wendell Berry, *It All Turns on Affection: The Jefferson Lecture & Other Essays* (2012).

A NOTE OF APPRECIATION

Editing is collaborative work and several people have offered assistance to help *Distant Neighbors* reach completion. It is important that they are recognized with a word of appreciation. St. Jerome's University supported the book with a Faculty Research Grant, allowing me to travel to special collections libraries and to meet with Gary Snyder, Wendell and Tanya Berry, and Jack Shoemaker along the way. I am fortunate to teach at a place where my colleagues embody a spirit of intellectual dialogue and the administration supports meaningful research.

Speaking more broadly, I am also indebted to a number of librarians and archivists at special collections libraries across the United States. Daryl Morrison and Jenny Hodge at the University of California at Davis helped me locate materials in the Gary Snyder Papers. From the other side of the country, Louise Jones and Jennifer Duplaga at the Kentucky Historical Society, along with Deirdre Scaggs and Ruth Bryan at the University of Kentucky, offered assistance with finding materials in the Wendell Berry Papers. In addition, James Maynard at the University at Buffalo helped with correspondence related to Snyder and Berry in the Sand Dollar Collection. I also appreciate Doug Sikkema's research and editing assistance at the University of Waterloo.

It is difficult to adequately express my appreciation to Jack Shoemaker, Wendell Berry, and Gary Snyder. When I approached Shoemaker about compiling and editing this book of letters nearly two years ago, I did so as a new scholar and a total stranger. His willingness to support my vision and to patiently work with me through each stage of the book's production is something I will not soon forget. To have the opportunity to bring these letters into print with the staff at Counterpoint Press has been the highlight of my work as a literary critic. I am particularly thankful to Emma

Cofod and Julie Wrinn, whose publishing experience, hard work, and insight made this a better book than I first imagined. For many years, I have considered myself a careful and admiring reader of Wendell Berry's and Gary Snyder's work. Their hospitality and willingness to discuss questions and share stories about their lives and work has made this a collaborative project and a joy to complete. My thanks to them is offered through the book itself.

My deepest gratitude goes to Crissa, my wife, and our two children, Luke and Hannah. Our life together is a beautiful journey that speaks beyond words. We have so much more to do.